Advance praise for Frank Spinelli and *Pee-Shy*

"This is one of those horrific, true stories that Dr. Spinelli so courageously reveals. With raw honesty he makes us understand that monsters do exist and a child's innocence is precious. His story is one of too many, but maybe this one will help open our eyes a little more and shine a light on a taboo subject that many choose not to see or believe."

—Whoopi Goldberg

"*Pee-Shy* is a devastatingly heartbreaking look at life after childhood abuse, with wit and piercing insight that can only come from a place of brutal honesty. Dr. Frank Spinelli's quest to bring his abuser to justice, at the risk of his own recovery, shows a courage rarely encountered. That he does so to save others from suffering is beyond admirable—it's inspirational."

—Josh Kilmer-Purcell, author of *The Bucolic Plague: How Two Manhattanites Became Gentlemen Farmers: An Unconventional Memoir* and star of *The Fabulous Beekman Boys*

"Passionate, enormously insightful, and deftly humorous, Dr. Frank Spinelli's memoir recounts a riveting, frightening, and often amusing story of growing up gay in the 1970s amid the shame and fear of childhood sex abuse. *Pee-Shy* is a story of searing importance, one which no one should have to endure, but one in which humor and grit helped a young man find justice. Provocative, intense, and funny, this book is a page-turner that makes you think, cry, and laugh."

—Michelangelo Signorile, author of *Life Outside* and Sirius Radio Host

Please turn the page for more advance praise for *Pee-Shy*!

"A suspenseful page-turner that repeatedly made me laugh and cry. Spinelli poignantly recounts his childhood sexual abuse as well as a courageous struggle to come to terms with that experience as an adult. *Pee-Shy* is a powerful dose of non-sugar-coated reality, skillfully written with wit, humor, and much human feeling. Anyone wishing to see how one takes control of one's life and moves beyond victimhood status should read it."

—Jack Drescher, MD, Emeritus Editor of the *Journal of Gay and Lesbian Mental Health* and author of *Psychoanalytic Therapy and the Gay Man*

"His first-person narrative illuminates the psychological, medical, familial, and legal aspects of this pressing social problem as no academic approach could do. We are fortunate that Spinelli possesses the extraordinary courage that justice in this realm requires."

—Kenji Yoshino, author of *Covering*

"Frank Spinelli joins the ranks of courageous survivors of boyhood sexual abuse who have gone public about their trauma. The book, both evocative and chilling, makes us rethink how as a society we deal with those who hurt our vulnerable children."

—Richard Gartner, PhD, author of *Beyond Betrayal*

PEE-SHY

FRANK SPINELLI

KENSINGTON BOOKS
www.kensingtonbooks.com

The names and identifying details of some characters in this book have been changed.

KENSINGTON BOOKS are published by

Kensington Publishing Corp.
119 West 40th Street
New York, NY 10018

All Kensington titles, imprints, and distributed lines are available at special quantity discounts for bulk purchases for sales promotion, premiums, fund-raising, and educational or institutional use.

Special book excerpts or customized printings can also be created to fit specific needs. For details, write or phone the office of the Kensington Special Sales Manager: Kensington Publishing Corp., 119 West 40th Street, New York, NY 10018. Attn. Special Sales Department. Phone: 1-800-221-2647.

Kensington and the K logo Reg. U.S. Pat. & TM Off.

ISBN-13: 978-0-7582-9132-5
ISBN-10: 0-7582-9132-9
First Kensington Trade Paperback Printing: January 2014

eISBN-13: 978-0-7582-9133-2
eISBN-10: 0-7582-9133-7
First Kensington Electronic Edition: January 2014

10 9 8 7 6 5 4 3 2 1

Printed in the United States of America

For Chad

Contents

Part III

PROLOGUE

BILL CAME BACK TO ME IN A DREAM during the winter of 2008. I saw myself as a little boy standing in the doorway of my parents' home with my nose pressed against the screen waiting for him. As soon as his red truck appeared, the one with the storage shed built on the back that looked like a little house, I bolted outside. A warm spring breeze caressed my face as I raced across the lawn. Just as I reached the car, I woke up.

Alone in bed, I could still see his bearish face, the receding hairline, and those soft blue eyes as clearly as if he was sleeping there next to me in the dark. Soon more memories seeped out from the crevices of my brain, and it was 1978 again—the year I turned eleven and was first introduced to Bill. Over the years I tried to forget, but I can still see his bedroom with the drab wood paneling on the walls, the gunmetal-gray desk in the corner, and that iconic poster of Farrah Fawcett over his bed. *Too many teeth,* was my first impression when I saw it. I was nervous then. Why wouldn't I be? I had been called to my Scoutmaster's home for a private meeting. I never expected to be taken up to his bedroom, especially when I saw his old mother sitting stone-faced in front of the television downstairs.

Then suddenly, a growing uneasiness developed in my groin, and I knew that I would have to pee soon. That was easier said than done. I tossed and turned, postponing the inevitable for just a few minutes more.

PART I

CHAPTER 1

Careful What You Wish For

IT WAS A CHILLY, rainy day in June. I was standing in the foyer of my parents' home dripping wet and shaking in my Doc Martens combat boots. My mother was holding the ladder as my father changed light bulbs on the enormous chandelier that hung over the dining room table. When my mother noticed me, she let go of the ladder and firmly planted her hands on her hips. "What happened?" she asked.

My father wobbled unsteadily. "Hold the ladder," he ordered.

But my mother had something more important to deal with now. "What happened?" she asked again, inching menacingly toward me. My father climbed down the ladder. Together they stood in silence, waiting for me to explain why I was home early from college.

I remember exactly how I looked that day: blue-black dyed hair, tattered Billy Idol T-shirt, rosary beads around my neck, vintage oversized herringbone coat, and my trustee boots that I wore almost every day even in the summer. I was a parent's worst nightmare, and all because I was cursed.

For many years, I thought my life was plagued by bad luck, or what my Italian family called *il malocchio*. Growing up on Staten Island, I lived in fear that I had been cursed. Even my mother said I had no luck because nothing came easily for me.

As a little boy I was bullied at school for being a sissy, and in high school I embraced this feeling of alienation by dressing completely in black and listening to punk rock. In college, I continued my rebellious ways and cut class to draw in my notebook and write bad short stories in the student center. After failing chemistry, I lost my scholarship to New York University.

The day I saw that F next to my name, I felt this peculiar sense of detachment because I had never flunked a class before in my life. Leaving school, I walked in a daze to the diner across the street and ordered a Spanish omelet, but I couldn't eat a bite. It took hours for me to get up the nerve to go home. Once I got back to Staten Island, I walked all the way up the hill to my house in the rain. As soon as my parents saw me dripping all over their white marble tile, they knew something was wrong.

"I failed," I said.

Then they began hurling questions at me in rapid fire. *How did this happen? What were you thinking? How will you get into medical school?* And my favorite: *How could you do this to us?*

I wasn't shocked by their response.

Ever since I was a little boy, I always dreamed of being a small town doctor. It began when I was eight years old and my parents bought me a doctor's bag for my birthday. Unlike their previous gifts—baseball mitt, toy rifle, Tonka truck—which were completely useless to me, here were the most peculiar instruments I had ever seen. Much like Felix the Cat, my favorite cartoon character, I now had my very own lucky bag of tricks.

Looking back, I know that *il malocchio* had nothing to do with it. I wasn't cursed. I was sexually abused at age eleven, and all the "unlucky" events that followed stemmed from being molested. But that was something my parents never talked about, like premarital sex or abortion. Then, in the midst of all their shouting, I realized I needed professional help—the kind my parents should have provided for me when I was a little boy.

My best friend, Victoria, referred me to an art therapist named Olga Koniahin, an edgy woman with an auburn Mia Farrow pixie who wore long skirts with bold prints and lots of jewelry. I met with her on Tuesday nights in a small office in the basement of her house, but I kept this a secret from my parents, knowing that they didn't believe in therapy. Telling family secrets to a stranger for money was considered foolish, especially since we had priests who heard confessions for free.

My sessions with Olga were the emotional outlet I needed. Within a matter of months, she concluded that being sexually abused had left me traumatized. This was complicated by the fact that I was also struggling with being gay. My rebellious behavior as an adolescent was a reaction to the shameful feelings I suppressed at having succumbed to my Scoutmaster—a man I'd grown to trust—and the unresolved anger I harbored toward my parents for the way they reacted after I told them. For years I suppressed these emotions, and throughout high school I denied my sexual impulses. Once I started college, these conflicting emotions became too much for me to manage. Losing my scholarship, according to Olga, was a cry for help.

Week after week, I marveled at how Olga was able to make sense of my life in such a short period of time. She felt I needed an outlet to express my feelings. I told Olga I liked to draw. She suggested I paint "in order to begin the healing process." I started off small at first and then moved on to bigger canvases. I presented each to Olga so that we could discuss its hidden meanings, and then I stored them away in my own little studio in the basement of my parents' house. I left a little piece of my unfortunate past in every painting, and over the course of the next three years, I graduated from college with Olga's help and eventually went on to medical school.

My parents were delighted that my life was back on track. Of course they took all the credit for my progress, but they were also conflicted, knowing that I was about to move out of their house for the first time. My mother never got over the NYU fiasco. If she had her way I would have commuted every day to medical school, but I was determined to prove them wrong. So for the next four years, I lived like a Jesuit priest, dedicating myself exclusively to my studies and remaining completely celibate.

That all changed once I moved into Manhattan to begin residency in 1996. My cousin Alex took me to my first gay bar, called Uncle Charlie's. Within a matter of months, I was dating men and partying in dance clubs on the weekends, high on life and something called Ecstasy and carrying on as though I was making up for lost time. Except once residency was over, I wasn't so interested in dancing in a sea of shirtless men, and I was faced with the bigger problem of finding a job.

Lying in bed, jobless and single, I wondered where life was going to take me next. Then it occurred to me that I needed to rediscover the strength I'd gained with Olga, because I wasn't going to find love or a job in a dance club. Luckily, I was offered a position in the HIV clinic at Cabrini Medical Center, and eventually I was promoted to clinical director. Meanwhile, I built up a private practice seeing patients in a very small office, which I dubbed the rat cage since it was located in a basement. Over the next six months, I saved up enough money to put a down payment on my very first apartment on West Twenty-third Street. Now I was a homeowner. It appeared as though my life was going in the right direction again.

Later that same year, I began dating a Russian named Ivan, who lived one block away from my new apartment. Fascinated by his background, I immersed myself in his culture, studying *Russian for Dummies* and reading novels by Tolstoy. He was very regimented and spent hours at the gym. Each night, I'd meet him after his workout and we'd eat sashimi at a local Japanese restaurant. Ivan was very strict when it came to his diet, and he hardly ever ate carbohydrates. On weekends, he treated himself to a glass of red wine. That was his only vice.

Ivan was also a nester and insisted we stay at his apartment. Most nights he'd watch CNN from his white leather bed eating unsalted almonds from a bowl on his lap. He often talked out loud to the television, commenting on the news. Ivan had strong opinions when it came to religion, politics, and relationships.

Several months went by, and we were sitting in our favorite Japanese restaurant. As always, Ivan took it upon himself and ordered for the both of us. "Just tuna and salmon," he told the server. "No rice!" It never occurred to him that I might have wanted something else for once. In that moment, I imagined what my life with Ivan was going to be like—the two of us together, eating raw fish and no carbs.

After dinner, still haunted by the revelation I'd had at the restaurant, I scanned Ivan's studio with new eyes. Suddenly, it occurred to me that he had decorated his apartment to reflect his myopic point of view. Everything was either stark white—including the painted brick walls, the parquet floors, and his leather bed—or jet-black, like his leather couch and replicated Barcelona chairs. Unnerved, I walked around in a trance. Was it possible that Ivan was as black-and-white as his apartment? The one saving grace was that Ivan introduced me to Eric. Once we met, we became best friends.

Eric was my age but looked much younger. He had wide-set green eyes, fair skin, and brown hair with blond highlights that he straightened with a flatiron. We both grew up in New York. Eric was born in Roslyn, Long Island, and I was from what he called the "other" island. In late November, Eric invited Ivan and me to a lovely dinner at Ruth's Chris Steak House, where he held a position as director of sales. That night I met his partner, Scott, a tall, lean man with dark hair, who was much more reserved than Eric. They were both Jewish and had been a couple for over fourteen years. At dinner, we discovered our shared fondness for television shows, particularly popular ones produced by Aaron Spelling during the 1980s and '90s, like *Dynasty* and *The Colbys*. Scott and I were also obsessed with entertainment award trivia. Throughout dinner he quizzed me on the Academy Awards (a topic I considered myself an expert on).

"Who beat out Glenn Close the year of *Dangerous Liaisons?*"

"Jodie Foster in *The Accused*," I said.

"Very good, Frankie," said Scott. Looking over at Ivan, he asked, "Where did you find this one?" Ivan just focused on his filet mignon.

After dinner we walked down Fifty-second Street trying to hail a cab. It was late, and all the Broadway shows were letting out. Ivan stood at the corner with his hand held out, cursing the cabs as they drove by while Eric and I huddled together, arm in arm, for warmth. "Do you remember the lyrics to *The Electric Company*?" I asked.

Eric jabbed Scott in the ribs. "Frank apparently doesn't know who he's dealing with yet." Then Eric pulled me toward him. "I am an expert on children's television. So if you want to go toe-to-toe with me, you'd better be prepared to go the distance."

After too many cosmos, I was feeling up for the challenge. "Oh really?" I said. "Well, do you know the lyrics to *The Magic Garden*?"

With an impertinent look, Eric said, "Do you want me to sing Paula's part or Carole's?"

It seemed I'd met my match. Right there on the street, heading down toward Times Square, Eric and I began belting out the theme song. The louder we sang, the more irritated Ivan became. "You sound like a couple of hyenas," he said as a cab finally pulled up to the curb. Eric and I ignored him and laughed so heartily that we could barely finish the song. That night felt magical: the glow of the neon signs seemed to loop around us like a tilt-a-whirl.

Later Ivan scolded me. "You were acting like a child," he said. "You should be more of a man."

Throughout my thirties, I spent most of my time trying to have it all—boyfriend, career, success—and feeling like a failure. Nothing changed because I hadn't changed, and as I saw it, there was only one solution. I had to get off the ride. After a year and a half with Ivan, we broke up just before my thirty-seventh birthday.

I told myself I would be strong without him. Now it was time to focus on one thing—my career. I promised myself I wouldn't date anyone seriously for at least a year. I dedicated myself to building my practice by day; and at night, instead of searching hopelessly for yet another relationship to consume my time, I decided to write.

Eventually, *Instinct* magazine hired me to write a health-care column. That led to a monthly appearance on a gay radio show, *Twist*, where I offered health tips. Several months later, I had amassed enough information for a book proposal on gay men's health.

Then something amazing happened. One spring morning in 2005, I woke up as usual to go to the gym. It was a typical New York day. The air was thick with humidity, and I could see the sun coming up over the East Side. As I strolled down the three long tree-lined avenue blocks toward the gym with my back-pack over my shoulders, I decided to stop off at a Korean deli on the corner of Twenty-third Street and Ninth Avenue to buy a protein bar. I never ate before working out, but for some reason I was starving that day. While I paid the woman behind the counter, something caught my eye. There was a sign in the win-dow of the building across the street. It read: DOCTOR'S OFFICE SPACE FOR RENT.

The perfect place for my new office, I thought to myself. It had everything I was looking for: it was on the ground floor, it was in Chelsea, and it was on the same block as my apartment. The Korean woman behind the counter coughed politely to get my attention. In her hand she held my change. That's when I re-alized there was a line of impatient people behind me. Immedi-ately, I grabbed the money and ran out the door. I never made it to the gym that day. After I copied down the phone number off the sign, I ran back home and called Eric to tell him the news.

When I inquired about renting the office, I discovered that that building was actually part of a twenty-acre complex and all the ground-floor units were designated for medical purposes only. I scheduled an appointment to see the office that after-noon. Eric joined me. He thought it would be a good idea to tell the Realtor he was my lawyer, so he showed up in character, dressed in a suit and a long raincoat even though it was very sunny. Since he had a master's in dramatic arts, he played it up, walking from room to room, asking the Realtor questions about price per square footage and negotiating a five-year lease once he heard the office was rent stabilized.

I watched Eric, trying my best not to chuckle as he paced around the room, hunched over with his raincoat trailing be-hind him like a cape. As the Realtor explained the building's rules for occupancy, Eric furrowed his brow intently. I had to walk away to avoid laughing. Leaving them to talk in the front room, I wandered off by myself, imagining what it would be like for me to finally realize my dream of practicing medicine in my own Chelsea office. Two weeks later, I signed the lease.

Since the office was small, even by New York standards, I consulted with a carpenter to discuss renovations. To maximize the space, he built a small alcove desktop to house my computer in the corner of the second exam room. Above that, I stacked the shelves with textbooks, journals, and research binders. It was my own private little nook, and every day thereafter, I researched ideas for my book once the last patient was gone. It was easy for me to become consumed with work and writing. Avoiding the dating scene, I stayed true to my vow not to get into a relationship with anyone for a year. Three years later, I was still single and about to turn forty. Although love had eluded me, I no longer believed that luck or *il malocchio* had anything to do with my future success. I proved to myself that hard work mattered more. As it turned out, the *Advocate*, the oldest gay publication, agreed to brand my book once I completed writing it.

On the verge of my fortieth birthday, I decided to embrace the new decade: I said good-bye to my thirties by throwing myself a small party with my closest friends in April. Eric helped me organize the dinner at STK, a trendy new steakhouse in the Meatpacking District. The party was held in a private room upstairs from the main dining area. There was a fireplace in the center surrounded by white leather couches configured into a small seating area.

We dined on petite filets and drank bottles of pinot noir. Toward the end of the evening, my guests sang "Happy Birthday" just as Eric carried out a red velvet cake. Before I blew out the candles, he whispered, "Careful what you wish for." It was then that I realized I had accomplished nearly everything I'd set out to do. I was a doctor in a solo private practice. I owned my own apartment and was about to become a published author. The only thing missing was someone to love.

Chapter 2

An Old Fixer-Upper

THE WEEK AFTER MY PARTY, I was in my office working when I received a phone call from Eric pretending to be a man from India who needed to see a doctor immediately about a hernia. Eric often made prank calls to the office. He had a large repertoire of characters and voices, but over time I'd grown keen to his various accents and it was becoming increasingly difficult for him to fool me. Most times I'd just let him go on until one of us broke out laughing. That afternoon, we were laughing so hysterically that my assistant, Gloria, had to intervene. "Doctor," she said, poking her head into the exam room. "Could you try to be a little more professional?"

I first met Gloria years earlier. She was the receptionist at the first practice that hired me out of residency. Having saved a good deal of money working in the clinic and the rat cage, I was able to offer her a full-time position. Gloria was a petite woman in her forties and a single mother born in Puerto Rico. To me, she looked more Mexican with her long, dark, pin-straight hair, round face, and down-curved nose. We had a wonderful relationship. She was very dedicated and enjoyed my sense of humor. Patients loved her because she was kind and remembered them when they called. However, she also had a fiery temper and had no problem showing it when patients became aggressive or when drug representatives insisted on seeing me without an appointment. I often referred to her as "my little Puerto Rican pit bull" because she ran my practice entirely by herself.

"Tell Eric you have to go," she instructed. "Ginny is waiting for you."

"Got to go, Mr. Gupta," I said to Eric. "Mama Gloria is making me work."

"But what about my hernia?" insisted Eric, still using that awful Indian accent.

"Good-bye."

Ginny entered my office holding a large cup of coffee. "Hi," she said. "I come bearing gifts."

"Well, then, come right in, pretty lady," I said, standing up to take the cup from her. "You brought me coffee? You can have anything you want."

"I just wanted to check in and wish you a belated happy birthday."

Ginny was a pharmaceutical representative who worked in the HIV division. I'd known her for years and met her while I was chief resident. She was a pretty, fair-skinned girl with long, straight blonde hair who always smelled like lilacs. I always made time for her because she was a genuinely sweet person. Unlike some of the other drug representatives who were all about business and the hard sell, Ginny was more like a friend.

Over the course of the past year, her life had changed dramatically. She had gotten married to a man from Ireland, moved to the suburbs, and was thinking about having a baby. Today, there was something different about her. Her cheeks were flushed, and she appeared eager to tell me something. I suspected she was pregnant. I was right.

"Wow," I said. "You really didn't waste time. You straight girls have that checklist down. Get married. Check. Get pregnant. Check. It's like once a girl finds a guy who's willing to settle down, they immediately become this other person. My sister Maria was the same way."

"Oh, come on," she said, playfully swatting her hand at me. "You know I've always wanted kids."

"Okay, Ginny, you can drop the act," I said sarcastically. "Remember when I was chief resident, and we used to go out on Fridays? I don't recall you talking about kids then. All we talked about was sex. But it's okay. I get it. *Yous a married lady now, Miss Scarlett.*"

Ginny dramatically flipped her hair behind her back. "So, what about you?" she said, trying to change the subject. "Are you dating anyone?"

"Me?" I said, sitting back in my chair. "No way. Men suck."

"You know," she continued, leaning in. "I know this really nice guy who used to work for my company. I'd love to set you two up."

"Why is it that when a straight girl knows two gay guys, she automatically assumes they'd be perfect together?" I asked. "There's more to it than just being gay, Ginny. Sorry, but no thanks."

"But why?" she insisted. "You'd really like Chad. He's such a nice guy."

"*Nice,*" I repeated. "That's code for *unattractive* or *out of shape.* I don't want nice."

"No, you want a bad boy."

"Ah, yes," I said, standing up to open the door. "That was true years ago. I've changed. I no longer desire the bad-boy type."

"So why not give a nice guy a chance?"

Grabbing her arm gently, I escorted Ginny out of my office. "Thank you for the coffee, but you're going to have to stop thinking of me as some old fixer-upper," I said, kissing her on the cheek. As lilacs filled my nostrils, I saw Ginny's face turn dour.

"I'm not giving up on you."

"I appreciate that. Congratulations on the baby. Come back soon now, ya hear?"

Ginny's visit left me wondering why I hadn't dated anyone since Ivan. Later that afternoon, I sat down by Gloria's desk and asked her the same question. She was one of the few people other than Eric whom I confided in routinely. She knew all about my dating past and was one of a handful of people I told about my history of sexual abuse as a child. I was drawn to her because, like me, she felt disassociated from her family, having also grown up with strict, religious parents. She described herself as a rebellious young girl who chose to have her baby without marrying the father. I thought she was incredibly strong and admired her choices.

Her answer was simple. "Love will come," she'd say. "You just have to be patient. In the meantime, keep writing."

For some inexplicable reason, I valued her opinion more than any high-priced therapist's. I took her advice. Over the course of the next several months, I devised a new routine for my weeknights: return home from work, eat Chinese takeout, and write. Since the deadline to submit my manuscript was quickly approaching, I worked feverishly every night after work to get it done. I created a profile on BigMuscle.com in order to amuse and distract myself and flirt with other gay men. One evening in August, while I was eating egg foo yung from a carton, I noticed a message from a man named Chad.

In his e-mail, he referred to Ginny and mentioned that she had been trying to fix us up for months. He wrote that he was looking through profiles and coincidentally found mine. I remembered thinking back to when Ginny visited me after my birthday. She'd described Chad as *nice*. She neglected to mention he was also hot. Attached to his e-mail were two photographs. In the first, he was wearing a baseball cap, a University of Arizona T-shirt, and jeans. The second was a close-up of his face. Unlike all the other men I ever dated, Chad had wholesome good looks, a perfect white smile, and the most brilliant blue eyes I had ever seen. He looked as if he belonged in a commercial for mouthwash or an ad for sugarless gum.

Unfortunately, Chad no longer lived in Manhattan. He worked for a pharmaceutical company in Boston and was in New York just for the weekend attending a business meeting. He wrote to ask whether I would meet him for a drink. I accepted willingly, but reminded myself that it was just a date and nothing more. As a rule, I never dated anyone who lived out of state.

I showed Chad's pictures to Eric on his laptop that night while we were watching television in his apartment. "Another blind date?" he said out of the corner of his mouth. "I thought you said you would never go on another one as long as you lived?"

"I know, but I don't meet guys like Chad. No thanks to you."

"Remember the time you went on that blind date with that guy who played the guitar?"

"He wrote me a song."

"Yeah, and remember how embarrassed you got when he tried to pay for dinner using a coupon?"

"Chad is not some starving singer/songwriter."

Eric then adjusted himself in his seat. "Remember the time you went on that blind date with Jason, who came back to your apartment and took a giant number two in your toilet and flooded the bathroom?"

"He was a pig. I chalked that up to bad Mexican food."

"Oh really," he said, sitting up and drawing his legs under his buttocks. "Remember Larry?"

I turned my head away. "Enough," I said, holding my hand up.

"The dentist," he continued, "the one who brought you back to his apartment, and there was a man standing in the corner of his living room alone in the dark."

"Eric," I pleaded. "How was I supposed to know he had a slave?"

"Frank, he had a *slave*," repeated Eric, pulling on his hair. "Who has a slave?"

"I don't know," I yelled. "He seemed like a normal guy."

"That's my point. They all seem normal in pictures."

"Eric, I haven't been on a real date for over three years. I deserve it. Besides, what are my options?"

"I'm not saying you shouldn't go," he said, reaching out and placing his hand on mine. "You should. It's just I don't want you to set yourself up again. Remember, he lives in Boston."

"I know," I said. "I've completely prepared myself for that, and I'm not going to fall for him. It's just a date."

Eric flashed me a sideways look. "Just don't say I didn't warn you."

I sensed Eric's disapproval was partly selfish. Since the day we met, we had become inseparable. Once my relationship with Ivan ended, Eric and I grew even closer. Although he was in a long-term relationship, Eric's nights were mainly unoccupied because Scott was a retail manager at Bloomingdale's and worked until the store closed. When I wasn't busy writing, Eric and I spent nearly every evening together. And even when Scott was home, we acted as if he wasn't there, carrying on like schoolgirls, gossiping about the people we knew from the gym or what was going on in the world of celebrity tabloids.

Scott often grew bored with us and retired early. On weekends, after Scott went to sleep, Eric and I stayed up with their dogs talking and laughing well past midnight. Inevitably, Scott would come out of the bedroom to scold us. "Girls," he'd say. "You're going to wake the neighbors with all that laughing." That earned him the nickname "the Governess."

On the rare occasion when I did go on a date, Eric was often cautiously optimistic, but with Chad, I suspected he felt threatened. I think even Eric realized that a guy like Chad didn't come by very often.

I ARRANGED TO MEET CHAD at a bar on Ninth Avenue called Kanvas. That Saturday night I arrived early and selected a seat up front so I could watch him walk in. I purposely picked a straight bar so that there would be no distractions. The last guy I'd gone on a date with had a serious case of gay attention deficit disorder. His name was Brett. We met on Fire Island after I resuscitated him from a GHB overdose. As we carried him to the ambulance, he woke up and stared right into my eyes. "You're beautiful," he said, before passing out again. Two weeks later, Brett called after he tracked me down through a mutual friend and asked me on a date. I knew rule number one of medicine was to never date your patients, but I reasoned that Brett was simply showing me his appreciation for saving his life.

We met at an Italian restaurant on Eighth Avenue. Before we were even seated, Brett called the server and ordered a gin and tonic. I asked for the same even though I hated gin. Brett then proceeded to talk and talk until our drinks arrived. Within ten minutes, I realized that this was the worst idea I had ever had because Brett kept staring over my shoulder. I watched as his pinpoint pupils followed each passerby until they were out of sight, and then his head shot back like an old-fashioned typewriter only to latch on to someone new who was probably more beautiful than me.

Glancing at my phone at Kanvas now, I noticed Chad still had ten minutes. Outside, the sun was setting, and the air was heavy with moisture. The windows to the bar were wide open, and tables were set up along the sidewalk with people enjoying drinks in the light of the early evening. I sat there at the bar wondering whether I'd worn enough deodorant and anxiously sipping watered-down vodka and cranberry from a straw.

Just after 8 P.M., a cab pulled up at the corner, and a tall, athletic man stepped out. When he turned around, I saw that it was Chad. He looked exactly like his pictures, yet in the dim light of the August sun his eyes appeared even bluer than in his photographs. My heart quickened. Before Chad entered the lounge, he checked the address against a folded piece of paper he was carrying, and I took the opportunity to swig the rest of my cocktail. Then he walked into the bar, and we looked straight at each other and smiled.

"Chad?" I said, standing up and reaching out my hand.

He nodded. "Hi, nice to meet you."

I sat down immediately because I was intimidated by his height. At nearly six foot, he was five inches taller than me. Chad apologized for being late and went into the details. While he spoke, I felt drops of sweat sliding down my back. The bar suddenly seemed very crowded, and I could feel the heat radiating from my body like steam. Then I remembered why I hated blind dates. Of course, it had nothing to do with Chad. He seemed perfect. The reason why I stopped going on dates was because of my own crippling insecurities, which always found a way to manifest themselves at the most inopportune times.

Then, without warning, I felt a tingling sensation in my bladder. I had to pee. Unfortunately, I knew the men's room at Kanvas had two urinals and only one stall. The bar was unusually crowded, and Chad had just arrived. There was no way I was going to attempt to urinate under these conditions. To distract myself, I remembered Eric's first rule of acting: always maintain eye contact. The trick was to stare at one eye in order to give the appearance of being focused. This helped me, because I was also flustered by how handsome Chad was. His smile was perfect: straight, white, and tartar free. With his buzzed hair, I imagined him sitting in a lifeguard chair, wearing aviator sunglasses with a whistle around his neck and rubbing suntan lotion on his body. "Do you come here often?" Chad asked, looking around.

"Not really," I replied. Just then, a group of girls gathered directly behind me at the bar. Their shrill laughter sent shock waves through my body directly toward my bladder, almost to the point that I thought I might pee my pants if another one erupted into hysterics. "It's really loud in here. Do you mind if we go somewhere else?" I asked.

"You read my mind," he said. "Let's go."

I sighed with relief.

Outside, the sky was orange and purple. It was still quite humid, and the streets were busy with people. Since I had to pee badly, I quickly scanned the neighborhood. Across the street there was a new Austrian restaurant, Klee. I had been there a few weeks ago and remembered they had a private restroom. I suggested we sit at the bar and have appetizers. Chad agreed.

Klee's décor reminded me of a lounge at a ski resort, with dark wood walls and a white tiled bar. Soft music played in the background, and the lighting was warm and dim. It was a refreshing change of atmosphere from Kanvas. Once we were settled at the bar, I excused myself to use the restroom.

"What would you like to drink?" he asked as I hurried off.

I was slightly tipsy by then, so I asked Chad to order me a cosmo, though I knew that even gay men considered it a girly drink.

Live a little. What do you care? He lives in Boston.

The restroom at Klee was exactly as I remembered: a single-occupancy toilet. Plus, there was a bolt lock on the door, not some cheap hook. I hated restrooms where only some tiny latch inserted into a little metal loop and anyone with the strength of a toddler could burst through. A good restaurant, in my opinion, should have a private bathroom with a proper lock. That's just common courtesy.

Once inside, I began the ritual: I unbuttoned my pants and pulled them down to my ankles. Then I began chanting, "Olga Koniahin, Olga Koniahin." When no urine came, I reached out my hand and pressed it up against the door, even though it was sturdy. This relaxed me. Meanwhile, I continued to chant, but still no urine. Beads of sweat collected on my forehead. I kept imagining Chad waiting for me at the bar, wondering what was taking so long. My chanting quickened. "Olga Koniahin, Olga Koniahin, Olga Koniahin." Years of experience taught me that there was a small window of opportunity before this escalated into a full-blown panic attack. I had to urinate now, so with my free hand, I began to twist my nipple, gently first, then harder, tighter, until I felt a surge of electricity shoot down from my nipple to the tip of my penis. All at once, like magic, a switch flipped and the urine flowed.

When I returned, Chad was waiting. His smile didn't fade the entire night.

"Here's your cosmopolitan," he said, sliding the pink drink over to me.

"Thank you. I know what you're thinking. He's gay and drinks cosmos. How cliché?"

"I drink cosmos all the time. Besides, being gay means you don't have to apologize for liking them."

"Good answer, Chad," I said, motioning for the bartender. "Do you eat carbs?"

He laughed. "Of course."

"Good, because they're known for their pizza here. I hope you like bacon?"

Chad made a yummy sound. "I love bacon."

Now I noticed Chad was drinking wine. "Are you a wine person?"

"I like white wine. I know red wine is better for you because it contains tannins, which are good for your heart, but I find red wine stains my teeth. Would you like to try it?"

"What did you swallow, a wine encyclopedia before you came out tonight?" I joked as I sipped from Chad's glass. An immediate wave of relief washed over me once I tasted the alcohol. I felt relaxed, realizing Chad wasn't crazy, or at least he hadn't shown me that side of himself just yet.

"Do you taste the buttery notes?" he asked. I shook my head. He laughed. "Don't feel bad, neither do I. I'm just repeating what the bartender told me."

"What is a buttery note anyway?"

"I'm not quite sure, but this wine tastes delicious." While Chad spoke, I felt myself leaning in toward him. Our legs were inches apart on bar stools. As the conversation went on, I lightly brushed my knee up against his. He continued, "I've been single for a while now. I actually don't mind being alone, but that's not to say I wouldn't want to be in a relationship if the right guy came around." Unlike the other men I'd dated recently, Chad seemed unpretentious, and his honesty was endearing. When the bartender approached us for refills, I placed my hand over my glass. I asked for water.

Our server arrived with our pizza and set down two small white plates. "This looks delicious," said Chad, serving each of us a slice. Throughout the rest of the evening, we carried on as though we'd been friends for years, but this false sense of security was short-lived: we'd soon paid the bill and left the restaurant.

Walking home, I remembered that Chad didn't live in Manhattan, and that made saying good night even more difficult. Before we reached my apartment, I quickly ran through a mental checklist of all the reasons why I shouldn't date Chad:

1. I would have to commute up to Boston every other weekend to see him.
2. I'd worry he was cheating on me if we were apart for long stretches of time.
3. I'd just started my own practice and needed to be in New York.
4. I won't move to Boston!

By the time we arrived at my building, I still hadn't persuaded myself why I shouldn't date this single, smart, handsome doctor. Anyone with an IQ above 50 would have jumped at the opportunity or left the right man for the wrong reasons. Yet I was not like everyone else. In the past, I'd often dated the wrong man, so how could I tell when a good one came along? In the end, I kissed Chad in front of my building in a dark corner where even the doorman couldn't see us. Chad smiled and said good-bye. I rushed upstairs to my apartment and burst through the terrace door. Leaning over the rail as far as I could, I watched Chad walk back to Tenth Avenue and hail a taxi. Standing there as it pulled away, I wondered whether I'd ever see him again.

Chad returned to Boston that Monday. We e-mailed each other sporadically, but I never offered to visit him. Several weeks later, he wrote to ask whether I was interested in going on another date. My actions must have been confusing. In an e-mail, I wrote: "I'm sorry. It's just that I can't begin a long-distance relationship right now." I hesitated briefly, remembering those blue eyes, that perfect, beautiful smile, and his easygoing nature, but in the end, I bit my lip and pressed SEND.

CHAPTER 3

Kitten Tartare

IN NOVEMBER 2007, a cardiologist named Ed offered to introduce me to a best-selling author whom I will refer to as Dean. "He's a great guy, a little eccentric but very sweet. He could give you advice on your book. I'll talk to him if you like?" I didn't refuse this opportunity because I was a fan of his writing. His offer also helped to lift my spirits. It had been three months since my last conversation with Chad, and I was worried I'd made a big mistake.

My cousin Alex had presented Dean's first book to me years earlier, and in handing it to me, said, "Read this. It's the story of our lives." Of course, it wasn't exactly, but Dean and I did share one thing in common—we were both victims of childhood sexual abuse. What interested me most about his books was that he didn't shy away from the grotesque reality of life, and best of all, he was openly gay. This made him even more accessible to me because my sexuality was something I'd struggled with until my late twenties.

Ed fulfilled his promise and made the introduction online. Later that afternoon, I received an e-mail from Dean himself. I was sitting in my office when I read it. I could hear Gloria in the reception area arguing with a patient who was refusing to pay his bill. Quietly, I pushed away from my desk, whirled across the floor on my chair, and closed the door gently so that I could read Dean's e-mail again without being disturbed.

My first reaction was to print his e-mail so that I could enlarge it on the office copy machine and then hang it in my waiting room like a piece of art. Immediately, I called Eric to brag. "Oh, look at you," he quipped. "I guess you think you're gonna have fancy new author friends to go along with your fancy new book? Well, I don't think so. You tell Dean that the job of best friend is already taken."

"Get serious," I replied.

But later, as I reviewed lab results in my office after hours, I glanced over at my dark computer. Gently nudging the mouse awakened the screen to reveal Dean's e-mail still open from earlier that day. I hadn't yet responded. Wanting to impress him, I'd agonized for hours, making several attempts but deleting them once I'd read them aloud. Finally, I settled for something succinct. "Thank you so much. I'm very excited. Any advice you can offer me would be greatly appreciated."

The next day, I arrived at work and discovered another e-mail from Dean waiting for me. I was like a child on Christmas morning as I opened his message and read through it with the giddy anticipation of getting exactly what I wished for.

Over the next few weeks, we exchanged e-mails regularly. His recommendations on how to promote my book were very helpful, but it was his outrageous comments and inappropriate suggestions that interested me more. Dean thought I should get as much publicity as possible. He subscribed to the notion that there was no such thing as bad publicity, even if it included pictures of me getting hand jobs from patients.

His e-mails had a frantic, maniacal quality, as though he was writing in a desperate race to empty his in-box. Words were often misspelled. Others were in all caps for emphasis. Sentences ended abruptly, while others ran on without punctuation. With each new e-mail I read, his words began to take shape in my mind. After several weeks, I could actually hear his voice in my head, shouting at the keyboard, as his hands failed to type fast enough to keep up with his dictation.

I, on the other hand, struggled over each response, checking my spelling and grammar as if he was going to correct it. Then, each time I sent off an e-mail, my pessimism kicked in, and I prepared myself for the possibility that he wouldn't write back. To my surprise, in a day or two another e-mail always arrived. It was easy for me to fall into this trap. I didn't really know Dean, except for what I'd read in magazines and in his books. To me he was a celebrity and now someone who had taken an interest in me. I found that very exciting. Yet, there was a little voice in the back of my head warning me not to put so much trust in someone I'd never met, but I didn't listen. After several more exchanges, I began writing to him every day. Eventually, he asked me more direct personal questions such as, why was I still single? (A question I despised.)

I wrote back my standard response: "I guess I haven't met the right guy yet."

He wasted no time telling me that finding a husband should be my first goal. When he was single, that was all he thought about, but as he put it, he was more high-maintenance, so I should have an easier time finding someone.

With each new correspondence, I felt a thin connective tissue forming between us, like an invisible umbilical cord. I found myself telling him secrets I had told only my previous therapists or Eric. I was convinced that if I was completely honest—revealed my most personal details—then he wouldn't become bored with me and stop writing. So, without ever discussing this with Dean, I embarked on my own quid pro quo in the hopes of maintaining his interest. My scheme was that he would then confide in me, and I would slowly reel myself into his world, clinging to and collecting that connective tissue like a ball of yarn.

I wrote, "I find myself attracted to the same big, hairy, domineering guys. All I want to do is get them to like me, and, then, once I do, I end up feeling trapped. Once my last boyfriend and I broke up, I decided to take a break from dating. I gave myself one year to be single. That turned into three. Now I've resigned myself to the fact that I'm not good at maintaining a relationship. And please don't call it a fear of intimacy. I go on dates. It's just that I find myself wishing I was home watching television before I'm finished with my appetizer. I know it's hard to have it all, but then again, I don't think I'm asking for too much. The last date I had was with a terrific doctor named Chad, but he lives in Boston. Are there no decent men in Manhattan?"

The next afternoon, while eating sushi at my desk, I nearly choked on a California roll when Dean's screen name popped up in my mailbox. According to Dean, honesty, bluntness, and the brutal naked truth were all he cared about. He appreciated my frankness, and for that, he presented me with his own personal e-mail address, which began with the words *kitten tartare*, on the condition I promise never to share it with anyone, including my best friend, agent, or even the pope. If I did, he said he would cut me out of his life forever.

The wasabi inflamed my nostrils as it seared through the lining of my esophagus, but I didn't feel anything except bliss. Dean agreed that "on paper," he didn't think I was asking for too much. Unfortunately, in Manhattan—specifically in the gay community—there was always another guy who was hotter than the one you just dated. Manhattan could be a revolving door. He pointed out that when you meet a guy and it's going well and things begin to feel real, something happens. A first fight, for example. That's when you see a side to him you hadn't seen before, and so begins the process of compromise. In Manhattan you don't have to compromise. You just get rid of him and find another guy who doesn't have that particular problem. You trade up—and that becomes addictive. Everybody says, "I'm not looking for a perfect guy," but that's a lie. Everybody is. Dean predicted I would meet someone through my book. Whether a reader or someone I might meet promoting it—he bet this would happen.

"Predictions," I wrote. "I love it. Do you have a crystal ball or do you see visions? I use a Magic 8-Ball myself. I don't think love is in the cards for me. I'm damaged goods, have been ever since I was molested by my Scoutmaster. After two years, I told my parents, but the assistant Scoutmasters advised them not to go to the police. Even after I stopped seeing him, I still rode my bicycle past his house, hoping to run into him. Isn't that fucked up? Now as an adult, I just keep repeating this cycle of dating men who initially pay me little attention and then disposing of them when they finally do."

That evening, I returned to my apartment after a tedious day at work and began my nightly ritual: ordering Chinese takeout (roast pork egg foo yung), opening a bottle of wine, and chatting on the Internet. Once I'd finished writing my book, I spent most nights sitting on the edge of my bed and flipping through my favorite websites designed to entice desperate, single gay men. I returned to these sites nightly with mounting hopelessness, yet once I logged on and the parade of eligible gay men appeared on my screen, I was suddenly filled with anticipation.

Maybe tonight that special someone is waiting for me?

It was an addiction, but I convinced myself it was just a distraction that kept me away from bars and dance clubs. Framing it that way helped me to look past my loneliness, which was as cold and palpable as the congealing egg foo yung sitting on my lap. Slowly that loneliness grew bitter with each passing day, until eventually, as I scrolled through the seemingly endless photographs of men, I found myself passing judgment. Although I wanted to remain open-minded, it was impossible, particularly when someone's main photo was a close-up of his penis or, better yet, his anus. It struck me as peculiar that someone would want to introduce himself in such a way. So I was left to assume that Musclestudtop's penis was his best attribute as was Hungrybottomboy's anus. I was sure I was searching for men in the wrong places.

Often, I thought about registering on a legitimate dating site, but I always abandoned the idea, telling myself I was too good for that. Subconsciously I knew that if I enrolled on a site where you couldn't post a naked picture of your genitals, then I might possibly meet someone normal. Opening myself up to that possibility was terrifying.

That night, I was slightly more irritable than usual because Dean hadn't responded to my last e-mail. By 11:00 P.M., I signed off my computer, saying good night to all the men I had been chatting with. I threw the remaining egg foo yung in the trash, stacked the dirty bowl in the dishwasher, and dropped the empty bottle of chardonnay discreetly into the recycle bin down the hall. Once again, it was off to bed after a night of Chinese takeout and online dating, both of which left me feeling at first satiated but then tired and famished a few hours later.

The next morning, it was raining. I didn't wake up early enough to go to the gym, so I took my time getting dressed for work. Once I arrived at my office, I began another ritual: signing on to the computer, collecting the lab reports from the printer, and sipping coffee at my desk. In my in-box there was an e-mail from Dean. Sitting back in my chair, coffee in hand, I closed my eyes and smiled.

CHAPTER 4

Second Time's the Charm

B Y THE BEGINNING OF JANUARY 2008, my life continued to change dramatically. My book, *The Advocate Guide to Gay Men's Health and Wellness*, was finally published, and I was about to embark on a book tour. My publicist, Len, informed me that I was going to be on the cover of several gay magazines, and nearly everyone who knew me shared my enthusiasm that I had achieved my lifelong dream of becoming a writer. The day I received the first bound book from the publisher, I held it in my hands and thought, *If I die at this very moment, then at least I have something more than just my medical license to leave behind.*

That year also marked Chad's return to New York. He wrote me after New Year's, saying he'd moved to an apartment two blocks away. His e-mail also included an invitation to dinner.

We agreed to meet the following Thursday at my apartment. Luckily, this was the same day the cleaning lady came. After work, I raced home to adjust the lights and draw the blinds to three-quarters in order to create a romantic mood. Then I checked myself out in the mirror. Concerned that I wasn't as tan as I had been in August, I dimmed the lights even lower. After a debate over whether to light a candle, I decided instead to open the terrace door to allow the fresh air to flood my small living room. When the doorman buzzed, I jumped nervously. Within a minute, there was a knock at my door. I inhaled, waited five seconds, exhaled, and then opened the door, smiling at Chad. His summer buzz cut had grown nearly an inch, and he had a scruffy five-o'clock shadow. He was wearing dark blue jeans and a flannel shirt under a well-tailored wool coat with multiple pockets and zippers. Only his eyes were the same: blue, decisive, and penetrating.

"Well, hello," I said, breathing heavily as though I had just run across the room.

Chad walked in past me. We exchanged an awkward moment as I leaned in for a hug and he put out his hand to shake mine. Then, recognizing our misstep, we attempted the opposite gesture but failed miserably. I shifted gears and offered him a tour. Chad nodded politely as I led him into the bedroom, the bathroom, and then back into the living room. He reserved his only remark for when he noticed the door to the terrace. "Wow," he said. "You don't come across one of these every day."

"I'm very lucky. This terrace is the reason I bought the apartment."

As we stepped outside, the cold air nipped at our cheeks. Chad immediately craned his body over the railing to admire the view of Twenty-third Street. In the distance, the traffic lights twinkled green, red, and yellow. Overhead, the sky was a mass of thick charcoal clouds. The moonlight peeked in through the cracks. Looking over his shoulder at me, Chad smiled. "It's beautiful up here."

From where I was standing, I completely agreed.

WE ATE AT A NEARBY MEXICAN RESTAURANT, a quick walk from my apartment. Before I sat down, I reminded myself not to drink excessively.

One or two cocktails, and only if he orders one first.

From the beginning, it was clear that I was not going into this date with the same carefree attitude I had the first time. The stakes seemed higher, because now I didn't have the excuse that he lived out of town to deter me from becoming invested. Once our waiter arrived, Chad immediately ordered a margarita, and I nodded eagerly for the same.

"So what brought you back to New York?" I asked, as the server handed us our menus.

"The pharmaceutical company didn't get FDA approval for the drug I was working on. So they offered me a severance package, and I took it. Luckily, I was able to get another job with a medical education agency here in New York. Honestly, I was happy to move back. I didn't really like living in Boston."

Just then the waiter returned with a basket of tortillas, salsa, and our drinks.

"Oh, and here I thought you moved back for me," I said.

Chad's smile faded.

"I'm kidding," I added quickly. I noticed the waiter roll his eyes as he set down our drinks. I grabbed a chip and scooped up some salsa, but before I could get it into my mouth, the salsa fell onto my pants. The waiter grabbed a napkin off an empty table and discreetly laid it on my lap. I winced, then thanked him quietly.

"Well, cheers," I said, offering up my glass in a toast. As our glasses clinked, I noticed my hand quivering. That same hand placed my drink down, grabbed the napkin off my lap, and held it tightly under the table as my other hand began to twist it into a taut knot.

Chad decided quickly what he was going to eat. He seemed very comfortable with the menu. I reminded myself that he probably grew up eating Mexican food. So I asked whether that was true. His eyes lit up. "For Christmas Eve, my mother makes a traditional Mexican dinner with homemade tacos, chips, salsa, and my favorite: cheese enchiladas." Then he made that same *yummy* sound I remembered from Klee, and it made me giggle. "Why are you laughing?"

"The way you described the holidays with your family was very cute. Christmas Eve at my mother's is completely different. She makes seven fishes. No meat of any kind is served. It's very traditional, very Italian."

"It sounds delicious. Are you very close to your family?"

I thought about his question for a moment and replied, "Yes, I am. We're very close. In fact, my mother still makes each of us a birthday cake every year."

"That's sweet."

"It can be."

Dinner went by quickly. Afterward, we walked back to my apartment. I refrained from inviting Chad up. I was nervous, and sex would have been disastrous in my current state of mind. Instead, I kissed Chad good night and walked up to my apartment alone.

Later that evening, I found myself, as usual, on the corner of my bed, wearing only my underwear, and writing to Dean. "Chad looked even hotter than I remembered. I was a wreck tonight. Hopefully, I didn't make a complete ass of myself. He paid for dinner, but I think that's because he felt sorry for me."

The next day, Dean wrote back and told me not to play games with Chad. He suggested I call him to thank him for dinner. Then I should ask him out.

"Okay, Dad," I replied. "I'll call him in a day or two. I'll suggest another date this weekend."

Dean wasted no time replying. He was adamant that I shouldn't wait to call Chad. His feeling was that too many guys play games. All too often, even people who say they don't play games play them anyway because no one wants to look like a loser. Always be you, he encouraged, as clingy as you are, as damaged as you feel, and as hungry as you desire.

Unfortunately, I didn't take Dean's advice. Instead, I called Chad three days later to thank him for dinner. I invited him for drinks, but he politely declined, saying he already had other plans. Anxiously, I began throwing out several other possible dates, hoping to get Chad to commit to one. Finally, he agreed to a movie the week after the next. Once I hung up, I realized I should have listened to Dean. I blamed myself for playing games. And even though Chad agreed to another date, I was concerned that he had already started to lose interest.

That night as I tossed and turned in bed thinking about Chad, little did I know, my life was about to change irrevocably.

Chapter 5

Confessions of a Priest Stalker

"There he is," said Paul, rising from one of the waiting room chairs. "The man of the hour himself." He gave me a warm, loving, powerful hug. I looked over and saw his partner, Luke, was with him. He was holding a copy of my book. They had been together for ten years and had been my patients for nearly four. I always looked forward to their visits.

"We are both so proud of you," said Luke, placing his arms around us and kissing me on the cheek. I protested sheepishly, trying my best to sound as if the attention was embarrassing.

"Come inside—we have so much to catch up on." I led Paul and Luke into one of the exam rooms. As soon as I closed the door, Paul sat on the exam table and Luke took the seat in the corner. "Did you guys come in for a visit, or do you just want an autograph?"

"Both," said Paul with an impish smile. He was just slightly older than me but had the facial features of a cherub. Paul had taken it upon himself to act as my matchmaker in exchange for medical advice. He was frustrated that I was still single, and being a self-proclaimed relationship expert, he wanted me happily married by the end of the year. In many ways I felt as though he was the older brother I never had. "How does it feel?" he continued, referring to the publication of my book. "You must be so excited!"

"Truthfully," I replied, "it's everything I anticipated and more."

"Well, that's wonderful," said Luke. "You really deserve it." Luke had a warm, reassuring voice. Whenever he spoke, I thought he should be on the radio selling insurance, or urging you to make sound investments.

"Well, we have some exciting news," said Paul.

"You're pregnant," I interjected.

"No, but close," he laughed. "We were at choir practice last Sunday, and your name came up."

"How did my name come up?"

"Well, Luke and I were talking about you and your book."

"Wait a minute. You were talking about a gay men's health book at a Catholic church choir rehearsal?"

"Of course," said Luke. "You know Paul has a thing for priests."

He wasn't joking. Paul had confided in me years earlier that in high school, he used to flirt with priests during mass. Paul described how he made seductive gestures at the "cute young ones" from the front pew. Several times, his flirtations led to actual sex. "I was shameless," he admitted. "But if they stared back or did a double take, then I knew I had them. Then I'd check the schedule to see when they would be hearing confession."

"You were a priest stalker?" I asked.

"I was. I admit it."

The first time he told this story, I reacted casually, listening to Paul not as a victim of sexual abuse but as his doctor. I tried to temper my outrage because I genuinely liked Paul, but it was unimaginable for me to see him as this Sharon Stone character in *Basic Instinct*, sitting in the first pew, crossing and uncrossing his legs. Of course, he didn't know anything about my past, and there was a part of me that believed he was masking his history of sexual abuse with humor, as most victims do.

The second time he brought it up, I was treating him for an abrasion he'd sustained after falling off his bicycle on the way to choir practice. He was telling me about a new priest assigned to his parish. "He's so cute," he said as I dabbed Betadine onto his wound. "If only I was younger . . ."

Anger bubbled up inside me like hydrogen peroxide on a cut. This time I couldn't contain myself. "Paul," I said, "I don't mind you telling me that you find a priest attractive, but we've been friends long enough now that I have to say that it really bothered me when you told me that you had sex with priests as a boy."

"Oh Frank," he said. "Trust me. I was the aggressor. They were the victims."

"Listen to me," I said, wrapping the gauze around his knee and securing it with tape. "I don't care how precocious you may have been, it still doesn't make it right. Those priests were adults. They should have known better."

"I'm not condoning sex with minors," he said, getting up off the exam table. "I'm just saying that I wasn't a victim."

"I still think it's disgusting. I was molested by my Scoutmaster when I was eleven years old. I know you think your situation was different, but I'm sorry, there is no circumstance that makes it okay for an adult to have sex with a minor."

Paul's smile faded as he hugged me. In my ear, he whispered, "I'm sorry that happened to you. Now I understand. Please forgive me if I sounded insensitive."

From then on, we refrained from talking about priests, until now.

"Okay, explain to me, how did my name come up at choir practice?" I asked.

"Luke sings in the choir, and I play the organ at this parish in Long Island," continued Paul. "For some reason your name came up because we told the priest that our doctor wrote a book on gay men's health."

"I'm still trying to envision how that came about."

"I know it sounds bizarre, but this priest is very cool," said Luke. "He knows we're gay and everything. Anyway, we were at choir practice last weekend, and Father Roberts said that he remembered a boy with your name when he was assigned to a school on Staten Island thirty years ago."

"His name is Father Roberts?" I asked.

"Yes."

"Of course I remember Father Roberts," I said. "He was my altar boy instructor at my grammar school, St. Sylvester's."

Luke turned to Paul. "Yes, it must be him."

"There was also a woman who played the accordion . . . I can't remember her name," I said, knocking on the counter to stimulate my memory.

"Lucy!" they sang in unison.

"That's her. She also taught music when I was in sixth grade."

"How could anyone forget Lucy with the big tits," added Paul, swinging his arms in front of his chest.

"That's her," I laughed. "My sister Josephine thought Father Roberts and Lucy were having an affair."

"People still say that," muttered Luke under his breath.

"Some things never change."

Father Roberts was a tall, slender man with long salt-and-pepper hair and a thick beard. He was probably in his early thirties when he joined St. Sylvester's parish in the late 1970s. He was considered quite handsome, which was proven by the disproportionately large number of women who attended his sermons, crammed into the first few pews—that is, except for my sister Josephine, who called him the "Jesus Priest."

"Why would you say that?" I asked her once.

"Because he tries to look like Jesus up there on the altar," my sister replied, striking a pose with both arms outstretched to mimic the crucifixion, except her eyes were rolled up in her head and her tongue was hanging out to one side. "That Father Roberts really knows how to pack 'em in, if you know what I mean."

I disagreed. Unlike the other priests who were old and strict, Father Roberts had an effortless way about him. But it was his youth and conviction, not his good looks, that enabled him to be a maverick at such a stringent Catholic school, and he certainly made no apologies for being one. I liked that about him and looked up to him not only as a mentor, but also as a friend.

On one particular occasion, I stumbled into him behind the rectory. He was leaning up against a wrought-iron gate that led to the garden where Father O'Neil grew his famous red roses. I had just finished serving the early morning mass and was racing home to watch *The Partridge Family.* "Slow down, Frank," said Father Roberts as I nearly collided with him. He quickly raised his right hand above his head, but even in my haste, I noticed the crimson glow of a burning cigarette there. It was shocking to see a priest smoke, particularly Father Roberts.

In school, we were told that smoking was a sin, but we were also taught to revere our elders, especially priests and nuns, because they were accountable to a higher authority. I felt so conflicted standing there before Father Roberts that my face must have flushed the color of the roses he was standing in front of. Father Roberts, on the other hand, didn't flinch. The sunlight caught the smoldering fumes from his cigarette and outlined his languid torso dressed casually in monochromatic black. He appeared saintly among the roses. And even when he sensed my chagrin, he didn't correct his posture or snuff out his cigarette. Instead, he simply shrugged and said, "Frank, priests have vices, too, you know."

I scurried off and took the back road to my house just over the hill. Suddenly, watching *The Partridge Family* reruns wasn't so pressing. As I marched through the woods, Father Roberts's words echoed in my head. By the time I arrived home, I had reconciled that Father Roberts, like all the other parishioners, was not without sin, and it was comforting to know that he was human just like everyone else.

AFTER PAUL AND LUKE LEFT THAT AFTERNOON, I couldn't stop thinking about Father Roberts. I began to count how many boys he must have taught over the years. The fact that he had any recollection of me left me stunned and, oddly, flattered. It filled me with a sense of accomplishment and meant I left some impression on him.

That night I dreamed of Bill.

It was a knee-jerk reaction to think of both men when either's name came up. They were once considered youthful role models to the boys who made up the parish of St. Sylvester's School. Father Roberts and Bill Fox were two components of a very important team. As a priest, Father Roberts taught us the significance of family, religion, and community service, while Bill, a police officer and Scoutmaster, instructed us on discipline, self-defense, and honor.

In those days, I wore a uniform to school—blue slacks, white shirt, and a tie monogrammed with three S's running diagonally down the center, which always had to be perfectly aligned with my belt buckle. Since I was chubby, my uniform had to be custom-made, and my belt bore holes that my father made with a knife.

In the dream, my parents and I were wandering around the Staten Island Mall trying to find Billy the Kid brand jeans. The Boy Scouts were holding court in the center of the mall. Across the square, I saw a large man standing with his arms folded across his chest. It was Bill. He turned and looked directly at me.

I woke up with a start.

The next morning I was sipping coffee on my terrace thinking of Olga. She was the one who encouraged me to paint as a way to deal with my history of sexual abuse. Years later, I rediscovered the strength I gained through my sessions with her by focusing on my career and avoiding men who were versions of Bill. But now, I was tingling with the realistic possibility that I could face this trauma, not as a boy who stored paintings in a basement, but as a grown man who didn't want to hold on to the past. Suddenly, I felt compelled to find Bill Fox and understand why it happened.

But before I could do that, I had to pee.

CHAPTER 6

The Cop and the Kid

THE NEXT MORNING I SKIPPED THE GYM. After I finally got out of bed, it took me nearly fifteen minutes to pee. I spent that time standing over the toilet, chanting Olga's name and twisting my nipples.

The spasming that caused my urethra to collapse upon itself was something I'd suffered with most of my adult life. My urinary retention was often brought on by situations of extreme anxiety. This usually involved a fear of using a public urinal, especially when other men were standing next to me. I considered this a handicap. Not being able to urinate in a public restroom made me less of a man, displayed my weakness.

Standing side by side, leaning up against a piece of porcelain, spaced at very close intervals to other men—all of them conditioned to the humiliating urinal—I stood in many bathrooms, trying to look casual, waiting for a stall to open while I watched in amazement as other men went about their business, urinating effortlessly, even conversing with one another, all the while ignoring the fact that they were performing an extremely private act. Over the years, I took mental notes as they strode up to those mounted fixtures of masculinity and wondered how they did it.

I made multiple attempts throughout my life to use a urinal. Each time I walked up to one, I felt overcome with a peculiar sense of the unknown, as if I'd never seen one before or didn't know how it worked. Suddenly, I felt as though I was in a school play and had forgotten my lines. Then, I became extremely anxious and imagined everyone was looking at me. In my delusion, stares drilled holes into the back of my skull. I tried to temper my breathing to avoid hyperventilation. I concentrated on the cold tile before me or let my gaze follow the sweaty pipe as it disappeared into the wall.

Positioning myself in a tall stance, one trembling hand on the lever and the other practically choking my member, which I had pulled out through my zipper, I waited, idled, hoped, prayed, and then rationalized when nothing happened. Maybe a flush would trigger a response? I practiced this once, then twice, hoping that it would provoke a reaction. When it didn't, I felt a twang of terror, and I hung my head in shame, staring pathetically at the marble tile under my feet.

I could have counted on two hands how many times I'd successfully peed in public. The majority of those times occurred when I was inebriated: I was once so intoxicated at a nightclub that I pushed my way into the restroom, and noting a long line for the stalls, fearlessly walked right up to an empty urinal. Even with countless strange men standing there alongside me, I urinated effortlessly—and triumphantly. Most times, however, I was left to mimic urination by standing dumbly until two or three men had come and gone. Humiliated, I'd make a show of flushing and then walk over to the sink to rinse my hands—only to return moments later for a go in the stalls.

In childhood, this manifested itself initially as bed-wetting. I was eleven when it began. The same year I met Bill. My mother should have been furious with me when she discovered the urine-soaked sheets stuffed into the back of my closet. I was foolish: The stench of urine permeated the bedroom. My mattress was drenched, and even my Evel Knievel comforter hadn't been spared. Instead of going on one of her usual rampages, my mother quietly opened all the windows, washed the sheets, and carried on as if the entire incident had never happened. My bed, stripped down to the mattress, bore the only remaining piece of evidence—a yellow stain. My accident was covered up instead with a fresh set of linens and a spare down comforter.

Two weeks later, it happened again. When I awoke in my own urine that morning, I decided not to hide the sheets. Instead, I lay in my own wet, punishing myself. This time my mother confronted me. I was sitting at my desk, studying for a social studies exam. Standing in the doorway, she said, "Is there something wrong?"

"No," I whispered, staring down at my book.

"I thought I was done with babies. Only babies wet themselves. You're supposed to grow up, not down." I listened, tapping my pencil on my desk. "You sure there's nothing you want to tell me, Frank?"

"No."

Of course, my young brain couldn't comprehend that I had begun to wet the bed as a way to tell my parents that Bill was molesting me. Worse still, no one in my family thought that this sudden profusion of bed-wetting was a sign that something was wrong with me. The next evening, I even heard my mother arguing with my father about it. She blamed it on him, mentioning that it ran on his side of the family. Even my two sisters understood what was going on, and it became a family secret always referred to as "Frank's problem."

By fourteen, I stopped wetting the bed for good, but then something happened in my freshman year at Xaverian High School, an all-boys Jesuit preparatory school in Brooklyn. It was November 1981, and I was in my first-period Italian History class. My teacher, Mr. Sansone, had just begun lecturing when I felt the sudden urge to urinate. I tried to hold it in, but there was no use in pretending that I could wait until the end of class. Initially Mr. Sansone refused my request for a lavatory pass, but after watching me squirm nervously for several minutes, he finally gave in. I hurried down the empty hall, holding my groin and praying I wouldn't leak.

Inside the powder-blue restroom, I quickly unbuttoned my pants, unhooked my belt, pulled my aching penis over my white Fruit of the Loom underwear, and waited. Luckily, the lavatory was deserted and peaceful, with a faint smell of chlorine in the air. The window must have been open, because it was very cool. Standing at the urinal, staring at my penis, I sighed heavily, waiting for the urine to flow. But nothing came. Suddenly, a tangy scent filled my nostrils. Then I heard a hiccup echo from the nearby stall, followed by a relentless dry, hacking cough. A thick veil of smoke wafted over the stall and clouded me in that pungent scent. Someone was smoking pot. Footsteps clicked on the tile behind me. I turned my head around to look over my shoulder and saw Vincent Consalvo standing there, eyelids heavy, a sardonic grin on his lips and two long plumes of thick white smoke flowing out of his nostrils.

"Spinelli," he said. "What the fuck are you doing in here?"

Consalvo was a tall, dark-haired senior, who looked as if he'd never exercised a day in his life but was naturally skinny. For some odd reason—probably genetics—he was thick around the middle, so his body looked misshapen.

"Answer me," he said now. I ignored him while I stared down at my penis, willing it to function. Consalvo had paralyzed me. There was a pause, during which I felt his presence looming behind me. "You're not thinking about telling anyone, are you?" he whispered in my right ear. I glanced over. His dark brown eyes scanned my face. I wondered whether he could see how stunned I was. I held still and let Consalvo look.

"No," I blurted out. "I swear on a stack of Bibles."

"Then get lost."

"I—I will," I stuttered. "Just let me finish."

"Finish then," he said. The acrid smell of his dragon breath caused my stomach to churn.

"I really need to pee," I begged. "Please, just leave me alone, and I promise I won't say anything to anyone."

"No way," he said, pointing his long, bony finger at my nose. "Pee right now with me standing here."

"I can't!"

"Why not?" he shouted. "Are you some kind of fag or something?"

I turned to run away, but Consalvo grabbed me by the back

of the neck. The next thing I felt was a warm rush of wetness run down my leg. I froze, allowing Consalvo to discover what had happened. Then I heard a high-pitched cackle. As Consalvo's grip loosened on my neck, I ran out of the lavatory. In the distance, I heard the wheeze of the pneumatic door closing behind me. Faster, I headed down the hall toward my locker so I could get my coat and escape. My wet pants leg slapped against my cold thigh as the sound of Consalvo's laughter followed me home, and after that I was left unable to use a public urinal ever again.

It wasn't until I began therapy with Olga that I learned sexually abused children often start wetting the bed again as a call for help. Even though the bed-wetting stopped on its own when I became a teenager, I became profoundly pee-shy (in medical terms, *paruretic*).

Paruretic for nearly three-quarters of my life, I've become something of an expert in the field. It affects the urinary systems of nearly 17 million adults, many of whom were molested as children. Typically, paruretics are unable to urinate in public places. As an adult, I was resigned to the fact that I could not use a public urinal. Even in the confines of a public stall, there was always the possibility that my bladder might hold me hostage, negotiating with my brain to relax so that I could simply pee.

The morning after Paul and Luke visited my office and told me about Father Roberts, I couldn't even urinate at home. Was this handicap no longer just a part of me I could conceal by ducking into a vaultlike stall when I was in public? Something beyond my control was giving strength to my affliction. I worried that in time it would take over. Standing over my toilet, I stared helplessly into the medicine cabinet mirror. In that instant, I saw myself in the future being forced to wear a catheter or, even worse, bound to a dialysis machine for the rest of my life.

THAT MORNING I GOT DRESSED and headed to my office. The sky was clear, but the air was ice-cold. As soon as I stepped outside, I realized I wasn't wearing warm enough clothes. I bought coffee at the Dunkin' Donuts on the corner. Cup in hand, I practically ran the entire way. Once I unlocked the front door, I felt the rush of warm air as I stepped into the vestibule. It had been a cold winter, and I'd been leaving the heat running in my office overnight. That particular morning, it was draftier than usual. I left my coat on and headed straight to my little nook in the back of the office. My teeth chattered as I sat at my desk and waited for the computer to awaken. Even with the warm coffee cup in my hands, I shivered so hard it felt as if someone was shaking me. I looked at my watch. It was just after 7:30. Once I was online, I googled William Fox.

First, I checked the obituaries.

Twenty years ago, while sitting around the dinner table, my mother informed my sister Josephine and me that Bill Fox had died of AIDS.

"Get out of town," said Josephine.

"When did you hear that?" I asked in disbelief.

"This morning at church," replied my mother. "The priest said it at mass. You know when they ask everyone to pray for those who are sick or passed away."

Josephine was unable to hide her skepticism. "Why would a Catholic priest say that one of their parishioners died from AIDS? There's no way they would ever mention that word in church."

"I'm telling you, Josephine, the priest . . . he said it," insisted my mother, slamming her hand on the table so hard it rattled the silverware. Startled, we looked at each other with surprise. For a second, I almost broke out in laughter. My mother's anger always brought out her thick Italian accent, making it very difficult for us to hide our smirks. Unfortunately, laughing only inflamed my mother's fury, but Josephine had been right to question her. My mother had a reputation for making up stories. Whenever anyone tried to poke holes through her thinly constructed tale, she'd defend herself wholeheartedly, because as any good Catholic knows, it's not a lie if you believe it's true.

When I was six years old, I found my pet rabbit Snowball floating in a pot of water on the kitchen stove. His white fur had been skinned off and his pink eyes were still open. My mother swore he ran away, but that was a lie. That night when she served chicken for dinner, I knew it was fried Snowball. After that day, I never trusted my mother again.

Sitting at my desk trembling with cold that morning, I remembered the night I finally admitted to my family that Bill had molested me. It was 1981, just before my fourteenth birthday. The confession—which was how I saw it, despite the fact that I was the victim—finally came after I struggled with whether they would blame me. Ultimately, I confessed only because I wasn't willing to go on another hiking trip with Bill.

Over the years, my family's response to my abuse has become a great source of guilt for them; however, neither my parents nor my sisters ever thought to correct their error in judgment. Bill's death was the best resolution my mother could offer up as consolation, even ten years too late, and despite my disbelief, I wanted to believe Bill had died. Eventually, I accepted this information willingly, like a child clinging to the hope of Santa Claus.

AFTER SEARCHING ONLINE FOR NEARLY AN HOUR, I was unable to locate Bill or even a reasonable match—dead or alive. This didn't surprise me. Logically, I assumed most pedophiles would try to maintain their anonymity.

I heard the *click* of the front door lock followed by the stomping of boots on the tile floor in the vestibule. Gloria had arrived. I looked at my watch. It was nearly 9 A.M. I scanned the remaining links that came up under Bill's name, and clicked on a *New York Times* article written in March 1982. I sipped the remainder of my cold coffee and waited for my computer to bring up the story.

My computer was slow that day. I stared at the screen as my

leg shook up and down. Then the images began to click on one by one, and the headline appeared, "With Policeman, Boy's Lot Is a Happy One." It was about a seventeen-year-old named Nicholas who climbed onto the roof of a Bowery flophouse. Someone in the gathering crowd notified the police. Officer William Fox was called onto the scene. While the crowd chanted, "Jump, jump," Fox told the homeless boy he cared and offered him the spare room in his house.

I stared unblinking at the screen and reread the entire first paragraph. There was no photograph attached to the article, but I knew it was him. The cold coffee sat uneasily in my stomach.

I couldn't get the image of a suicidal teenage boy standing on a ledge out of my head. Bill must have been reassuring to Nicholas on that awful day. From experience, I knew that all it took was one look into those soft, pale blue eyes, and Nicholas would have trusted the man behind them, just as I had thirty years ago. His decision was easy: kill himself or allow this man, a police officer, to take care of him. Anyone in his situation would have done the same and reached out his hand to take Bill's, once he saw those eyes.

The article went on to say that the main reason Fox was able to take Nicholas in was because he lived with his widowed mother, Beatrice. Fox called her the "overall ruler of the house." My interactions with Beatrice would never have led me to believe that she was much of a matriarch. Several times I visited their house; Bill would have me sit in the living room with her while he finished working downstairs or made phone calls. Almost a fixture in her lounge chair, she always wore the same frumpy housecoat and stared blankly at the television. She remained catatonic whenever I was there, as if Norman Bates's mother from *Psycho* had developed an interest in game shows.

The article mentioned that a writer named Noel Hynd was writing a book about Bill and Nicholas with plans for a two-hour CBS television movie to be shown in the fall. I searched online and located a used copy of the now out-of-print book. Frozen by this sudden bombardment of information, I remembered another name from my past—Jonathan, my best friend from childhood and a fellow Boy Scout. We lost contact after graduation, but we had stopped being friends even before then.

"Doctor, your first patient is here." Gloria poked her head in. "Excuse me, but does someone have to go make pee-pee?"

I looked up. "What?" Gloria was staring at me with a comical expression. I realized that I was squeezing my crotch and bouncing up and down in my seat. "Oh yeah, I do have to go."

"Well, go now before you get backed up with patients," she said.

"I'll be right there."

Once Gloria returned to her desk, I quickly rummaged through my briefcase and located my wallet. Typing in my credit card information, I wondered where Jonathan was now. Then I remembered what he said to me that last time he'd slept over my house, months after I had confided to his mother about what went on during those afternoons with Bill. Though Jonathan had adamantly denied that Bill had ever touched him, that night he confessed everything to me. We were bunking in my parents' den and stayed up to talk well past lights-out. There in the dark he disclosed all the details of his experiences with Bill. "No matter what," he whispered, "we will always be friends, right?"

"Doctor!" Gloria called out. "The patients are waiting."

"I'll be right there!"

Chapter 7

The Blame Game

It was Wednesday night. I was sitting on the edge of my bed in my underwear reading e-mails when I saw one from Chad. He wrote to ask what I wanted to do on our upcoming third date. Up until that very moment, I had completely forgotten that we'd made plans.

Since the day I'd discovered Bill's book, I'd felt propelled through my week in a cyclone of memories, collecting mass until I felt weighed down by them. I worked each day, forcing myself not to think of Bill (even though he was all I thought about). Each afternoon, I rushed home to check my mailbox, waiting for Bill's memoir to arrive. It hadn't.

Stunned by Chad's e-mail, and our impending date, I felt overwhelmed with anxiety. I read the last line again, "What would you like to do tomorrow? You decide." This time I had to take charge. Immediately, I thought we should see a movie. I had this romantic notion that seeing a film, as a couple, would be something substantial we could mark our relationship by. In years to come, if we were still dating, whenever that movie played on television or if someone mentioned it in passing, Chad and I would recall it fondly as the movie we saw on one of our first dates.

My body relaxed as I checked the movie listings. My eyes scanned the films and stopped at a comedy called *Juno*. Purchasing the tickets online, I reassured myself that this was an excellent idea. Then I wrote back to Chad, "Meet me at the movie theater on Twenty-third Street and Eighth Avenue at 7 P.M." Once I hit SEND, I shut down my computer and fell back onto my bed. Staring up at the ceiling, I felt some of the heaviness of the past few days lift. In its place, I allowed some excitement to creep in. Lying there, I listened to the hum of the computer motor and made a snow angel in bed.

Thursday flew by. After work I checked the mail: still no sign of Bill's book. I directed my focus back to my date with Chad. In deciding what to wear, I layered a dark gray sweater over a black T-shirt and paired them with dark boot-cut blue jeans and black boots. Stepping outside that night, I noticed the rain had washed away most of the snow from the last storm. The sidewalks were still littered with mounds of residual ice blackened from passing cars and trucks. I marched steadily across Twenty-third Street with my head held down. The wind whipped violently overhead, mussing up my hair, which had been matted down perfectly with gel.

Inside the theater lobby, I was comforted by the combination of warmth and the smell of popcorn. Eating popcorn at the movies was one of my favorite pastimes. When I was growing up, my father popped huge quantities in my mother's spaghetti pot. On Friday nights, we watched television in the den. The aroma of kernels frying in olive oil crept up from the basement kitchen, making my mouth water, until my father arrived holding several bowls of hot, buttery popcorn.

I was early that night. The lobby was crowded even for a weeknight, mostly with gay men, flirting when their boyfriends weren't looking. I ignored them and searched for a mirror so that I could check on my hair. Glancing at my reflection in a candy counter window, I was horrified to see a mass of salt-and-pepper swirled on top of my head like a mound of cotton candy. I licked the palm of my hand and tried to mat it down again. I noticed Chad's reflection as he entered the lobby behind me. He was dressed in a fitted black snow jacket with gold zippers, black jeans, and charcoal-gray lace-up leather boots. He was rubbing his hands together and blowing on them. When I turned around, our eyes met and he smiled.

We crossed the crowded lobby. I took his arm, trying to navigate him past flirtatious eyes. I felt his body twinge with surprise at my touch, but he didn't pull away. "Wait!" I said, coming to a halt. "I forgot. Do you want anything from the concession stand? How about some popcorn?"

Chad flinched. He looked at me and began shaking his head violently, as though I had suggested liver and onions. "No thanks," he said. "I'm not a big fan of popcorn. It sticks between my teeth." I must have recoiled because Chad quickly followed that up with, "But go ahead. The chewing won't bother me."

In life there are three things that make me suspicious of someone:

1. People who don't drink coffee.
2. People who don't like Chinese food.
3. People who don't eat movie-theater popcorn.

I don't know what bothered me more: the fact that Chad didn't want to share a bucket of popcorn or his insinuation that chewing it might annoy him.

Skipping the concession stand, we took the escalator to the screening room on the second floor and found seats in the middle section on the aisle. In the dark theater, I stared at the outline of Chad's head against the light from the screen. I noticed the way his eyes sparkled as they caught the light. He was sexier to me now more than ever. Throughout the movie, I found myself leaning in toward him, wishing he'd reach out his hand and place it on mine. I tried to brush my knee up against his, but he didn't reciprocate.

I remembered the first night we met. Sitting at the bar, sipping cocktails and eating pizza at that Austrian restaurant, our legs had intertwined. That evening tingled with exciting possibilities. Back then, Chad seemed eager to get to know me, just as I tried to convince myself that he was too good to be true. Over the past five months, that energy still seemed to flow between us, but now in the opposite direction. After the movie, we left the theater and walked out into the cold and desolate night. By the time we reached the corner of Twenty-third Street and Tenth Avenue, several awkward silent moments had passed.

Kiss him.

I ignored the nagging voice in my head, worried that if I made any advances, Chad would reject me.

"Okay," he said finally. "Thanks for the movie."

"No worries. Hope you liked it?"

"It was different."

Kiss him.

We stood there, shivering uncomfortably for several more seconds before we finally said our good-byes.

That evening, I sat on the edge of my bed staring pathetically at Chad's picture—the one he'd attached to that first e-mail he'd sent five months earlier—blaming myself for everything that had gone wrong, feeling the frustrating need to recall what it was that excited Chad about me, and wondering how I could get him to feel that way again.

⎯⎯⎯∞⎯⎯⎯

LATER THAT MONTH, my publicist threw a book party for me at a restaurant in Hell's Kitchen. There was a private space in the back with a long staircase that led to a rooftop terrace. That night the sky was dark with heavy clouds and a crescent moon. My entire family came to support me. Even my sister Maria surprised me by flying up from Alabama. It looked like a scene from a Martin Scorsese movie. My five-foot mother was wearing a chocolate-brown wool suit with a bejeweled gold-lapel jacket and a pencil skirt. Maria wore a tight-fitted leopard-print dress, and Josephine had on a shimmering black-sequined top. They even managed to convince my father to put on a suit and tie. I wore the black suit Maria and her husband had bought me for Christmas.

Standing at the entrance, I greeted people as they arrived. Lounge music played in the background. On the far wall, a projector flashed images of me taken by the photographer Aaron

Cobbett. Eric and Scott arrived early. Seeing them calmed my nerves. Earlier my publicist had suggested I say a few words later in the evening. Usually I had no issues with public speaking, never have, but I was nervous that night. Though I wanted desperately to soothe my anxiety with alcohol, I decided to drink water instead. I knew that if I had even just one or two drinks, I'd end up slurring my words. Nothing would have been more embarrassing than to hear my inebriated voice amplified throughout the room. So I convinced myself to hold off on the cocktails until after my speech.

As more people arrived, I stood in the same location, accepting their congratulations. For so much of my adult life, I'd compartmentalized people, placed them in buckets: family, friends, business associates, people I slept with. Tonight they were all here, intermingling and having fun.

Nearly everyone I invited showed up. Initially, Dean thought he might attend but later cancelled. Since Chad and I hadn't spoken since our movie date, I decided not to extend him an invitation. That was one compartment I was not prepared to share with everyone else just yet.

When it came time for me to speak, I stood halfway up the staircase that led to the roof deck. Once the microphone was in my hand, I felt relief from the nervousness that had been brewing inside me up until that moment. Staring out and seeing all those familiar faces beaming with pride, I paused, wanting to savor this moment. I scanned the room. I saw my mother with tears in her eyes. There was Eric, giving me a wink. Even my cousin Alex appeared mesmerized, looking up at me. Then something more happened. I felt triumphant. And in that moment of joy, I remembered sitting in my office, googling William Fox and discovering his book.

I was overcome with shame. My eyes found my father staring up at me. I smiled at him, hoping to resurrect that feeling of pride, and then I remembered his face that night at dinner when I admitted to my family that Bill had molested me. His face had been as impassive as a corpse's. It hurt me to think of that now. I took a slow inhale. Everyone was waiting. Then I began to perspire. What had started as a fun, successful night was now erased by the memory of Bill. When the jarring sound of the microphone's feedback through the speaker system shook me from my trance, I began to speak. Ten minutes later, it was over. I was relieved. Once I was done and the applause faded away, so did any residual feeling of happiness, and in its place I felt empty inside.

When I returned home that night, I e-mailed Dean. "The party was great. I'm sorry you missed it. I made sure that not an ounce of alcohol touched my lips before I took the microphone. I wanted to be completely sober. I don't remember what I said, but it was wonderful to see a room full of people there to celebrate this accomplishment with me. I wish there was a way to put that moment in a pill so if I ever wanted to remember how all that love felt, all I would have to do is swallow that pill and all those warm feelings would return. I'm embarrassed to say that there was a point when I thought of Bill. He nearly ruined the evening for me, but believe it or not, I didn't obsess over the negative. Normally, I would fixate over this, but not tonight. Tonight it was all about me. I felt proud of myself, and that's something I'm not used to. Sorry I didn't get to meet you."

To my surprise, Dean wrote back immediately. First, he congratulated me for not obsessing over the negative. He was shocked because he thought of me as someone who usually obsesses over the bad stuff, and I should let the party mark a profound change in my personality. Regardless of everything else that had happened to me, Dean felt I was a genuine, kind person who had worked hard to become a doctor. Being single was the last piece of the puzzle that needed to fit into place. He ended by suggesting we meet the first week in February.

I got into bed and stared out the window, which was rippling with rain. I couldn't explain to myself the mixture of feelings I was experiencing: pride that I had written a book, shame that I let Chad get away, anger with Bill for destroying my party, and stupidity for lying about it to Dean. We didn't meet the week Dean was in town. He didn't mention it once in any of the e-mails that followed, and I simply convinced myself that he was too busy to make time for me. Of course, I was disappointed. Over the years, I've met other victims of child molestation. We're attracted to one another like moths to a bug zapper, picking up on the insecure cues we give off: being overly flirtatious, thriving on our desperate need for attention, and relying on self-deprecation to entertain others.

Initially, we're excited to learn about this commonality we share, but eventually it repels us from one another. We see each other as a mirror, reflecting our worst characteristics, and that becomes too unbearable. I called this the blame game. This was how I rationalized why Dean and I should never meet, and I convinced myself that it was better to know him online than not to know him at all.

CHAPTER 8

Out Like a Lyon

Two exciting things happened in February: My publisher arranged a book signing at Barnes & Noble in Manhattan later that month (a dream come true for me) and another in San Francisco at A Different Light in March. Even better, Chad asked me on another date.

It was a Thursday, what Gloria called "Tushy Day," when I received Chad's text. I was in my office, performing anal Pap smears. That afternoon, I was in consultation with a young man from London named Donovan. "Why don't you get undressed and I'll take a look down there?" I said. Just then, my cell phone jingled in my lab coat. It was a text from Chad. He wrote: *Hey, it's been a while. I've been traveling like crazy for work. Any chance you want to come with me to the Chelsea Art Tour on Saturday? It starts at 10 A.M. Let me know and I'll buy tickets.*

I responded immediately. "That sounds like a great idea. Where shall I meet you?"

That Saturday, it was unseasonably warm, but the wind, coming up from the Hudson, made it feel ten degrees chillier. I waited for Chad at the corner of Twenty-sixth Street and Tenth Avenue. Down the block, fifteen gay men gathered outside one of the galleries, but there was no sign of Chad. Standing there at the corner, I felt a sudden convulsion of embarrassment thinking about our last date. I promised myself that this time I was going to listen to my inner voice and be more spontaneous. When Chad suddenly appeared across the street, I quickly shook off that memory and smiled as he approached. He was wearing a dark brown suede jacket and blue jeans. And someone was with him. Suddenly it occurred to me that perhaps Chad didn't intend for this to be a date. By the time they reached me, the smile had faded from my face.

"Hi," said Chad, kissing me on the cheek. "This is my friend Michael Lyon." Michael was a tall man with pale skin and black hair. He was wearing a long, dark coat and tight black-and-white-striped pants that looked like Spandex. "Michael is a friend of mine from Arizona."

"Oh, are you visiting?" I asked.

"No, Michael lives here. He's retired but produces gay films." I looked at Michael, who nodded in agreement. "We should hurry," Chad continued. "Otherwise we'll be late."

We made our way over to the crowd. A short, balding man identified himself as the tour guide and asked for our tickets. In exchange, he handed each of us an itinerary of galleries and exhibits that were part of the tour.

On our way to the first stop, I asked Michael, "So which movies have you produced?"

Michael smiled and remained silent.

Chad stepped in between us and said, "Have you heard of *Slutty Summer*?"

"Can't say that I have."

Chad began to describe the story. All the while I kept glancing over at Michael. There was something suspicious about him, even more peculiar than his Freddie Mercury pants. Then I realized that he hadn't said a single word, not even "hello" or "nice to meet you," and I found that very bizarre. As soon as we entered the first gallery, I pulled Chad off to the side, and when I was sure Michael was out of earshot, I asked, "Is your friend okay?"

"Yes," he said. "Don't worry about Michael. He can take care of himself."

At the second gallery, we were directed to the third floor.

Since the elevators were out of service, we took the stairs. I felt as if I were back in grammar school, marching along with the others for a fire drill. Chad followed behind me as we ascended. When we were momentarily detained on the second-floor landing, I accidentally backed into Chad and our fingers touched. Feeling his warm skin against mine, I instinctively heard the voice inside my head urging me to be spontaneous, and I grabbed ahold of his hand. Better still, he didn't pull away, and our hands remained clasped tightly together until we reached the third floor. We lost contact walking through the entrance where the crowd funneled into the gallery. I didn't mind letting go because I knew he was mine. As I glanced over my shoulder, Chad entered the gallery and smiled. In that moment, I knew he felt the same way.

When Michael found us, he put his arms around our shoulders and said, "Hey, kids, what you say we cut out of here and go get some champagne?"

"You can talk!" I said.

Michael rolled his eyes. "Oh, of course I can talk. Honey, I was a lawyer, for Christ's sake. Chad said I could come along only if I promised to act like a mute so that I didn't monopolize the conversation."

"I knew it wouldn't take long," said Chad. "Guess you're paying for drinks."

—⚬◆⚬—

"Keep it coming." Michael tossed his Platinum American Express on the bar. I noticed the way the young, spiky-haired bartender's eyes widened when he saw that card. Within minutes, the bartender filled an orange bucket with ice and opened a bottle of Veuve Clicquot. Michael immediately began to engage him. "What's your name?"

"Michael likes them young," Chad whispered in my ear.

"I heard that," said Michael without looking backward. Chad reached over and grabbed two glasses off the bar. Michael swiftly turned around. "Don't even think about drinking one sip without a toast."

"Michael always has to make a toast."

"To my good friend Chad," said Michael. "And to my new friend, Dr. Frank . . . may you make beautiful babies together."

"Thank you," I said.

"You don't happen to have your prescription pad with you?" asked Michael.

"No. I don't usually carry it around with me."

Several hours and four bottles of champagne later, Michael was telling us about a trip to Brazil for Chad's fortieth birthday. He was simultaneously talking to us and the bartender, whose name we were told was Dylan. I felt myself swaying as I tried to maintain focus. "So our tour guide was driving us through the favelas when we got pulled over by some drug lords with automatic weapons," said Michael.

The day had somehow unexpectedly taken a turn for the better. Michael's presence brought Chad and me closer together, closing the gap we had been unable to fill on our own. Unfortunately, I didn't know how much longer I could hang on. In the fog of inebriation, all I heard were remnants of Michael's story mixed with Chad's laughter. Discreetly, I leaned over and whispered in Chad's ear, "Hey, I don't mean to be rude, but I've got to go before I pass out."

"Oh, okay," he said. Then he turned and interrupted Michael. "We're gonna head out."

Michael looked over at us, stunned. "Leaving so soon?"

"It was so nice to meet you, Michael," I said. The room felt like it was on a tilt. I didn't even wait for him to say good-bye. I grabbed my coat and exited the bar, clutching the edges of bar stools and random men's shoulders as I teetered out the door and into the welcoming brisk air.

That day Chad came home with me. Inside my apartment, we kissed. I maneuvered him into the bedroom as he unbuttoned his shirt. Clumsily, I kicked off my boots and pulled down my pants. I threw him down on the bed and we had sex, awkward but intriguing, exciting sex. Afterward, we lay quietly for a long while, side by side, naked and breathless. Finally, I asked, "So did you really tell Michael to pretend he was a mute?"

Chad laughed loud enough that it filled up my bedroom. "No, that was his stupid idea. I went along with it, knowing Michael couldn't keep it going. You heard him at the bar. He doesn't shut up."

"I feel awful leaving him there," I added. "Will he be all right?"

"Don't worry about Michael Lyon." Chad turned over and put his arms around me. "He probably convinced Dylan to go home with him by promising him a part in his next movie."

"I suppose you know him better than I do," I said, stroking Chad's arm with my fingertips. I felt the coarseness of his hair bristle against my touch. Then I had an idea. "Hey, what are you doing next week?"

"I'm not sure. I might be traveling again for work."

"Well, if you're in town, I'll be at Barnes & Noble on February twenty-eighth. My publisher arranged a book reading."

Chad sat up. "How cool is that? I've never been to a book reading." Then he stood up and walked into the bathroom.

While Chad showered, I slipped on my jeans, walked across the cold floor, and collapsed onto the couch. As I listened to the shower run, I began to worry about what would happen next. I suspected Chad would get dressed and come up with some reason to leave: busy day tomorrow, need to prepare for some big meeting, have to feed the cat. Whatever it was, I told myself not to appear disappointed. It bothered me that I wasn't a stronger person. Someone who could take charge and say, "Hey, you want to grab a bite to eat?" or "You know, that was fun, but I have to get up early tomorrow." For once, I wanted to be the person who navigated the relationship instead of waiting for someone else to tell me what was going to happen next.

The shower turned off. Chad opened the bathroom door. Steam flooded out, and he appeared in the doorway with a towel around his waist. His bare, white skin glistened. "Do you like Chinese food?" he asked.

"Yes, of course. Why?"

"There's a great Chinese place on the corner of Ninth Avenue. Are you hungry?"

"That sounds like a good idea."

"Great," he said, smiling, "let me finish getting dressed and we'll go."

Before he closed the bathroom door, I asked, "By the way, do you like coffee?"

"With Chinese food?"

"No, of course not. It's just a question."

"Sure. Who doesn't drink coffee?"

I shrugged. "I don't know, but whoever they are, I don't trust them."

Chad returned to the bathroom and got dressed. He may not have liked popcorn but two out of three wasn't bad.

THE FOLLOWING WEEK, I focused on the upcoming event at Barnes & Noble. Chad and I exchanged a few texts, but he never mentioned whether he was coming. Unwilling to ask him again, I decided that his appearance at the book signing would be a litmus test.

That night Eric and I agreed to meet at the bookstore on Eighty-second Street and Broadway. When I got out of the cab, I saw a poster with my book and my picture in the window. Instantly, I thought back to the night of my book party and remembered how I sabotaged that evening by thinking of Bill. I told myself that wasn't going to happen again. "Tonight is all about you," I whispered to myself, staring into the storefront window. Then I caught a glimpse of my reflection in the glass. I saw a little boy with a backpack wearing a green Boy Scout uniform and a red beret.

Rushing into the store, I found an employee, who directed me upstairs to the reading area and told me to look for Phil. On the second floor, I noticed chairs had been assembled and there was a lectern with a microphone. Surprisingly, there were several people already waiting. In the back there was a small room. Inside, I found Eric talking to Phil, playing the part of my agent and manager.

"There you are," said Eric, standing up to greet me. He was

wearing a dark suit. His blond highlights spiked up from his forehead.

"Were you at the salon earlier?" I asked.

"What are you talking about?" said Eric. "Are you referring to my hair? This is natural." Then he redirected my attention and continued, "Phil, this is Dr. Frank Spinelli, our speaker this evening."

Phil was a short, balding man wearing chinos and a striped blue-and-white shirt. "We'll begin just after seven o'clock. I'll make the introduction, and then you're on. Are you nervous?"

"Oh, don't worry about this one," injected Eric. "He's probably been in rehearsals for weeks. Am I right?"

I nodded.

"Great," said Phil. "Let me go check on things. I'll be right back."

When we were alone, Eric put his arm around my shoulder. "How are you?" he asked.

"Nervous."

"It's okay to be nervous," he whispered. "But you got nothing to be nervous about. Everyone is here to support you, especially me."

I felt my heart racing as I tried to assure myself that Eric was right. I was still haunted by the memory of Bill at my book party and could think of nothing else at that moment. Eric sensed there was something more than nerves bothering me. He grabbed my shoulders and spun me around to face him. "Hey," he said. "What's really bothering you?" He was staring into my eyes, searching for something. I hadn't told Eric that I'd discovered Bill's book, because I'd been so preoccupied with preparing for this night. Now didn't seem like the right time to tell him.

"I'm just feeling emotional today," I said. "I'll be fine once it begins. Go out there and tell me there are at least twenty people."

"Okay, I'll be right back."

I stood there, alone in that small room, looking around at the stacks of books. Then I remembered Bill's bedroom and a bookcase behind his bed where he hid his pornographic magazines.

When Eric returned he was smiling. "It's a packed house. I'm not kidding."

"We're ready to begin, Dr. Frank," interrupted Phil.

I nodded and followed after him. Eric looked me in the eyes one last time and gave me an assured nod. Then he left to take his seat. Phil instructed me to wait for his cue before I stepped onto the stage. From where I was standing I couldn't see the audience, but I felt their presence. Once I heard Phil's voice echo throughout the store, I panicked, thinking about everyone in Barnes & Noble listening to me.

When I heard my name, I walked out to a room full of applause. Standing up at the microphone, I saw so many familiar faces: My parents were in the first row. Josephine was behind them, sitting next to Eric, and to my left were Gloria and my cousin Alex. Everyone was there except Chad. Then, I noticed all the seats taken by people I didn't know, and that filled me with such an unexpected sense of pride that when I began to speak, the words came easily. There were no ghosts that night. I didn't see Bill or remember myself as a little boy sitting on his bed. I felt no wave of shame staring at my father, only gratitude that he had worked so hard to get me to this point. And then before I knew it, I was done. It was over. Then came more applause, followed by questions. There were so many, and it felt rewarding to answer them. For the first time, I felt I had achieved some level of professional acknowledgment.

Just as I was about to leave the lectern, I heard someone ask one last question. I looked up and searched the audience. With his hand held up, my cousin Alex asked jokingly, "Who's gonna play you in the movie?" The audience laughed, and Alex winked at me.

I smiled and said, "Mario Cantone, of course."

Phil then stood up and offered some closing comments. I sat at the table by the lectern and greeted everyone who bought my book. The crowd gradually dispersed. Eric suggested we go out for drinks after I was done signing books. As he disappeared down the escalator, I saw Chad standing in the back of the room. He waved. My litmus test was positive.

CHAPTER 9

Airplane Jeopardy

STEPPING OUT OF THE BUILDING, Eric waved his arms frantically overhead. We both had been looking forward to this trip for some time. Once my book became available, my publisher confirmed the date for a reading in San Francisco. I suggested Eric accompany me, knowing his mother and stepfather lived there. "This will be perfect," I told him. "I won't have to travel alone, and we can visit your mom."

"I don't see why we have to ruin a perfectly good trip by involving my mother," he muttered.

The driver helped Eric with his bags and opened the door for him.

"Oh, excuse me," said Eric, poking his head in. "Am I allowed to sit back here with you or should I ride up front with the driver? Or better yet, would you like me to get in the trunk?"

"Shut up," I laughed. "Do you have everything? Tickets, wallet, identification, cell phone?"

"Yes," he groaned.

"I don't think I like your tone."

"Well, you'd better get used to it," he said. "Because I'm not going to act like one of your groupies now that you're a published authoress."

Once we made it through the Holland Tunnel and I realized

there was no traffic to hold us up, I thought it was tim
Eric about Bill's book. I pulled it out of my carry-on and
it to him. "Speaking of books, look what I bought."

He stared at it with an expression of wonderment and shock.
"What's that?" he asked, taking it from me. He studied the
black-and-white picture of Bill and Nicholas standing side-by-
side on the cover. Bill was in his police uniform. Nicholas wore
a white button-up shirt under a winter jacket. They both smiled
in that awkward way people do right before someone shouts,
"Say cheese!"

"Who is this ugly man?" insisted Eric.

"That's Bill, the man who molested me. He adopted a boy
and wrote a book in 1983."

"What!" he barked. The driver looked back at us through the
rearview mirror. "When did you get this? Or better yet, why
would you buy this?"

"I had to," I said. "Before my book party, I spoke with two
patients who work with a priest who gave me altar boy instruction in grammar school. Since then, I can't stop thinking about
Bill. Then I went online and found out he not only adopted a
boy, but he also wrote a book about it. Eric, I know you. If you
were in my shoes, you would have done the same."

"Did you read any of it?"

"I read a little bit, but I decided to save it for this trip."

"Does he talk about molesting children?"

"Of course not, but I can tell from the first few pages it's
going to be one of those heroic-cop-saves-boy stories."

Eric stared at me with the most curious expression. Then,
suddenly, his demeanor shifted quickly to one of concern.
"Frank, I know this man hurt you," he said, taking my hand.
"But honey, why do you want to put yourself through this?"

"Because if all the adults involved back then had done what
they were supposed to, then maybe he wouldn't have been able
to adopt this boy."

"Reading this book and getting yourself all worked up is not
going to change any of that," he said, tapping his finger against
his skull. "Hello, Earth to Frank."

I felt my ears burn. "You don't think I know that?"

"Then why put yourself through this? Now, of all week-ends!"

"Eric, they let this man go free, and he adopted a boy. I have been living with the repercussions of his abuse for nearly three-quarters of my life." I paused to lower my voice. My ears were throbbing. "Bill took something from me that he had no right to. Are you trying to tell me that you wouldn't read this book if you were in my position?"

Eric grew quiet. His eyes shifted from left to right, as though he was scanning my face for some hidden truth. Then he replied, "Yes, I would read it, but be very careful. Don't jump feet first into something you don't fully understand. You need a plan."

I OPENED BILL'S MEMOIR as soon as the plane took off. Eric swallowed a sleeping pill and passed out with a *Star* magazine on his lap. After reading the first few chapters, I started to get angry. It was worse than I anticipated; it was a hagiography. Bill described his life in stages that ranged from dutiful son to heroic police officer, then dedicated father. Throughout adulthood he struggled to find a higher purpose. He wrote, "I think back on everything I ever learned in my religious instruction and everything I learned as a cop. Life is rarely a series of easy decisions. But I already know what I must do." Although engaged twice, Bill never married, and he even considered joining the priest-hood. It was his fateful encounter with a sixteen-year-old boy that finally satisfied the longing he needed to fulfill, however. "Cops develop a certain sense about children. You can tell a troubled good kid from a punk just by looking."

Halfway through the memoir I realized I was no longer just reading it—I was studying it. Over the course of the next two hours, I converted his book into a resource, taking notes in the margins and writing names on the back cover. I dog-eared pages I considered incriminating and circled sections that coincided with events I remembered vividly. Reading Bill's book was excruciating. With each page I heard his voice in my head, narrating his journey of self-righteousness.

In one passage, Bill described how Nicholas was considered for adoption by several people, one of them a "queer" man. Upon discovering this, Bill reassured the boy, "Don't worry. I won't let them get you." As I read this, heat rolled up toward my head, and I felt tiny pins and needles in my groin. Crossing my legs, I kicked Eric and woke him from his near coma. He stared at me, bleary-eyed. "You're still reading that book?" he asked, almost incoherent. "Are you sure you want to open this can of worms?"

I ignored him at first because I was intent on finishing the book before we arrived in San Francisco, but when he reached to pull it out of my hand, I snapped, "Why don't you take another Xanax and leave me the fuck alone?"

"I don't think I like your tone now," he said. With an appalled, injured expression, he got up from his seat, stepped over me, and marched down the aisle.

I should have gone after him to apologize, but I didn't. Instead, I opened the blind and stared out the window.

Throughout my life, I've suffered from loneliness and depression, but even during those dark periods, I sometimes wondered about Bill's loneliness. I reasoned the isolation a pedophile must endure was the most profound of all. Except now it was obvious to me that Bill was unlike any other child molester I'd read about. With this book, he'd rewritten the past so that he would forever be remembered as an honorable cop who gave a wayward boy a home. He converted his secret into an inspiring story. Bill was a sociopath. At his core was a repressed, deep-rooted rage. He appeared charming on the outside, but inside he was hostile and domineering; he saw his victims as merely instruments for self-gratification.

I closed the blind and got up. At the back of the plane I saw Eric talking to a male flight attendant and sipping a Diet Coke. I gazed down at my seat and Bill's book. Immediately, I felt the urge to urinate. Closing my eyes in dread, I walked hurriedly toward the back of the plane, past Eric, and into one of the available restrooms.

———⊶∞⊷———

THE TURBULENCE MADE IT IMPOSSIBLE FOR ME TO FOCUS.

Airplane restrooms are small, awkward, and claustrophobic even for someone my size. Usually, I'd wait until everyone was asleep so I could pee in private, without the threat of being interrupted. I didn't have that luxury this time. Frustrated, I began the ritual: I pulled my pants down to my ankles and hoisted my shirt above my chest. I stretched my arms out in front of me, held onto the wall, and braced myself as the airplane shuddered through the black sky. I looked at my reflection in the mirror.

Pathetic.

The last two episodes of urinary retention had been the worst I'd ever experienced. Recalling them only intensified the problem. I felt as if my bladder were being held up under a running faucet. I felt it expanding, growing heavy with fluid, as gravity pulled it down into my pelvis. My eyes focused on the wall, searching for a distraction to relax my urethra. A NO SMOKING sign caught my eye. I stared at it, took a deep Lamaze breath while chanting, "Olga Koniahin. Olga Koniahin." When nothing happened, I began rubbing my nipples.

Male nipples develop along the milk line, which extends from the armpits to the groin. Manual stimulation of the nipples relaxes the urethra and facilitates urination. In some men, this can cause vigorous orgasms. In this instance, I simply wanted to pee.

After five minutes, I began to relax. One or two drops of urine had even leaked out by the time I heard the fasten-seat-belts chime and my urethra immediately clamped down.

"Damn it!" I shouted.

Over the years, I had come up with two rules to deal with an airplane crisis.

Rule number one: if the flight time was less than two hours, I went back to my seat, crossed my legs, and hoped there were no delays.

Rule number two: if the flight time was longer than two hours, I had to weather the storm and remain standing over the toilet until I finished urinating.

I looked at my watch to determine the time change from East to West Coasts, but in my panic, I couldn't remember whether the West Coast was three hours ahead or behind New York. As the seconds ticked by, I heard the theme music from *Jeopardy* play in my head.

I'll take paruresis for a hundred.

More than anything, I was concerned that passengers were congregating on the other side of that flimsy metal door. I began to picture them as they lined up one-by-one, their concern growing with each passing second. Inevitably, they'd begin to look around and then at one another, worried that something was very wrong. Their imaginary conversations played out in my head while I stared down at the empty metal bowl.

"I saw him go in there at least twenty minutes ago," I pictured a heavyset woman in black leggings and a tight purple sweater saying.

"Really?" an older but much thinner woman, wearing low-rise jeans and a white T-shirt, would chime in. "Did you knock to see if he's still in there?"

The overweight woman would stare back, insulted. "I think I would have noticed if he came out of the bathroom," she'd say, pulling her sweater down over her hips.

While I ignored them (because I was chanting), they'd ask an older, female flight attendant with twenty years' experience for help. In unison they'd explain the brewing situation to her. "I know exactly who you're talking about," she'd say, scratching the back of her bleached updo. "He was so engrossed in his book that he completely ignored me when I came around with the beverage selection."

In reality, I was able to urinate that day, but only after repeating Olga's name fifty or more times. It started to flow, slowly at first, but at least I was peeing. I breathed a heavy sigh of relief. Regardless of everything that happened in my life, the one thing I was unable to control was my urinary system. During that flight, I vowed to take back that part of my body. I'd been tortured for far too long—and all because of one man.

Then, there was an actual tap at the door.

"One minute," I barked. Beads of sweat dripped from my forehead as I clenched my pelvic muscles to squeeze out the last remaining drops of urine. Along with it came a fart. Then I laughed out loud. The plane jolted through turbulent air. A thick braid of urine whipped up and down like a golden lasso. I laughed even harder. Once I finished, I pulled up my pants and flushed the hydraulic toilet. I opened the door and found several irate people waiting, just as I'd imagined. As I passed these passengers, I mouthed apologies. An angry older man brushed past me, entered the restroom, and slammed the door. I turned to an actual flight attendant and said, "I'm so sorry."

Saying I'm sorry had become my epithet in any uncomfortable situation. For one reason or another, I had been apologizing most of my adult life, even in situations like this, where I clearly was not culpable. How could I explain to these strangers that the reason I was detained in the bathroom was because I was molested by a man who went on to adopt a son? That only infuriated me further. My anger now propelled me back up the aisle. When I returned to my seat, Eric was unconscious again. I eased myself back into my chair, but I was unable to sleep, even with the quiet hum of the airplane motors outside.

Against my better judgment, I picked up the book and read on.

⸺◦∞◦⸺

NERVES COMPLICATED MY ALREADY ERRATIC MOOD on the day of the book event. A Different Light was much smaller than Barnes & Noble, and the location of the reading area was confined to a few folding chairs and a lectern by the store's entrance. It was not the grand debut I experienced in New York.

Beginning Bill's book on the plane had left me on edge. I decided to abandon the lengthy speech that I had prepared and simply read a few excerpts. Then I took questions. When it was over, I remembered little of the event itself, except for a nagging expectation that Bill was about to walk in the store at any moment. Later that evening, we dined with Eric's family. Throughout the meal, I had only one thing on my mind: get back to the hotel and finish reading Bill's book.

In the hotel room, Eric watched television from the king-sized bed and ate potato chips from a can. In the adjoining dining area, far enough away so that I couldn't hear the television, I was busy copying names from the book onto a small, complimentary hotel notepad. I cross-referenced these names with addresses and phone numbers I found on the Internet. Once I'd established a legitimate list of contacts, I picked up my cell phone and began dialing.

Eric bolted up in the bed. "Hang up, Nancy Drew," he ordered. "You just can't go and call people out of the blue and expect them to tell you where to find this guy. Are you out of your mind?"

Sitting there at the desk with my laptop, notes, and Bill's tattered memoir strewn everywhere, I saw how obsessed I'd become.

Eric got out of bed and knelt down beside me. "Listen, I can't imagine how painful this must be for you, but you need to be careful. If you're really going to do this, then you need a plan. This trip is supposed to be a proud moment in your life, and you're shitting all over it."

When I looked into Eric's eyes, I saw my old friend Jonathan, and I began to cry. Eric put his arms around me. I rested my head on his shoulder and let loose with tears.

"Honey, you were in love with this man," he said.

I pulled back, appalled by that thought, but Eric held me closer.

"You were a little boy, but you still loved him. He rejected you, and that hurt. Reading this book now will only hurt you more." We stared into each other's eyes again.

"I know, but I still have to do this."

When he nodded, I knew he understood.

"Okay, then come hang out with me for a while. Enjoy this weekend for a brief moment, and I promise I will see this through with you until the very end."

I felt torn. When Bill molested me at age eleven, I became two different people: I was a boy who went to Catholic school, but I was also a boy who had sex with a man. Over the years those two boys grew up to become both a man who was a doctor and a man who was split off from himself emotionally. Now I was divided again, but this time I knew what I had to do: I had to find Bill. Staring into Eric's eyes, the panicked look on his face, I made a decision to listen to his advice. I stood up from the table and walked back into the bedroom with him.

"Do I smell sour cream and chives?" I asked.

"Yes," he answered defensively. "But they're fat free."

"Did you save me any?"

"Only if Nancy Drew can take a break from solving her next mystery."

Chapter 10

Wheels Are in Motion

Back from San Francisco, I found myself staring in the bathroom mirror, rehearsing lines as if I was in a play. Bill's sister was in the White Pages. She still lived in the same house on Staten Island, just as Bill described in his book. Finding her couldn't have been any easier had Bill simply drawn a map of her neighborhood with a big red dot over her house.

I knew she'd lead me to him. I just had to strike the right tone.

Hunched over the vanity—a gargoyle dressed only in black underwear—I repeated my lines: "Hello, this is Dr. Spinelli. I was a Boy Scout many years ago in Staten Island, and my Scoutmaster's name was Bill Fox. I recently found his book and wanted to get in touch with him. Is this man your brother?"

I had to know whether Bill was involved again with the Boy Scouts, and I was more than curious to see whether—and what—he remembered of me. After all, I was the reason he left the troop in the first place. Mr. Castro and the other assistant Scoutmasters may have protected my identity, but surely Bill figured I was the one who'd told on him.

Staring at myself in the mirror with the phone in my hand, I saw that same little boy who ran to Bill every time he pulled his truck up to my house on Endor Avenue. *But you're not that little boy anymore*, I told myself. I dialed her number before I could change my mind. Then I gripped the receiver tighter and breathed deeply in anticipation of her greeting. My plan was simple: engage her as much as possible and lead her to believe that all I wanted to do was thank her brother for inspiring a young boy from Staten Island.

She's going to be tough as nails, a real firecracker.

The phone continued to ring.

You can do this.

Then it hit me. Eric's second rule of acting: stay committed to your character. Play the part with genuine passion, and you will be resolved of any nervous energy.

After the fifth ring, the answering machine clicked on. It was a prerecorded greeting provided by the manufacturer. Once the beep sounded, I exhaled and delivered my well-prepared, deliberately paced message: "Hello, this message is for Wendy. My name is Dr. Frank Spinelli. I'm looking for your brother, Bill Fox. He was my Scoutmaster from Troop Eighty-five in Staten Island thirty years ago. I recently read his book and thought I'd look him up and say hi. If you could give him my number, I'd really appreciate it. Thank you." I hung up, pleased with my performance but somewhat concerned I hadn't reached Bill's sister.

The next afternoon, I was in my office when I heard my cell phone ring in my lab coat pocket. I picked it up to silence it. Glancing at the number, I noticed a Pennsylvania area code. I stared at it briefly before dropping it back into my pocket.

Later, I listened to the message over lunch in my office. Even though thirty years had passed, I knew who it was as soon as I heard that voice. The low register of his tone, the slight lisp—it was all still there, only fainter, older, more distant. "Hey, Frank. This is Bill Fox. Gimme a call when you get this . . . I'll be up late."

A lump formed in my throat. I pressed PLAY again and listened to the message three more times. All I wanted to do was crawl under my desk, but Eric's voice chimed in my head. "You have to be careful. You need a plan." Knowing I still had patients to see, I decided to wait until the end of the day before I thought about my next step. An hour later, my cell phone rang again, only this time I recognized the number as Bill's. I stared at the phone as if paralyzed.

"It's either your boyfriend or your mother," laughed my next patient.

"Excuse me?"

"I only look at my phone like that when it's my boyfriend or my mother," he explained with a wry smile. "Just let it go to voice mail."

"You know what? That's exactly what I'm going to do."

This time Bill didn't leave a message.

At the end of the day, I sat down at my desk and planned my next move. Before I returned Bill's call, I asked myself what I was hoping to accomplish by speaking to him. What did I want? An apology? A confession? I didn't know.

LATER THAT NIGHT, I WAS ON THE COUCH napping when my phone startled me awake. When I leaned over to pick it up, I saw Bill's number again. Now I was certain he was more than just curious. I let it ring. Once again he didn't leave a message. I picked up the phone off the coffee table and saved his number under the name CHILD MOLESTER.

A twinge of electricity zapped me in the groin. Earlier that day, I'd had trouble urinating at work. For some reason, it was getting worse. Usually, I didn't have a problem using the restroom in my office or the one in my apartment. It seemed the closer I got to Bill, the more pee-shy I was becoming. That night I marched straight into the bathroom, pulled off my shirt, pushed down my pants, and began chanting.

"Olga Koniahin, Olga Koniahin."

Whispering her name over and over with my eyes closed, my thoughts drifted to a home out in the woods in rural Pennsylvania. I saw a red truck parked around back. The grass was overgrown. The gutters were rusty and water leaked from the roof. Faded, cracked green shingles lined the outside walls. Somewhere inside, probably in the kitchen, an old man nervously hung up the phone. His heart, pounding.

Then, like magic, the urine flowed effortlessly, but I kept my eyes closed and savored this image a few seconds more.

—∞∞∞—

ON HOLD FOR A PHARMACIST THE NEXT DAY, I heard my cell phone ring in the second exam room. Seconds later, Gloria walked in holding it up to my face. She looked terrified. The caller ID read CHILD MOLESTER.

I hung up on the pharmacist and took my cell phone from her. We exchanged concerned glances. I decided at that exact moment to answer it.

"Hello?"

"Yeah, hi, is this Frank?"

"Yes."

"Frank! This is Bill Fox."

"Hey, Bill, how are you?" I looked up at Gloria. She gave me a nod of encouragement.

"Good, how are you?" I heard him pause, as though he was drawing in an excited breath.

"Great." Then I paused. "Hey, listen, Bill. I'm in the middle of seeing patients. Would it be all right if I called you after work?"

"Sure," he said.

"Okay, talk to you later."

When I hung up, Gloria walked silently back to her desk. The rest of the morning, I could barely focus on work. Reviewing labs during lunch, I kept glancing at my phone, expecting Bill to call back again. I spent most of my lunch hour in the bathroom trying to pee.

At 1 P.M., I resumed seeing patients, but I felt distracted. Even one of my oldest and dearest patients, Wylie, a writer from Louisiana, wasn't able to hold my attention. "Okay, what's wrong?" he demanded, pounding his fist firmly down on his own knee.

"Nothing. Why?"

"Frank, I've been coming here for over ten years. I know

when you're not paying attention to me, because Lord knows, it doesn't happen often."

In the distance, I heard my cell phone ringing on my desk. This time, I jumped up and ran out of the room. Picking up the phone, I was relieved to see Eric's name.

"What's up?" asked Eric.

"Nothing," I said. "What's up with you?"

"Why are you out of breath? Is everything okay?"

"Yeah, I'm just busy."

"I just want to remind you that Scott is going to meet you at the train station on Twenty-third Street and Seventh Avenue at 7:30 P.M. Don't be late, because my husband, Alexander Graham Bell, doesn't own a cell phone."

"Oh my God, I forgot all about the show."

"You forgot about *Xanadu?*" Eric's surprise gave away to shock. "I don't believe it! You've been talking about this show since it went into previews. Wow, you really are overworked."

I rubbed my temples. "No problem. Tell Scotty I'll see him later."

Once I hung up, I noticed Gloria standing in the doorway. "Is everything all right?" she asked.

"Yes," I said. "Tell Wylie I'll be with him in a minute."

Gloria arched her brows. For the rest of the afternoon, her face retained that same uneasy expression.

THAT EVENING, I PACED MY APARTMENT, humming the music to the song "Suddenly" and trying to get up the nerve to call Bill. The lyrics seemed to say everything: *Suddenly the wheels are in motion.* It seemed ironic that I would talk to Bill the same night I was to attend *Xanadu* on Broadway.

In 1980, Maria took Jonathan and me to a matinee of the film starring Olivia Newton-John. Later that night, Jonathan slept over, and we stayed up late talking. In the dark we whispered stories about the times we spent alone with Bill. Jonathan finally admitted the truth, as well as that awful secret. My memory of that magical afternoon seeing *Xanadu* was forever tainted by what Jonathan told me. I was no longer the same boy after that night, and I never saw Jonathan again.

Impulsively, I picked up the phone and dialed Bill's number.

It rang three times before he picked up. "Hello?"

"Hi, Bill, it's Frank."

"Frank!" he repeated, drawing out my name as if it had two syllables. "How the hell are you?"

"Is this a good time?"

"Sure."

"You're probably surprised to hear from me?"

"Well, yeah," he said. "But a lot of boys from Scouts have called me over the years." The mere sound of his voice—low and husky with that lisp—was startling and confusing, yet slightly arousing. Initially he sounded distant, but with each breath, I heard the resonance in his voice growing closer as if he was approaching. I maintained my composure. "You really scared my sister, though," he added.

"Well, tell her not to worry. It's just that I found your book recently, and I wanted to talk to you."

"Oh, that's nice." He sounded sincere. "Well, if I can be frank, Frank? After my sister gave me your name, I looked you up in some of the old photos I have. Honestly, I can't put a face to the name. You were in Troop Eighty-five, you said?"

I flinched. I felt as though I had been smacked across the face. "Yes, I was."

"Hmm," he grumbled. "I think I remember you. After I got your message, I pulled out the ol' scrapbook. Did you go on that trip to DC?"

I felt a pulse of excitement. "Yes."

"Did you go on the three-mile hike or ten-mile river trip?"

"Yes," I repeated.

"You know, I remember your name. I'm just having trouble placing the face."

Do you need a picture in your ol' scrapbook of me wearing my uniform with my pants pulled down to my ankles? Would that jar your memory?

"Maybe you'll remember this," I began. "One time, I was left behind in the school parking lot because there was no room in the cars. My mother made such a big stink that you offered to drive me up to camp yourself the next day after you got off work."

He paused. "Yeah, maybe."

"Do you remember a boy by the name of Jonathan Duran?"

"Hmm, name sounds familiar."

"His father and mother were very involved in Scouting."

"Yeah, I think I remember him. You have to understand that three hundred boys went through my time as Scoutmaster. That's a lot of kids."

"You don't remember taking me on errands after school?"

Bill was silent for a moment. "I'm gonna have to go back and look at those old photos again." I sensed sincere regret in his voice.

Instantly I felt like that little boy again, anxiously waiting for him by the door of my parents' house. I decided to change the subject. "How's Nicholas?"

"Oh, Nicholas is all grown-up now," he said proudly. "Got married and has kids. They live in California. He's a police officer in Santa Barbara."

"Wow, you must be so proud. After I finished your book, I kept thinking what a great thing you did, adopting him. Do you see him much?"

"Not really. He didn't live with me very long, went back to live with his mother."

"That's interesting. Reading your book, I just assumed that you were still very much a family. You must have felt awful once he left to go back, after all the trouble you went through to adopt him?"

"You're not going to believe this." He chuckled. "But I've adopted a total of fifteen boys over the years."

I felt light-headed. "Fifteen."

"Yeah," he continued. "I still have three living with me, but they got what you call mental disabilities."

A sharp, stabbing pain struck me in my lower abdomen so

abruptly that I nearly dropped my cell phone. I grabbed my belly as the pain changed. It felt as though my bladder was twisting upon itself like a magician's cheap balloon animal. Without uttering a single word, I ran to the bathroom still holding my phone.

In the mirror, I saw myself as a surgical resident again, working in the emergency room at St. Vincent's. The paramedics had brought in a man in the late stages of AIDS, suffering from severe urinary retention due to metastatic lymphoma. The urologist came down to the ER immediately, took one look at the distraught man writhing in pain, and ran to the supply closet. He returned with a surgical tray. "We have very little time," he said. Opening the tray, he revealed a funnel-shaped object. "Put some gloves on, and get the Betadine solution." I obeyed, watching him pull back the patient's hospital gown to reveal an emaciated abdomen. What looked like a small beach ball pushing against his skin was actually his bladder. Taking the sharp, pointed end of the funnel, the urologist etched an X several times into the patient's skin directly below the belly button—as though he were engraving his initials into a desk with a protractor. "Go ahead. Do it."

"But without anesthesia?"

He glared back at me and slapped the instrument into my palm. "Now!"

I positioned the sharp edge of the funnel over the X. Beads of sweat dripped down my forehead. My heart was pounding in my chest. When I looked up at the man's agonized expression, I squeezed my eyes shut, whispered an apology, and plunged the instrument through his skin with all my might. After an audible *pop*, urine rushed out of the funnel like a fountain. The urologist slapped me proudly on the back and walked away.

Standing over my toilet, I now knew how that patient felt.

"Well, listen, if I ever get to New York," said Bill, "I'd like to meet up for a cup of coffee."

"Wait," I said. "Are you still involved with the Boy Scouts?"

Bill chuckled again. "Yeah, I'm still part of the Explorer Post in Staten Island."

"But you live in Pennsylvania?"

"I'm not supposed to since I don't live in New York, but I get up there about once a month. So they let me keep my position."

I eyed my watch. It was just after 7:30 P.M. I was already late, and Scott was probably worried. He knew I was obsessed with being punctual, but I couldn't break free. I held on, asking more questions, clinging to Bill like that eleven-year-old boy with his nose pressed up against the screen, ready to bolt out the door when his hero's red truck pulled up.

"Well, if I am ever in the city"—he said a second time—"let's get together and have a cup of coffee."

Let him go.

"Definitely."

"Well, talk to you soon."

"Good-bye, Bill."

I hung up and began chanting. "Olga Koniahin. Olga Koniahin." *Xanadu* began at 8:00 P.M. I was supposed to have met Scott ten minutes ago. My chanting accelerated. I knew I had to urinate at that very moment, before I left for the theater; otherwise I would have to suffer through the entire first act. Most Broadway theaters have few stalls in the men's room. Prior to showtime, the restroom would be overwhelmed with audience members waiting to pee before the curtain went up. Being late already meant I had to be lucky enough for a stall to become available when it was my turn to go. The equivalent of winning the lavatory lottery.

I couldn't chance it. I had to pee now. "Olga Koniahin, Olga Koniahin." Even the chanting wasn't working. My frustration was rising. I stared down at my penis, willing it to work. Looking up, I caught sight of myself in the mirror and turned away in disgust. I was furious with myself.

You're so pathetic.

"Let's meet for coffee," he said.

Sure, Bill, then we can talk about old times, like how you used to make me suck your dick?

"No!" I yelled out loud.

My voice resonated off the tile walls. Then I heard the neighbor's dog bark back. I was taken off guard. Miraculously, droplets of urine started to fall. One, two, then a steady flow. Air gurgled up in my bladder like a water cooler, and a cool swell of relief washed over me.

Scott was grinding his teeth when I arrived at the subway station. We made the show on time, but I was unable to concentrate. In the darkened theater, I replayed my conversation with Bill over in my mind, ignoring the performance entirely until I heard Kerry Butler sing that lyric: *Suddenly the wheels are in motion.*

I closed my eyes and saw Jonathan singing into his hairbrush. Now more than ever, those words rang true. I knew I could not dwell on the past or worry about whether Bill was going to come after me. Not after what I'd just learned. Now I was intent on exposing him. Not only for my sake but also for all the boys I believed he had molested, especially the ones who still lived with him.

It had begun. I had to find Jonathan.

Chapter 11

Something You Should Know

After *Xanadu*, I said good night to Scott at the subway station and walked home. Once I was in my apartment, I sat by my computer, wrote a detailed account of my conversation with Bill, and e-mailed it to Dean.

I stayed up for another hour, hoping Dean would write back. When he didn't, I went to bed. Splayed out in the center of the mattress, I stared up at the red light projected onto the ceiling from my router. When I fell asleep, I dreamed of Bill.

The next morning, when I signed on to my computer, I saw Dean's e-mail was waiting. He confirmed my suspicions: Bill had likely molested all the boys; molesters never do it just once. Bill had been doing it for years, over and over. Dean wasn't surprised Bill didn't remember me. If he were an alcoholic, I was just another glass of merlot to him. Dean's biggest concern was how far I was willing to take this. He suggested that I think things through and be careful. If anything, I should remember that Bill was not stupid. As far as my next step, Dean thought I should consult with a great lawyer and an excellent psychologist—the best that money could buy.

I signed off and got ready for work. I skipped the gym again. Walking to work, I felt shell shocked. Knowing that Bill had adopted fifteen boys was made worse by the fact that not a single one had come forward with allegations in almost twenty years.

The entire day passed like a bizarre dream. Patients arrived. I greeted them, listened to their complaints, and then wrote prescriptions. They were all faceless—one melded into the next without any clear distinction. When the last one was gone, I stayed behind. Alone in my office, I sat in the dark, not wanting to go home.

———

PER MY USUAL ROUTINE, I sat on the edge of my bed and wrote to Dean. "I had an awful day today. With his book, Bill has rewritten history. Now he will be remembered only as a decorated police officer and dutiful father. The more I think about it, the more it makes me sick. I can't live with myself knowing that boys still live with him. I couldn't pee tonight for over half an hour. All because of him. He has to know what he's done to me."

Later that night, Dean wrote back saying we needed to speak on the phone. He said he would call late the next night and that it broke his heart that I couldn't pee. When he read that line, he said the bottom of his chest fell out. He encouraged me to go to see a movie or get a facial. He insisted that I shouldn't be alone.

I was tempted to call Chad and tell him everything. But I was afraid of scaring him off. After my reading at Barnes & Noble, we'd started seeing each other regularly. Just last week, we ate takeout Mexican in my apartment. After dinner, we spooned on the couch, watching his all-time favorite movie, *Bad Romance*. During the movie, I asked him, "What day do you consider our anniversary?"

He didn't respond right away. I could feel his breath in my ear as he nestled his chin on my shoulder. "That's a good question."

I sat up to look at him. "We met in August, but then there was that period where we weren't really dating."

"You mean when you started seeing other people," he joked.

"No, I was working on my book, Mr. Smart-Ass. We started back up again once you moved to New York."

"Honestly, things really only started getting serious after your thing at Barnes & Noble."

I thought about that for a second. "Okay, then that date should be our anniversary."

Once I read Dean's e-mail, I picked up the phone to call Chad, but it went directly to voice mail. I didn't leave a message. Staring at the computer monitor, I contemplated my next move.

I have to find Jonathan.

Searching the White Pages online, I found a listing for *Duran, Anthony*. Was that Jonathan's father's name? The address was familiar. I picked up my cell phone and dialed the number. A man answered.

"Hello, Mr. Duran. My name is Frank Spinelli. You probably don't remember me, but I was good friends with your son, Jonathan, when we were in grammar school back at St. Sylvester's."

There was a pause. All I heard was the faint beating of my heart. In those few seconds, I prayed that this was the right man. "Oh, oh yeah," he said, his voice rising in recognition. "I remember you. What's it been, like thirty-some odd years?"

"Just about. Does Jonathan still live on Staten Island?"

"Oh no. He moved to Denver years ago."

"Really? Well, do you know how I can get in touch with him?"

"Why don't you give me your number? I'll pass it along to him when we speak on Sunday. Hold on. I need to find a pen and some paper." When Mr. Duran returned, I slowly dictated my cell phone number, repeating it twice.

"So how is Mrs. Duran?" I asked.

"Sharon? She passed away twenty years ago from lung cancer."

"I'm so sorry."

"It was sad, but we weren't married at the time. The smoking finally caught up to her."

"Jonathan must have been devastated?"

"He was. I don't think he ever really got over it, but he sure is going to be surprised to hear from you. I'll be sure to tell him on Sunday."

———

I SPENT THE NEXT NIGHT OVER AT CHAD'S APARTMENT. The first time he invited me over, I felt as if I'd walked into an art gallery. His loft had high ceilings, and everything was painted white. What I remember most about that day was that Chad's apartment smelled like it was brand-new. Everyone's home has a distinct odor. My neighbor's place reeked of peanut oil and curry. Kitty litter fumes hovered outside the young single girl's studio down the hall. My parents' house always smelled like an Italian restaurant.

That first time Chad invited me over, I was reminded of when I was younger and my mother and I would visit model homes for fun. I loved wandering around a home where no one had lived yet. It was like walking into a giant dollhouse, fully furnished, immaculate, and without odor except for the fresh smell of the brand-new furniture and carpet. Walking into Chad's apartment felt exactly like that.

Apart from all the white, there were hints of orange in the Native American rug and in some of the abstract artwork. There were several chrome sculptures on a far wall, which Chad had painstakingly hung. On the opposite wall, a sideboard that looked as if it belonged on the set of *Star Trek* was centered, with a fifty-inch flat-screen television on top. The only piece out of place was a carousel horse, which Chad had stripped down to its natural wood and refinished himself. I loved his apartment and told him it looked like a cross between a spaceship and the Playboy mansion. He was very pleased with my description.

I hadn't yet told Chad anything about Bill, his book, or my conversation with him earlier that week. As we relaxed on Chad's L-shaped couch, watching television, I nervously monitored the time, waiting for Dean to call. I had spoken to him only three or four times before: always brief, cordial conversations. Tonight was different. This was a serious matter.

"Is everything okay?" asked Chad. "You keep checking your watch."

I explained that I was waiting for Dean's call.

"You seem nervous," he said, picking up the remote control. He began flipping through the stations. "Is anything wrong?"

I took the remote back from him and began to systematically check the stations I frequently watched. Chad did not protest. "He's got some ideas he wants to go over with me on how to publicize my book." I settled on a program about the history of cinema.

"Does he have a boyfriend?"

"Of course," I said, rolling onto my back and placing my head on his lap. "He's been in a relationship forever. Why do you ask?"

"No reason," he said, reaching toward the remote again. I deflected his hand with my arm and moved the remote out of his reach. Then my cell phone rang. It was Dean. I jumped up and tossed the remote to Chad. Walking briskly into his bedroom, I answered the phone.

"Hi, Frank, sorry to keep you waiting. We just got home." His voice was unlike how I remembered. I detected a Southern accent, but I couldn't be sure. "So listen. I've been thinking about your situation ever since you said you talked to that motherfucker. First of all, you need to keep a journal every day. Write down details and how they make you feel. The next thing you need to do is find a lawyer and have him explain the law to you."

"I already did that. My friend, Peter Panaro, is a lawyer. He represented Jesse Friedman, who was accused of child molestation. The family was the subject of a documentary called *Capturing the Friedmans*. Peter said that the statute of limitations for my case has run out, but if one of those boys in Pennsylvania was to come forward, they could press charges against Bill. A victim in that state has until his fiftieth birthday."

"Then I suggest you contact Child Welfare in Pennsylvania."

"That's a good idea."

"The next thing you need to do is get a therapist. You need a very good female therapist. One who's not going to come on to you like the last one."

My previous therapist, Roger, had become so frustrated with me during our last session that he threatened to "hold me down and fuck me." I sat there stunned after he said it. I went home and e-mailed Dean. He wanted me to report the "fuckhead" and get his license revoked. Of course, I felt protective of Roger and defended him, even though, as a clinician, I knew he'd crossed the line. Dean insisted that I stop seeing Roger at once. I cancelled our next two appointments and ignored the messages Roger left. Finally, I decided to call him back. To bolster my confidence, I kept thinking about Eric's acting rule number three: listen and respond. I had to give Roger the chance to explain himself and then tell him how that made me feel. Except his explanation was that as gay men, our conversations often bordered on sexual. Even though Roger apologized, it didn't matter, because I swore I'd never go back to therapy again.

Lying on Chad's bed, I cringed at the thought of finding a new therapist. "I have been in and out of therapy my entire adult life. I'm tired of telling my story. It makes me sick to hear it."

"Well, then, that answers my next question, Frank. If you really wanted to do something, then you would take the necessary steps, but that's okay if you don't. This could potentially be the biggest thing you have ever encountered in your life."

"But even if I do this, do you really think I can put everything behind me?"

"No, but you can learn to move on. I still have a lot of holes in me, and no matter how hard I try, those holes won't close up. They get smaller, but they don't close. You told me that you have been angry for years over what happened, and how your parents reacted. Now is your chance to possibly correct those mistakes. But you have to be willing to go all the way."

In the darkness, I heard the television playing in the other room. "What about Chad?"

"What about him? Tell him everything. If he can't handle it, then good riddance. What you need right now is emotional support. Even if Chad was to hang in there with you, the reality is that he won't be able to give you the emotional support you'll need. It's too much to ask of him. You need a professional to guide you."

"Is that what you would do?"

"No, what I would do is wear a wiretap and visit that fuckhead. Then I would get him to admit that he molested me and throw his slimy ass in jail."

"Should I do that?"

"No," he said flatly. "To do that, you would have to have the skills of an Academy Award–winning actress. No offense, but you're no Meryl Streep."

I hung up and lay there in the dark, listening to my heartbeat. Five minutes later, I got up and walked back into the other room. I took the remote out of Chad's hands and sat down next to him. "I need to talk to you. It might be too soon for us to have this conversation, but there's something you should know."

Chapter 12

Sunday Dinner

The Sunday after I returned from San Francisco, I planned to talk to my parents about Bill at our monthly family dinner. Sunday with my family was a tradition like Christmas and weddings. Like most things Italian, they involved the Catholic Church and eating. Growing up, Sundays meant attending the ten o'clock mass, followed by an early dinner with the entire family, then a visit to my grandfather's house. When I was young, I remember waking up on Sunday morning to the smell of tomato sauce instead of bacon and eggs because my mother started cooking dinner as soon as she got out of bed.

Being brought up by parents who were from Italy didn't seem unusual to me as a child, because they were my parents, but eventually, as I grew older and saw how other families lived, I realized how different mine were in comparison.

My parents were from a small town called Teggiano in the province of Salerno. Michelina Cirone was just eighteen years old and studying for final exams when her cousin, Pep; his wife, Antoinette; and her brother Angelo, who was visiting from America, paid her a visit. Twenty-three years old and single, Angelo was under strict orders from his father to find a wife on his trip back to his hometown. But my mother had no interest in meeting him, even when Pep described him as a wealthy and handsome man from New York City. Of all people, it was

Michelina's best friend, Pina, who convinced her to have coffee with Angelo once she finished her exams. Reluctantly, she agreed out of respect for her older cousin, but the meeting didn't go well. Afterward, Michelina described Angelo as a pompous "*pseudo-Americano,*" whom she had no interest in seeing again.

When she returned home for the holidays, Michelina's parents coerced her into giving Angelo another chance. Pep had convinced my grandfather that, because his daughter was educated, she was going to be too smart for most men and therefore difficult to marry off. In the end, Michelina gave in, and seventeen days after their initial introduction, they were married.

When Michelina traveled to America by herself to meet her husband in New York that summer, she was horrified to learn she had been misled. Angelo was far from rich, and Michelina found herself alone in a new country, with a different language to learn and a husband to help support. For weeks she cried, cursing her family, her husband, and even God. Yet despite everything, she remained devoted to Catholicism and always respected her husband and her parents.

According to my parents, Italian children showed respect in the way they spoke and behaved. My parents expected their children to abide by their rules, regardless of whether we agreed with them. Disrespecting them was considered not only a sin, but it was disloyal and ungrateful. While I lived at home, I obeyed my parents. Once I moved out of their house, I found it difficult to visit them for years because I was still closeted. My parents considered homosexuality a sin, and returning home for Sunday dinners meant keeping this secret from them. Over the years, I grew to resent them for this, and before I told them I was gay, the thought of making that trip to Staten Island for dinner caused me so much anxiety that I could barely sleep the night before. In general, I avoided Sunday dinners as much as possible.

It wasn't until I was twenty-eight years old and living in Manhattan that I decided I needed to tell my parents I was gay. Until then, it was the secret we never spoke about, which was convenient for everyone at the time. Then I started dating someone and fell in love. Suddenly, coming out seemed so important: I wanted to share my newfound love with my family.

My plan was to tell my parents on my next visit home for Sunday dinner. It was customary for them to drive me back to Manhattan. That day, I offered to drive so my father could relax in the backseat. I didn't want the news to startle him into an accident on the Verrazano Bridge. As we passed the first of two powder-blue towers, I looked into the rearview mirror as my hometown faded away. It was time. I calmly and quietly told them I was gay. There was a long pause. For a while, I could hear only the car engine. I kept my eyes straight ahead because I couldn't bear to look at them. Waiting for their response, I drove their Cadillac across the bridge. It felt as if we were floating because an incredible weight had been lifted. Regardless if they accepted me, I was finally free.

Seconds ticked by. My father stayed silent, which was not unusual, while my mother started to ask questions, which was. Still, we were communicating. Had I not been an adult, I don't think my parents would have been as receptive. They were disappointed, but they understood. For now that was enough.

When the ferry pulled into the terminal that Sunday so many years later, I grabbed my knapsack containing Bill's book and made my way to the parking area where I knew my father would be waiting to pick me up. Once I stepped out of the building, a blast of salty air washed over me. Across the street, my father was standing outside his car, waving.

"Hey, Pop," I said. "Waiting long?"

"Long enough." I threw my knapsack in the backseat and got in the car. As my father pulled away, he asked, "So how's the doctor business?"

"Busy as usual."

"It must be nice to live off the misery of others."

"At least I get paid for it," I said. "How's retirement?"

"It's like waiting to die."

This banter—a mixture of gangster movie talk from the 1940s mixed with Henny Youngman–like one-liners—was the way we communicated.

"Pop, do me a favor and take the road over Grymes Hill. I want to see the Verrazano Bridge."

"Why?" he asked. "Are you planning on jumping?"

"Not today."

Driving the winding roads, I stared out the window at the large homes: ranches with bright green, sprawling lawns, and tall, Spanish-style houses peeking out behind neatly manicured shrubs. When I was young, I wanted to live on this hill one day. Now I could barely force myself to visit once a month.

"Is Josephine coming for dinner?" I asked.

My father continued to stare straight ahead. It was then that I remembered he was nearly deaf and always seemed to have trouble with his hearing aids. I didn't repeat the question. Instead I stared at him, thinking about how old he looked squinting through his glasses. He'd had a heart attack and undergone a quadruple bypass and an aortic valve replacement ten years ago, and after that, illness began chiseling away at his health, little by little each passing year. For the rest of the ride, I wondered whether I was going to look like this squinting old man when I turned his age.

It seemed inevitable. He was my father, and genetically I had half his chromosomes. But unlike other boys who had close ties with their fathers—throwing baseballs, watching sports, and washing the car on Saturdays—I was never very close to my dad. My father worked all the time. Then on weekends, my mother made us participate in Little League or basketball games. She thought it would be good for us, except my father wasn't very encouraging, because he didn't particularly like sports himself, having grown up on a farm in Italy. I'm sure my father didn't even know how the games were played, so our mutual reluctance to participate in these forced outings only strained what little relationship we already had.

Once we arrived at my parents' house, we entered through the garage. My mother was in the basement cooking. Like most Italians, she did not use the main kitchen. The first order of business assigned to my father when we moved into this house was for him to install an oven in the laundry room downstairs so my mother didn't have to get her "real" kitchen dirty.

Each time I came home, my parents' house seemed smaller, but now it did more than ever, since I had stayed away for so long. Walking down the hall toward the laundry/kitchen, I passed by the small makeshift studio where I used to paint. Two self-portraits were still propped up against the wall in the far corner. I followed the aroma of tomato sauce and cheese toward the kitchen. I stuck my head inside the doorway. My mother was standing over the stove with all four burners lit. "Hi, Mom."

"Is that my son?" she asked, setting down her wooden spoon. Over the years, my mother's appearance had changed little. Her once-dark hair was now dyed blonde, but other than gaining a few extra pounds, my mother was still a small Italian lady who wore Versace eyeglasses, lots of gold jewelry (even at the beach), and sequins whenever possible. Grabbing my face with both hands, she kissed my cheek and said, "You look tired. How was your trip? Where did you go, California?"

"San Francisco."

"Oh, that's nice," she said, picking up her spoon to stir the tomato sauce. The washer and dryer doubled as countertops displaying fresh baked loaves of bread wrapped in clean dish towels, a bowl of tomatoes picked from her garden, and a large block of Pecorino Romano. "Why did you go there? Was it for work or for the book?"

"It was a reading," I said, tearing off a piece of bread.

"You're hungry," she said. "Let me make you a dish because your sister and Joe are always late."

"No, that's okay," I insisted, dipping the bread into the boiling pot of tomato sauce.

My mother ignored me and placed two links of pork sausage on a plate. She cut a huge piece of bread off the remaining loaf and handed it to me. "Here. Sit down like a human and eat."

I reluctantly took the dish from her hand, knowing it was very easy to overeat at my mother's house. Over the years, I'd learned to pace myself.

"Did you sell a lot of books?"

"Not really."

"Oh." I heard the disappointment in her voice. My father walked in from the garage. "Angelo, go get your son a glass of wine."

"Huh?"

"Go get your son a glass of wine," she repeated, loudly.

He looked at me. "You want wine?"

"Of course he wants wine," yelled my mother. "Don't ask stupid questions. Just do what I say."

He shuffled back down the hall, mumbling under his breath as he waved his hands overhead. In the garage, my father stored his famous homemade wine in huge wooden barrels. Since it had a pungent, almost vinegary taste, Josephine had taught me to cut it with ginger ale. The soda diminished the acidic quality without compromising the quick onset of inebriation. When he returned with a glass, I didn't ask for ginger ale. I downed the wine and handed it back to him for more.

"Uh-oh," he said, staring into the empty glass. "Hey, Lina, I think your son has a problem."

My mother ignored him as she tended to her eggplant. Once my father returned to the garage for more wine, she looked over at me. "Come and help." She beckoned me with her wooden spoon. "Bring this basket of bread upstairs, but be careful. It's hot."

The kitchen on the main floor was brighter and larger than the one in the basement. My mother had already set the table and laid out slices of provolone and dried sausage for us to nibble on while we waited for my sister. My gaze wandered around the room as I chewed a thick piece of cheese. On the refrigerator, there was a photograph of a statue of the Virgin Mary. A scene from the Last Supper, carved in white marble, hung on the wall over the head of the kitchen table. Pictures of my niece and three nephews were everywhere. When my mother came up the stairs, she was balancing plates on both arms and in each hand like a seasoned waiter at a steakhouse.

"Did your father get you the wine?" she asked, setting the

plates onto the table. Before I even had a chance to respond, she began shouting down the stairs. "Hello, Angelo!" she yelled, flicking the light switch on and off. "Hello?" When he failed to reply, she walked back into the kitchen. "I don't know what to do with that man! He is completely deaf."

Realizing I was still wearing my knapsack, I removed it and set it down on my lap. Without hesitation, I pulled out Bill's book and placed it on the table. My mother stared at it as she wiped her hands with a dish towel. After several seconds, she looked at me blankly.

"Do you recognize him?" I asked.

"Who, this man?" she said, pointing to the picture of Bill. I noted a hint of recognition.

"It's Bill. Remember Bill, my Scoutmaster?"

My mother picked up the book to inspect it. Then she scowled. "He wrote a book?"

"Yes, he did. He adopted that boy in 1982 and wrote this book."

"I don't believe it."

"It's true," I insisted softly. Then I added, "I spoke to him on the phone."

"What!"

My father appeared in the doorway, holding a glass of wine and carrying a full bottle. I motioned him over. He raised his eyebrows. "Since when did you become such a drinker?" he asked, setting the glass down in front of me. I took another good swig.

"Do you recognize this man?" My mother waved the book in front of him.

"Huh?"

"It's Bill. Do you remember Bill?"

I gulped down more wine. It burned my palate like scalding pizza. I shoved a piece of sausage in my mouth to soothe the sting while my father stared silently at the cover of Bill's book.

"Did you hear me?" asked my mother. "He was your son's Scoutmaster at—"

"I know who he is."

"He wrote a book!" she shouted. "Your son called him."

My father flashed his eyes in my direction, but he didn't say anything. Then he set the bottle of wine on the table and silently walked into the den. My mother placed the book back down on the table and returned to the basement. There was no further discussion, and I decided not to bring it up again, even once Josephine and her husband arrived.

After dinner, I stumbled into the den, drunk, and fell onto the couch. On the far wall, above the television, was a painting of a fishing pier my mother had made in art class. The year after I graduated from college, I created my largest and most personal work for Olga.

Inspired by Van Gogh, I painted a rowboat lost at sea. I imitated his swirling brushstrokes from *Starry Night* in the turbulent water and then repeated this technique in the blackened sky above. At the bow of the boat, a lone Boy Scout stood with his hands tied behind his back and a hood placed over his head like a scarecrow, fastened around his neck by a rope. Also in the boat were several nuns—wearing traditional, large-winged habits—inspired by the costumes worn in the television show *The Flying Nun*. In the water, nuns were drowning, and in the distance, their habits transformed into seagulls flying overhead in the dark, chaotic sky. It was overwrought and self-indulgent, but I painted it in 1990 when I was a very angry twenty-three-year-old punk. When I showed this painting to my mother, she made no comment. Instead she studied it suspiciously, wringing her hands with a dish towel as she always did before walking away without uttering a word. I never painted again.

When I returned home after my first year of medical school for summer vacation, I noticed the fishing pier painting hanging in the den. It was exactly the same size canvas I used to paint my masterpiece for Olga. When I confronted my mother, she didn't hesitate to confess she'd painted over it.

"You never liked that painting anyway," was her response.

I cannot describe how appalled I was, staring into my mother's eyes, searching for a glimmer of remorse and realizing there was none. My painting was simply another casualty of her denial.

Seeing that painting in my inebriated state that Sunday afternoon only fueled my anger. Once again my parents had refused to talk about Bill. My father had turned his deaf ear, and my mother had avoided the truth as she always had, though not with a fresh set of sheets or layer of paint this time; now she busied herself with cooking.

I'm still ashamed of what I did next. I stood up and walked over to that painting. I wanted to rip it down and throw it on the floor. Instead I picked off a small area of paint in the bottom left corner with my fingernail. I did it just so that I could see a remnant of my former painting underneath. But I couldn't control myself, and I ended up peeling off a section about the size of a quarter. Now there was a circular window of dark blue peeking through the fishing pier, as though someone was staring out of a peephole from the other side of the wall. I backed away, horrified that I had damaged my mother's painting, and ran up the stairs to my old bedroom.

My mother hadn't changed my room much. Gone were the movie posters, and all my first-edition Stephen King novels were stacked out of sight in the closet, their once-glossy covers faded and the pages yellowed. Rummaging through the closet for a shopping bag to pack them in, I found a shoe box of Boy Scout memorabilia, including my old merit badges, my Scout belt, and other patches awarded to me for completing hiking trips. After all this time, this box was hidden in the back of my closet. I placed it under my arm and headed back downstairs.

TWO DAYS LATER, JOSEPHINE CALLED.

"I just got off the phone with Mommy," she said. "You've got her all nervous because you called Bill. Are you crazy?"

"I wanted her to know. She's the one who insisted he was dead. Now we know the truth. Plus, I wanted to tell her he adopted a son."

"Are you trying to give them both a fucking heart attack?"

"No," I said. "But honestly, Jo, I didn't tell them everything."

"What else?"

"Bill told me he adopted fifteen boys. He still has three with him, and they're handicapped. God knows how many kids he's molested, and all because nobody ever wants to talk about it. Maybe you don't remember what happened to me, but I live with it every day. So don't tell me I'm crazy for wanting to get this out in the open now."

For once, Josephine was speechless.

My relationship with Josephine had been evolving since our childhood, when she treated me like an annoying little brother. Years later, Josephine retained a bad-girl edge that she felt stemmed from being a middle child; she often said what was on her mind, not caring what other people thought. Deep down, I knew she was a softy, and learning her little brother was being sexually abused by a man was too much even for a tough girl like Josephine. All these years later, those feelings of guilt had surfaced.

"Oh my God," she said. Her words sounded muffled, as if she was covering her mouth. "I know we let you down. I'm sorry. It's just that Mommy sounded so worried. She thinks he's going to come after you."

"What would you like me to do, Jo? Because I'm not going to live in fear. He has to be stopped."

"Okay. Just please don't talk to them about Bill," she said. "Call me instead."

"Do you really mean that?"

"Yes, from now on, I want to hear all about it."

PART II

PART II

CHAPTER 13

Evel Knievel versus Billy the Kid

It was a month before my eleventh birthday. My mother had us walking the aisles of the boys' clothing department at Korvette's, searching for the right size Billy the Kid–brand pants.

"Ma'am, we don't carry Billy the Kid," said the woman sorting through clothes in the fitting room. "Try Sears."

When she looked up at me, I quickly diverted my eyes to avoid her pitiful stare. Billy the Kid was the only brand with "husky" sizes. Other resourceful adjectives that applied to fat young boys included "stocky" and "rugged." These three words made up the holy trinity of large, extra-large, and too fat to fit into anything else.

I suppose the people at Billy the Kid wanted to maintain a strong, masculine perception when parents had to look beyond normal sizes for their sons. This sleight-of-hand marketing didn't work on me. I knew I was fat, and I was grateful Billy the Kid made pants that fit my build, or what Chris Reynolds, a classmate, described as my "girly curve."

We were in the school yard after lunch. I was talking to Matthew Seabream when Chris interrupted us. "You know, Spinelli, you have a girly curve to your body." Matthew giggled, then bit down on his lip when he noted the hurt expression on my face. I wasn't sure how to respond, but I prepared myself to be enlightened.

Chris was the class know-it-all (or so he thought). He earned this title in fifth grade after he callously explained to a small group of students where babies came from. Julie O'Connor's mother had recently delivered a baby girl, and the class was congratulating her on the arrival of her new sister. At recess, we were all standing around Julie, listening to her coo about the baby, when Chris walked right up to us and said, "You know where babies come from, don't you? They come out of a woman's hole." Then he gestured with his hands over his crotch. Julie grimaced so vehemently it caused her cheeks to blush all the way to her ears. I just stared at Chris in horror. For years, I thought babies hatched from their mothers' protruding bellies like chicks out of eggs. Chris's assertion, although crude, made much more sense. I suppose that's why his unprovoked observation about my body shape bothered me so much. "Spinelli, you have an hourglass figure," he continued, "just like a woman's." Then he motioned with his hands to outline the exaggerated curvature of my hips.

Even before Chris told me about my deformity, I already suspected there was something different about me. Unlike other boys who had narrow hips and straight legs, I had a small waist, thick thighs, a protruding behind, and freakishly large calves. In order for me to fit into boys' pants, my mother had to purchase them two sizes larger in the waist so I could get the pant legs over my thighs. Then I had to cinch my belt as tight as it would go, otherwise they would be too loose. The end result made me look like a garbage bag left out on the curb.

Billy the Kid understood boys with "girly curves" and made sizes that fit different body types perfectly. Looking back, their pants were probably cut from a pattern that would have fit an overweight woman. They just branded their pants with that signature red-white-and-blue label so no one would know.

"Ma'am, you really should try Sears. They carry Billy the Kid," repeated the woman from Korvette's. Suspicious, my mother scowled and then marched away.

"I don't believe her," she said to the air in front of her.

I grabbed my father by the hand and pleaded, "Can we go look at the toys now?" He wrinkled his brow and shook his head. I could tell he was frustrated, following after my mother, who had us searching up and down the aisles for nearly an hour, like Ponce de León for the mythic fountain of jeans. When she finally conceded defeat, I swiftly navigated my parents to the toy section.

Immediately, I went for the Evel Knievel foldout camper/recreational vehicle (also known as the "Scramble Van"). I'd had my eye on that Scramble Van for months, ever since I saw the commercial on television. It came fully equipped with a gasoline can, toolbox, cycle jack and grease gun, fire extinguisher, and a captain's chair to give it the "final touch."

I was a huge Evel Knievel fan, and I can recall the precise moment when my obsession began: I was watching a rebroadcast of his famous jump over fourteen Greyhound buses. Dressed in a white Spandex jumpsuit with stars and red and blue stripes that crisscrossed over his torso, he was a superhero come to life.

Right before the actual jump, Evel revved his engine to a fever pitch, silencing the roaring crowd as they collectively held their breath. Then he bolted up the ramp, leaving a cloud of gray smoke behind, and within seconds, he and his motorcycle took flight. I sat up on my knees, watching as if it were all happening in slow motion. Flashbulbs flickered like blinking Christmas lights in the stands as he sailed over the first, then the second bus. Evel leaned back in his seat, pulling the handlebars toward his chest, and soared even higher—over three, four, five buses. The entire journey was outlined in the air as one single perfect arc until he descended gracefully on the other side. The wheels screeched as they came in contact with the ramp, igniting a frenzy of cheers from the spectators in the stands and me at home. That day, I decided that I wanted to be just like Evel Knievel, flying through the air, but without the threat of a fiery crash or possibility of dismemberment.

"A mess," said my mother, pointing to the box with the foldout camper. "He will make a mess all over my rug if you buy that for him. He doesn't need that. He needs pants."

We were in a deadlock: Evel Knievel versus Billy the Kid. As my father listened to my mother, he glanced woefully at my face. I fought back with the most sincere expression I could muster and held his gaze in the hopes of distracting him from my mother's argumentative grip. He looked at me, my mother, and then back to me. Suddenly, it was all over: with one swift hoist, my father grabbed the box containing the Scramble Van, plucked an action figure from the metal hook, and proceeded to the checkout counter. It was a grandiose gesture, one that Evel Knievel would have been proud of himself.

While my father valiantly strode toward the cashier, I clenched my fist in quiet victory. My mother, however, wasn't ready to accept her defeat. Standing with one hand on her hip, she leaned in close so that our faces were barely inches apart. When my father was far enough away that he couldn't hear her, she said, "If I find just one of those pieces on my rug, I am going to throw the whole thing in the garbage." I glanced away and watched as my father paid the cashier. "Do you understand me?" she insisted. I nodded, knowing all too well the subtext of her warning. This entire situation had nothing to do with pants, Evel Knievel, or the Scramble Van. My mother was concerned that her husband had just bought his son a doll.

Six months earlier, my mother had discovered a partially amputated Barbie behind our couch in the den. I rescued her from my best friend Diane's garbage pail. Secretly, I played with her on several occasions. Dolls fascinated me. This Barbie was damaged. Her long blonde hair was matted, and she had only one leg. I was intrigued by the way her knee could be forced to hyperextend in the opposite direction, making her even more deformed.

Diane and her sister Karen lived directly around the corner from us, and our backyards met up perfectly. Had my father not erected a garish brick wall around the entire perimeter of our property, our two yards would have looked like a giant playground with sloping little hills of grass.

Of course, my mother did not approve of our friendship. She didn't think it was appropriate for me to have "girl friends," particularly when I didn't play with the other boys in the neighborhood. But they were the two nicest people I knew. Diane was my age and had fair skin and blonde hair. She wore cat's-eye glasses with light blue frames. Karen, younger but taller than Diane, had dark hair. Unlike Diane, who was gentle and reserved, Karen was aggressive. I remember she cried often and had fits of anger, which Diane explained was due to her being hyperactive. Their parents were divorced, and Diane and Karen lived with their older sister, Christine; their mother, Ellen; and her husband, Al, in a butter-yellow and chocolate-brown split-level duplex on Hewitt Avenue.

I was in love with Diane and hoped to marry her one day. She had the sweetest disposition of anyone I'd ever met and accepted me the way I was, unlike all the other kids at school. The day they moved in, I spied on them through the blinds of the sliding glass doors that looked out at their yard. I watched the way Diane and her family waved good-bye to the movers. When I saw her that first time, I knew I was in love.

To their credit, both Diane and Karen were not girly girls. We were adventurers and enjoyed trips into the woods nearby our homes. Beyond their street, a development of two-family houses had been under construction for months. We investigated the concrete foundations after the workers went home for the day, and we collected wood, which we used to make a fort near my house. That was a long time ago, a time when rabbits and lizards ran among the dirt roads beyond our neighborhood.

Diane and Karen probably played with dolls when they were alone together, but never with me. One day I walked into their room; Diane was listening to her Bay City Rollers' album. She loved the song "Saturday Night," and played it over and over. I found her sprawled out on her bed, piled high with stuffed animals and copies of *Tiger Beat*, a magazine of the latest teen idols. I always pretended I wasn't interested in listening to their boy-band albums. As Diane flipped through the pages of her magazine, I watched over her shoulder. Karen was cleaning out her closet, shouting the lyrics. "S-A-T-U-R-D-A-Y, night!"

I first discovered the dismembered Barbie in a pink tin pail underneath Diane's desk. When I fished her out of the trash and held her up by her hair, Diane stuck out her tongue. "Eww, that's Karen's. She broke her and stuffed her in the back of the closet."

"No, I didn't," yelled Karen, still rummaging through her clothes.

"Can I have her?" I asked.

They laughed. "Why?"

"So I can twirl her by the hair like a helicopter," I said.

Diane looked curiously at Karen and then back at me. "No. Broken Barbies go in the trash." Then she stood up, took it from my hand, and dropped it back into the pink can. Later, when neither sister was looking, I retrieved Barbie from the trash and stuffed her in my jacket pocket.

Barbie lived in between my mattress and box spring for days. Then one afternoon, when I was home alone, I took her down to the den and played with her as I listened to the Beatles on my sister's stereo. I was fascinated by her—the matted hair, that faraway stare, and those perfectly voluptuous breasts. But it was the articulation of her knee joint that had me obsessed, almost to the point that I wanted to dissect her to see what made her move. Just as I was about to get out my doctor's bag, I heard the sound of the garage door opening. I panicked and threw Barbie behind the couch. Just then, my mother and Josephine appeared on the landing. "Well, don't just stand there," shouted Josephine. "Help us with the rest of the groceries."

Obliging, I forgot about Barbie.

Then, one Saturday morning, I awoke to the sound of my mother vacuuming. Grabbing my pillow off the mattress, I molded it over my head to cover my ears. Suddenly I remembered that my mother always pulled the couch away from the wall to vacuum behind it. Just as I made that connection, I heard determined steps on the stairs. Without even a knock, my mother burst through the door, dangling poor Barbie by her hair. "What's this?" she demanded. I cowered pitifully under my Evel Knievel blanket, pulling it up and under my eyes. "What's this doing in my house?" My mother took two intimidating steps forward and waved poor Barbie in front of my face. "Frank, I'm not in the moon," she warned, as her Italian accent thickened with anger. She intended to say "mood," but I knew what she meant. "Where did you get this?"

"It belongs to Diane," I whispered. "She must have left it here when she came over."

Her eyes darted back and forth, staring directly into mine, as if she was searching for evidence of a lie there. I held her stare as long as I could, but my eyes burned so deeply I was forced to blink. Then the corners of my mother's mouth wrinkled upward in a crooked smile. Meanwhile, Barbie swung from side to side like some talisman my mother was using to will me into telling her the truth.

"I don't want you to see those girls anymore. Do you understand? And if I find another doll in this house, I am going to send you to military school."

After that day, my mother refused to buy me any toy that remotely resembled a doll, not even an action figure or army man. That was the price I paid for stealing a rejected Barbie doll from my best friend's garbage can. My act of thievery destroyed what little chance I had of convincing my mother to purchase that Evel Knievel action figure and Scramble Van. I was able to persuade my father only because he was as big of a fan of Evel's as I was.

Chapter 14

Charmed by a Fox

THE WEEK AFTER MY VICTORY AT KORVETTE'S, I found myself once again driving with my parents one Saturday afternoon in search of Billy the Kid pants. This time we were on our way to the Staten Island Mall. My mother had decided to try our luck at Sears.

The Staten Island Mall was located directly across the street from the Fresh Kills Landfill—a sanitation dump. This particular landfill had the distinction of being the largest in the world. As we stepped out of the car that day, the stench was overwhelming and worse than usual because of the humidity. A wall of dirt approximately twenty feet tall formed a barrier around the landfill, obstructing the view of the dump. Seagulls and other predatory birds gathered overhead like a shifting, menacing cloud, emitting high-pitched screeches.

During the spring and summer months, the sun baked the landfill. Fumes rose up from the enormous heap, distorting the air like a haze from a gasoline spill. Noxious vapors traveled across Richmond Avenue, enveloping the mall and blanketing the entire parking lot from spring well into fall. "How do people live near here?" asked my mother as she hurried ahead, clutching her pocketbook in the crook of her armpit while she held her nose. She said this every time we visited the mall.

Chris Reynolds told me that the Fresh Kills Landfill covered over two thousand acres. "My dad said you can see it from space because it's taller than the Statue of Liberty." I didn't share his enthusiasm. Having the bragging rights that we lived on an island with the largest dump in the world wasn't something I was proud of. It was, however, another reason why I felt I had to leave Staten Island when I was old enough.

Inside, my eyes were immediately drawn toward the center of the mall. Just three months earlier, this had been the exact location of Santa's Village. I could still recall the wads of white cotton that blanketed the perimeter of the square. Christmas trees of various sizes, adorned with colorful ornaments, candy canes, and sparkling silver tinsel, were placed in clusters at strategic areas, some reaching as high as the second tier of the mall. Garland hung from the railings above, scalloping the entire square like luscious gold icing on a giant Christmas cake. I loved visiting the mall during the holidays. The scent of nutmeg and cinnamon filled the air, in sharp contrast with the putrid smell outside. The square bustled with shoppers for weeks—as early as November and then right up until those last few days before Christmas.

Except now this once-hallowed place was occupied by the eerie presence of boys dressed in matching green uniforms, red felt berets, and neckerchiefs affixed to their eager necks with fleur-de-lis silver scarf rings. Instead of clamoring children, tethered to their parents' hands as they forged ahead for a chance to sit on Santa's lap, there were rowdy young boys, tying knots with rope and practicing oaths with their right hands held up at ninety degrees to display three stiff frozen fingers. These foreigners had infested the mall like an army of ants.

My first instinct was to run, to avoid being accosted by these boys, but my mother's eyes had already glazed over. Her pupils dilated to the size of pennies. Intuitively sensing my apprehension, she reached out to grab my arm before I had a chance to flee. As I was dragged helplessly toward them, I looked over my shoulder at my father following behind us. He did not intervene this time. My mother was on a mission, so I succumbed.

Just ahead, folding tables were set up with banners draped

over them, delineating the Scout troops by number. My mother walked up to the nearest one. Two seated men were dressed in similar adult-sized Scout uniforms. One wore wire-framed glasses and a hat that made him look like a state trooper. They smiled as we approached. "Here," said my mother, pushing me forward. "Sign him up." The two men looked at each other and smiled.

"Well, okay," said the one wearing the trooper hat and glasses. "Why don't you start by telling me your son's name?"

"Well?" she said, nudging me in the back. "Answer the man."

"Frank," I muttered with my head held down.

"Well, Frank, do you want to learn more about the Boy Scouts?" he asked.

My mother responded for me: "Yes, he does."

I turned back one more time to look at my father, pleading with the same expression I used on him at Korvette's department store, but he just stood there, resigned, his hands held behind his back.

"Is that your dad, Frank?"

"Angelo," yelled my mother. "Come here. Why are you standing all the way over there?"

My father obeyed.

"Pleasure to meet you, sir. Is this your son?"

"Yeah, he's mine."

"Well, that's great that you brought him here, because you know Scouting isn't just for your son. I'm the Scoutmaster of Troop 284 in Huguenot, and I thoroughly recommend that the fathers get involved, as well. Now, first off, what is your name, sir?"

"Angelo."

"Well, Angelo, I am Scoutmaster Hynes, and this is Assistant Scoutmaster Peterson, and like I said, we run Troop 284. Now, where do you folks live?"

"We live in Sunny Side near Clove Lakes Park."

"But more near Todt Hill," interjected my mother. That was the rich neighborhood next to where we lived.

"Okay, well, that's a problem. You see, you need to find the troop closest to your home. Troop 284 is all the way on the other side of the island. You see that table over there?" He pointed to a banner that read TROOP 85. "You need to speak to their Scoutmaster. His name is Bill Fox."

Without even a good-bye, my mother squeezed my arm and yanked me directly across the square. Standing behind the table was a formidable man wearing a Scout uniform with his arms folded across his chest. He maintained an attentive pose while three young boys, about my age, sat on the floor in front of him, tying knots. As we approached, he looked at my mother. He had deep-set blue eyes that peered out from under thick black eyebrows. His receding jet-black hair framed the crown of his head like an ebony laurel wreath. When his eyes fell upon me, I felt a tingle run down my back. He frightened me to death.

"My son wants to be a Boy Scout," announced my mother. "Are you the man in charge?"

He smiled. "That depends on who you're looking for," he said.

"That man over there told us you were in charge of the Boy Scouts for all of Sunny Side," she explained, pointing back to the man wearing the trooper hat. "He said we should talk to you." My mother was talking so loudly that the three boys stopped tying knots to look up at her. I wanted to crawl under the table.

"Let's try this," said the man with the blue eyes. "I'm Bill Fox, the Scoutmaster of Troop 85. We meet at St. Sylvester's School every Tuesday night. Do you know where that is?"

"My son goes to St. Sylvester's!" My mother had a hysterical look in her eyes. "Frank, did you hear that? They meet at your school!"

"I heard, and so did everyone else," I said. The three boys tying knots began to giggle. I wanted to run away.

"Fine parish, that St. Sylvester's," said Bill, "and Monsignor McGinn is a close friend of the family. He was a great mentor to me growing up. You know, I almost became a priest at one point, Mrs . . . ?"

"Spinelli. Michelina Spinelli."

"Italian, right?"

"Yes." She beamed.

As he continued to charm my mother, my eyes gazed around the center square at all the other boys dressed in those ugly green Boy Scout uniforms. It was at that moment that I realized I was about to become one of them.

For years, I'd heard about this organization but had no interest in becoming part of it. It was bad enough that I was forced to join the basketball team and Little League baseball. Scouting was completely different. It was more like a club that seemed frighteningly cultish than a team. You had to attend weekly meetings, wear a uniform made of stiff green material, and go on camping trips once a month. Nothing about Scouting interested me, yet by some cruel twist of fate, I was about to become one as payback for my Evel Knievel Scramble Van victory.

"Is this your son?" asked Bill.

"Yes, this is Frank, and that's my husband, Angelo," said my mother, motioning to us frantically. "We're shopping for my son. It's his birthday this month."

"Birthday!" said Bill. Then he walked around the table. He stood directly in front of me. That's when I noticed he was a large man, taller than my father, with even broader shoulders. Bill squatted down to my eye level. "Happy birthday, Frank. How old are you going to be?" His face was just inches away from mine, and his eyes never wavered. Although I found him genuine, I was still unnerved by his attentiveness and disregard for personal space. Unable to maintain eye contact, I stared down at my sneakers, wishing I was home, playing with my Evel Knievel action figure. When I didn't respond, my mother jabbed me in the back, and I mumbled something unintelligible.

"Eleven," my mother clarified.

"Eleven!" repeated Bill. "That's a great age. Do you know why turning eleven is so important for a boy?"

I shook my head, still staring down at my sneakers.

"Eleven is when a boy is old enough to become a Scout. It's the age when you are well on your way to becoming a man. So I'm gonna ask your parents to write down your name, address, and telephone number. I'll be expecting you and your dad the

Tuesday after your eleventh birthday at St. Sylvester's so that we can sign you up to become a Boy Scout. Okay?"

I don't remember responding, but I do recall thinking I'd been given a reprieve because I didn't have to join that day. In the end, we went to Sears and bought Billy the Kid pants. I didn't make a fuss in the dressing room and tried on as many pairs of pants as my mother chose. For the rest of the day and up until my actual birthday, I intended to maintain a low profile in the hopes that she would forget all about the day we went to the Staten Island Mall and met Bill Fox from Troop 85.

I SAVED THE BOX FROM THE SCRAMBLE VAN and used it as a ramp for Evel Knievel to jump from my nightstand to the bed. Seated on the plush navy blue carpet that lined my bedroom, I rolled Evel's motorcycle around the floor, sputtering my lips to mimic the sound of an engine.

That day, Evel was going to attempt his greatest jump—the Grand Canyon. As he waited, perched on the cardboard ramp, I heard my parents arguing in the living room just beyond my bedroom door. I tried to drown their voices out with my revving sound, but as usual, it was impossible to stifle my mother's voice, which could be heard over the propulsion engine of an aircraft.

"Well, you bought it for him," I heard her say.

My lips sputtered faster and louder. Evel took off, up the ramp and into the air with great speed, escalating higher and higher. Midway over the canyon, my bedroom door suddenly swung open.

"He's here," my mother exclaimed with wide eyes. There was a manic expression on her face. "Bill, the Scoutmaster, is here. He's beeping his horn outside. Go see what he wants. Go!"

I sighed heavily with frustration and stood up. Evel's jump had to be aborted. I abandoned him and his motorcycle on the floor of my bedroom. Even a picnic table, which I'd set up for his impending victory dinner, was left untouched. Walking down the stairs, I saw a red pickup truck idling outside. It had a storage shed built on the back that looked like a small house. Moving closer, I stopped to press my face against the screen door. A week had passed since we met Bill.

Slowly I pushed open the door. I noticed a blond boy licking an ice cream cone in the passenger seat. Bill leaned over him, thrusting his head out the passenger window. "Hey, remember me? Do you want to go for a ride?" The blond boy ignored him, consumed with his ice cream—a mound of strawberry—dripping down the sides of the cone and over his fingers. Bill noticed I was staring at it and said, "Come on. I'll get you one, too."

I shook my head.

"You mean you don't like ice cream?"

"I don't like strawberry."

Bill hung his head and laughed. The blond boy looked at him strangely. "Okay. You can have any flavor you want. Deal?"

I smiled and walked toward the truck.

Bill made the blond boy move over as I got in. "Do you like Carvel ice cream?"

"Yes."

"Okay then. We're off to Carvel."

Bill put the truck in gear. We headed down Endor Avenue and turned right at the corner. Up close, the blond boy was noticeably smaller than me. His hair was parted in the middle and hung uniformly in one length over his head. Not like mine, which was thick and curly. I would have killed to have hair like his. He didn't look familiar, but I assumed he was a Scout. His T-shirt displayed the word ZOOM across his chest, and immediately I recognized the font from the television show of the same name. I wanted to ask him whether he watched ZOOM, but he seemed disinterested in me and thoroughly engrossed with his ice cream.

"We just came back from Carvel," said Bill. "Then I realized we were in your neighborhood. So I thought we'd stop by." I half-listened to what he was saying because I was distracted by how different my neighborhood looked riding up front in his truck. It felt as though I was on a parade float. "Have you given any more thought about joining the Scouts?"

"Kind of," I said, looking out the window, hoping Diane and Karen were outside playing so they would see me. "I'm still not eleven. So I have time to decide."

"You haven't had that birthday yet?"

"It's next week. My mom is taking me to Farrell's Ice Cream Parlour with some friends from school. The waiters wear straw hats. When it's your birthday, they sing a special song and bang on a drum."

The blond boy, unfazed by my presence, remained focused on his ice cream, lapping up the sides of the cone.

"You have a nice mom. You know that? And she really wants you to be a Scout. I think that would make her really happy."

"And the person whose birthday it is gets a free hot fudge sundae," I continued.

Bill let out a hearty laugh and banged his hands against the steering wheel. "You really can't wait for that birthday, huh? Well, I'm gonna expect to see you one week from this Tuesday. Okay?" He turned the truck into the Carvel parking lot. Through the large windows, I could see a teenage boy behind the counter dressed all in white. A family was waiting patiently as the boy held down a silver lever, catching a thick, velvety braid of vanilla ice cream in a cone.

"Do we have a deal?" asked Bill.

I nodded.

⸻

THAT TUESDAY CAME QUICKLY. Suddenly I found myself being driven by my father back to school to attend my first Boy Scout meeting. Instead of boys and girls dressed in blue and white school uniforms, an army of ants was huddled together in those hideous green outfits. Bill was there, carrying on like the mayor with other adult men surrounding him.

One of the senior Scouts explained that the troop was divided into smaller groups called patrols. Each patrol had a leader. Senior Scouts were older boys who oversaw each patrol. They reported to the assistant Scoutmasters, and everyone answered to Bill. I was escorted over to the table where my patrol was gathered. The leader was Kevin Davis, an eighth grader from St. Sylvester's. The other members included Louis Minitoni, an obese boy who was in my homeroom; Joseph Longo, or "Pip Squeak," as he was also known because he was smaller than anyone else his age; and Achilles Salmone, who had to repeat the fifth grade and was one of the few black boys who attended St. Sylvester's. Except for Davis, we were a bunch of misfits. I felt even more out of place because I was the only boy not wearing a uniform. My parents didn't want to invest the money until they were sure I was going to stick with it. With my track record, that was reasonable.

My bedroom closet was a museum of artifacts from previous activities my mother had enlisted me in against my will. I owned my fair share of uniforms, baseball gloves, balls, and even an athletic cup, which neither of my parents knew how to explain. I spent years fighting my way off team sports because I wasn't athletic. I would have preferred my parents allowed me to spend the money on books or art supplies. But my mother was determined to make me a jock, and when that didn't happen, she turned her attention to the Boy Scouts.

Kevin greeted me with a hearty handshake. He instructed me to sit down next to Minitoni, who offered me a welcoming nod. Looking at the others, I felt trapped. How I wished I could have been home with Evel Knievel instead of sitting here with this hapless group.

At precisely 7 P.M., Bill strode up to the front of the gymnasium. The entire assembly came to order as a hush fell over the crowd. The meeting was about to begin. "Attention, everyone, please recite the Scout Oath," he instructed. With that one order, all the boys stood up with their right arms bent at ninety degrees, holding up their three middle fingers.

"On my honor, I will do my best . . ."

Silently, I watched the other boys. I was nothing like them, and worse still, I was now one of them.

CHAPTER 15

A Boy Like Me

HE DIDN'T SPEAK MUCH IN GENERAL, even when Mrs. Schiavone asked him a question in class. Hiding behind his Elemental Science textbook, only his tousled brown hair was visible.

"Mr. Duran," said Mrs. Schiavone. "We're waiting."

Craning his neck over the textbook he propped up to hide his face, Jonathan looked like a turtle peering out of his shell. His face was angular, and his tortoiseshell glasses were far too large for his face. Behind them, his eyes maintained a distracted far-off gaze. This boy spent a disproportionate amount of time in the library reading. I was sure he hadn't heard the question, because from where I was sitting, I could see Jonathan was hiding one of those creepy horror paperback novels he always read in class.

"Mr. Duran!"

This time Jonathan flinched, realizing Mrs. Schiavone was speaking directly to him. He looked around. Everyone's eyes were on him, and he began to shake like a wet puppy after a bath.

"Uranium," I whispered. "Just say 'uranium.'"

I don't know why I took pity on him that day. I hadn't reached out to him since he'd joined our class at the beginning of the year. Unlike the rest of us, who began as first graders, he was a transfer student. His sudden appearance that first school day in September raised quite a few eyebrows. Even before Mrs. Schiavone introduced him formally to the homeroom, the students were buzzing about in the school yard before the morning bell, wondering who the new kid was.

I distinctly remember overhearing Daisy Dickenson tell Angela Pascal that Jonathan lived next door to her. "He used to go to P.S. 48. Maybe he flunked out." This caused Angela to gasp, and soon news spread through the school yard like a virus on the breaths of the other children: the new boy was slightly retarded. That morning, after Mrs. Schiavone made a brief introduction, Jonathan darted directly toward his assigned desk, which was diagonally ahead and two rows away from mine. Within seconds, he dissolved into the background. He stayed that way for the next several months, occasionally popping up to answer a question in his high-pitched voice, but for the most part remaining invisible.

That was until now.

"Uranium," I murmured again through closed lips like a ventriloquist.

Jonathan returned a blank stare in my direction and for good reason: we had never spoken before. However, I knew that if I didn't intervene, this situation was going to escalate. Mrs. Schiavone was clearly on a warpath that day. I knew she was in a bad mood the minute I walked in that morning and noticed she was wearing slacks.

It was another of Chris Reynolds's observations. He told me once that Catholic schoolteachers had to wear skirts or dresses. "Just remember if you see a teacher in pants then that means Aunt Flo's in town," he said, "and they're going to be in a wicked bad mood." Of course, I didn't get the reference, so I asked Josephine what that meant.

"Who told you about Aunt Flo?" she asked.

"Some kid at school."

"Who's Aunt Flo?" asked Maria.

It was a Saturday afternoon, and my sisters were lying in bed reading magazines. They shared a bedroom, but very little else.

Maria was the eldest. She was taller than all of us and very pretty, with long dark hair and wide, chocolate-brown eyes. She was like a second mother, an instinctively nurturing person, who wanted to become a teacher. Throughout my childhood, Maria taught me many things, especially how to dance with a girl and how to order dinner on a date. I watched many young men come by the house to take Maria out while I sat on the stairs and spied as she introduced them to my parents. She never exuded the self-confidence I thought she should have, owing much to her being over-weight, and perhaps that's the reason why she never dated any boy for very long.

Josephine, on the other hand, was cute, with dark eyes and plump lips and a mole above her lip like me. She shared my fa-ther's sharp humor, and being the middle child and second daughter, she felt competitive with her older sister. She realized that if Maria was the pretty one, that left little room for any-thing else other than being the smart one, which she wasn't. So she became the street-smart daughter, the one who was thin, and the one who couldn't wait to move out of the house, re-gardless of whether she got married. When people used to ask me which sister I liked more, I always said Maria because she was nice, but in reality, I knew Josephine was more fun.

That afternoon, Maria had just returned home from working all day at the bank, where she was a teller. Still dressed in a white blouse, dark skirt, and black tights, she massaged her feet as she flipped through her latest edition of *Vogue*. Josephine sat up once she realized neither of us knew who Aunt Flo was.

"Seriously, Maria, you've never heard of Aunt Flo?"

Maria looked up from her magazine and shook her head. "I'm not in the mood for guessing games," she said. "Who's Aunt Flo?"

"You've got to be kidding me," said Josephine, bouncing on her bed. "Maria! You can't be that dense? Aunt Flo! Flow, like a river, flow. I just had a visit from Aunt Flo. You will see Aunt Flo next week. She comes once a month . . . We use napkins when she comes."

When it finally clicked, Maria blushed with embarrassment. "Oh," she said, rolling onto her side.

"What?" I said, stamping my foot. "I still don't get it."

"Aunt Flo means a girl is having her period, stupid," Josephine explained.

"Oh," I said, but I still hadn't made the connection between a girl's period and the need to wear slacks when Aunt Flo came to town. My knowledge of menstruation was limited to the extent that I knew a girl couldn't go swimming if she was having her period.

When I arrived in class that morning and noticed Mrs. Schiavone wearing gray polyester pants with a matching vest, I immediately caught Chris Reynolds's eye. He looked at me and winked. I giggled.

Mrs. Schiavone cocked an eye at me. "Silence when you enter the classroom, Mr. Spinelli." I quietly walked to my desk. Since the beginning of the school year, I had been the brunt of her fury many times. I had no intention of pissing her off that day. She enjoyed making boys squirm until their faces turned red. Often she chose one victim a day and picked on him relentlessly until he either cried or became so insolent that she made him stand in the corner.

"Mr. Duran!"

This caused Jonathan to shudder. When he refused to respond, she began to march down the aisle toward him. Jonathan's eyes bugged out of his head, but it was too late. Within seconds, she had descended over him like a giant float in the Macy's Thanksgiving Day Parade. Then, with one fell swoop, she reached down and ripped his Elemental Science textbook out of his hand, releasing that tawdry paperback into the air. For a few fleeting seconds, its faded yellow pages flapped desperately like a bird trapped in a cage, before it settled on the ground with a quiet *thud*. Now the entire class was privy to Jonathan's secret. The cover of his book displayed a voluptuous blonde being ravaged by a menacing figure with red eyes. The title, written in Gothic print with lime green letters, spelled out THE INCUBUS.

The classroom was silent except for a few quickly stifled

gasps. All eyes were now on Mrs. Schiavone, whose expression was a mixture of shock and disgust. This discovery catapulted the situation beyond simple disobedience into sacrilege. Being a Catholic schoolteacher, it was her duty to reprimand him to the fullest extent. Regardless of whether this was his first offense or not, Jonathan had done something morally wrong. He was reading a blasphemous book.

"What is this?" asked Mrs. Schiavone incredulously. As she bent down to retrieve it, her behind ballooned inside her polyester pants. A mild, yet discernible wave of giggles bubbled up from the far corner of the classroom. Immediately, Mrs. Schiavone stood up and continued. "What is this?" she repeated. Jonathan's face was the color of a glistening plum. "Don't you have better things to read than this filth?" she said, squeezing the paperback into a tight cylinder. "Go stand in the corner," she demanded. "Now!"

Jonathan oozed out of his seat and walked toward the back of the classroom with his head held down. Even though it was appropriate for Mrs. Schiavone to banish him to the corner, I saw a look in her eyes that made me think it hurt her to do so. If it had been anyone else—Bobby Staudinger, or better yet, Seth Connelly—Mrs. Schiavone would not have thought twice. But it was Jonathan, the quiet boy who never made trouble and always did as he was told, who now had to pay the price for Aunt Flo's visit.

I APPROACHED JONATHAN IN THE SCHOOL YARD DURING RECESS. Standing in the far corner by the convent, he looked defenseless without his paperback to shield him. From the other side of the yard, I estimated that a direct approach might draw the attention of Seth Connelly and his gang.

The aroma of soft pretzels being sold out of the eighth-grade homeroom window caught my attention for a second. Then, a trio of girls, led by Karen Rae, formed a kick line across my path. I heard them approaching: "If anybody's in my way, they're gonna get a kick, *boom!*"

I raced behind them, toward Jonathan. Breathless, I blurted out, "I have all of Stephen King's novels. Did you know that?" I noted a subtle sign of interest. "*Carrie* was the first book I ever bought. It's actually a lot shorter than I expected. I'm collecting all of Stephen King's books, in hardcover of course."

Jonathan, who always read paperbacks, seemed impressed.

"Did you know they changed the name of the gym teacher for the movie? Originally, her name was Desjardins. Betty Buckley from *Eight Is Enough* played her in the movie, but they called her Miss Collins."

Jonathan smirked. "Duh, I know that."

"So you're a Stephen King fan?"

"I love *The Shining* and *Salem's Lot* more than *Carrie*. Did you know that *Salem's Lot* started out as a short story called "Jerusalem's Lot," which was featured in the book called *Night Shift*?"

"Of course, duh." Then we both burst out laughing.

"I saw you last night," said Jonathan.

"Where?"

"At the Boy Scout meeting. You're in the group with Louis Minitoni."

"Yeah, but there is nothing *mini* about him."

Jonathan laughed again. He covered his mouth to hide his braces.

"I didn't see you. My parents made me join right after my birthday. I hate it."

Jonathan shrugged. "I like it. I started out as a Webelo."

"Ha, Weebles wobble but they don't fall down," I sang. "Do you want to come over to my house after school? There's a forest nearby that's supposed to be haunted with a burial ground set up by devil worshipers."

"Sure. Where do you live?"

———

THAT AFTERNOON, JONATHAN RODE UP to the front of my house on a white Schwinn bicycle with a banana seat. I watched him from the living room window as he released the kickstand with his foot. It was a slate-gray afternoon, and I was concerned that a storm was coming.

Jonathan wore stone-washed denim jeans and a red-and-white horizontal-striped T-shirt. He appeared leaner in street clothes, and as he walked up to ring the bell, I pressed my hand over my stomach, concerned that I was too overweight to be his friend. Opening the door, I stopped him before he could come inside. "Let's go before it starts to rain."

The block before my house was a dead end called Newbury Street, which led into a natural preserve called the Green Belt. The College of Staten Island ran along the entire course of the Green Belt, partitioned off by a fence. I took Jonathan into the woods beyond the fence heading north so that we could explore the forest without seeing the college parking lot. "There's actually a stream farther back that cuts a gorge into the ground. Clay lines the floor, and you can make cool sculptures. It's even better than Play-Doh because it gets soft again if you wet it. Do you want me to show you?"

"Sure," he said.

Jonathan was easygoing and acquiescent; he agreed to pretty much everything I said. That made him a perfect comrade, not because he was passive but because he was always eager to play along.

"Have you ever tried to test your telepathic powers?" he asked as we entered the woods.

"It's kind of hard to do on your own," I replied. "But I'm willing to try."

That afternoon kindled a friendship that lasted nearly three years. When I tried to analyze what made us friends in the first place, I can think of only one thing: we were exact opposites and yet exactly the same. At the time, neither of us knew we were gay, yet something inexplicable drew us together. It hid behind a love of horror stories and an interest in telepathy. For now, Jonathan and I were content with the notion that we had each found a buddy in a school full of bullies waiting to prey on boys like us.

CHAPTER 16

Camp Creeps

BOY SCOUT MEETINGS BECAME JUST ANOTHER RITUAL I had to endure, much like basketball and baseball practice. Instead of sitting on a bench every Saturday morning, now I attended weekly meetings and went on monthly hiking trips. I preferred spending my Saturdays watching cartoons and ignoring my mother's pleas to get dressed and go outside. Now that I was a Boy Scout, I was forced to sleep in a canvas tent or a musty wooden lean-to out in the forest. Since the age of five, I'd had my own bedroom. It wasn't an easy transition, sharing quarters with other boys.

My first trip took place at Pouch Camp on Staten Island, less than three miles from my home. My father dropped me off in the parking lot of St. Sylvester's Friday night. Once the troop had assembled, we filed into our individual patrols. Davis called out our last names. We responded by stepping forward, shouting, "Present, sir!" and saluting him with two fingers extended from our foreheads. I was wedged in line between Minitoni and Pip Squeak. Since Achilles was by far the tallest, he was made to stand in the rear. We waited in formation until we were assigned cars that would transport us to camp.

My mother packed my brand-new bright red backpack with enough clothing to last a week. It was weighed down severely by the unofficial mess kit she assembled: an old frying pan loaded with a blue plastic sectional plate, utensils, and mug we bought while on vacation in Maine. My mother refused to buy me the official Boy Scout mess kit, which was designed efficiently using featherweight stainless steel and included a dish and a pot secured together by a detachable frying pan handle. As she put it, everything I needed was in her kitchen. Unfortunately, the frying pan didn't fit properly in my knapsack, and the handle jutted into the small of my back, poking me with each step.

Once we arrived at Pouch Camp, we hiked for one mile to our campsite. I felt like a prisoner in a chain gang, being led in the dark to the state penitentiary. The forest echoed with the caw of crows overhead and the trudging of our feet over sticks and twigs. By this time, the sun had nearly set. Davis lit the kerosene lamp because flashlights were forbidden. Minitoni immediately began to tire, and that forced our entire patrol to lag behind the rest of the troop. Davis had to stop us on several occasions to allow Minitoni to catch up. Each time we waited for him, I saw Davis's jaw clench so tightly that the muscles in his face twitched.

Several minutes later, Achilles called out. "We lost Minitoni again."

"Are you shitting me?" cried Davis. He lifted the lantern and immediately began counting heads. "Goddamnit!" We stood in silence. In the distance, I heard a faint panting sound. "Spinelli, hold this while I go look for that fat fuck." I took the lantern by the handle while Davis reached into his backpack and pulled out a flashlight. Pip Squeak gasped. Davis flashed his eyes back at him. "You guys say anything about this," he warned, "and I'll personally see to it that you're on latrine duty for life." Davis disappeared into the darkness, the cone of light in his hand waving from side to side like a game of Pong.

Minutes later, Davis returned, dragging the puffing Minitoni behind him. "Just give me a second, you guys," huffed Minitoni. Davis and I shone a light on him. His pasty white face was now sweaty and red. His soaked hair clung together in spikes on the top of his head.

"What's weighing you down?" asked Davis.

"He's probably got a Thanksgiving dinner in his knapsack," said Pip Squeak.

"I'm gonna stuff my fist up your ass like a turkey if you don't quit it, Pip Squeak," countered Minitoni.

"Everyone shut up," yelled Davis. "Let's move it so that we can get to camp before sunrise."

I thought of my warm bed, my Evel Knievel Scramble Van, and all the television I was missing. Instead, I was marching in the dark with a bunch of nerds. Then it occurred to me. That was what Boy Scouts was—nerds in uniforms.

Up ahead, I heard voices. Davis switched off his flashlight and reached out for the lantern I was holding. Without thinking, I released the handle but grabbed the glass bulb. I heard the singe of my flesh burn, releasing smoke and a putrid smell, followed by the most exquisite pain I'd ever felt.

"Fuck!" I screamed.

"Goddamnit, Spinelli," growled Davis through clenched teeth. "What did you do that for? The glass is the hottest part."

From the darkness, a voice called out. "What's the holdup, ladies?"

In the distance, three shadowy figures emerged. As they approached, I could make out the faces of three senior Scouts: James Mendola, Stanley Metheny, and Chris Spivey.

"Nothing," said Davis. "We had a little holdup."

"Little?" mocked Spivey, "or *mini*?"

Mendola and Metheny laughed. I turned in time to see Minitoni hang his head in shame. "We should really get going before it gets too late," encouraged Achilles.

"Listen," warned Mendola. "You're not making the decisions here. Understand?"

Achilles nodded.

"I can't hear you!"

"Yes, sir," muttered Achilles.

"Now, why don't you ladies pick up your shit and march to camp before I make you sleep here!" ordered Spivey.

"Yes, sir," said Davis.

Our patrol followed silently behind Davis. We walked less

than ten yards before I saw the roaring flames of the campfire in a pit that had been dug into the ground and surrounded by stones. Tents were assembled in a circle around the fire but spaced far back enough to avoid stray sparks. Despite the chilly night air, my middle finger throbbed uncontrollably. I noticed a blister forming. Without thinking, I brought it up to my lip and bit into the fluctuant area, releasing the tangy fluid into my mouth. The raw skin underneath flared, and I sucked on it deeply to numb the pain.

"Spinelli, you want to suck my finger next or would you prefer something else to suck on?" asked Spivey. I turned around to see him standing there with his hands on his hips. His tall, sinewy body caught the light from the campfire, illuminating his long, flaxen hair. Stepping closer, he waved his index finger in my face. "Here. Suck this!"

Suddenly another voice called out from the darkness. "What's going on over here?" Behind Spivey I saw the large outline of a man. It was Bill. "Spinelli, is there a problem here?" Spivey slowly backed off. His eyes tightened to warn me.

"No," I said. "No problem."

"Spivey! Don't you have somewhere else to be?"

"Yes, sir," he said, turning to Bill. "It's just that we noticed Spinelli was hurting, so we came over to help."

"Really?" asked Bill suspiciously. "Spinelli, you want to tell me what's going on?"

Davis stepped in to offer an explanation. "Spinelli burned himself on the lantern, sir."

"Is this true?" asked Bill. I nodded. "Then come with me," he said. "The rest of you clowns find something to do and stay out of trouble." I picked up my backpack and followed Bill. Spivey's eyes stayed with me until Mendola patted him on the back, and then they both walked away.

Bill took me to a small cabin where the adults slept. He instructed me to remove my backpack. "Leave that filthy thing out here," he said. Then he went inside. I followed in after him. The room was dark except for the light from a lantern on the table. The room smelled like mildew with a faint hint of kerosene. There was a doorway that led into a large room, but it was too dark for me to see inside. "Sit down," he instructed. "Let's see what you did." I placed my hand on the table, and he grabbed my wrist while he inspected my fingers. Once he noticed the blister had ruptured, he asked, "Did you do this?" I stared up at his face, petrified. In that eerie, dim light, Bill looked deranged. "Goddamnit!"

All at once, he stood up and walked into the other room. I sat there alone, nervous, and in pain. Seconds later, he returned with a tackle box and a *Boy Scout Handbook*. He set the box on the table and began flipping through the pages until he found the one he wanted. Then he smacked it with the back of his hand. "Here," he said, holding it out in front of me. "Read this." My eyes desperately scanned the page, but before I had a chance to finish, Bill told me what it said: "You never, ever burst a blister. The fluid inside has natural healing properties." Then he slammed the book shut and set it down.

Next, he opened the tackle box and removed a small jar with white cream in it. Using a tongue depressor, he spread it on my burn. Immediately the magic frosting relieved the pain. With a roll of gauze, he wrapped my finger and secured it with white tape. "I want you to read your handbook, and don't ever let this happen again," he instructed. "Do you understand?" I nodded.

BACK AT THE CAMPFIRE, I FOUND MY PATROL'S TENT. Forced to settle down next to Minitoni, it was impossible to fall asleep that night on the ground. With each turn, I felt the jab of a twig in my side or the poke of a rock in my hip. Finally, I lay on my back, staring at the half-open flap of the tent's entrance as it waved in the breeze like a sail. The ambient light from the moon and the stars filtered through and illuminated the inside of our small confines so that I could almost make out the rolling curves of Minitoni's belly, heaving up and down in time to his breathing. Then, for the first time, I noticed the delicate features of Pip Squeak's angelic face: his small, upturned nose and dimpled chin. I felt safe again with my patrol, but still, I wanted nothing more than to be home in my own bed.

I counted stars to fall asleep and wondered where Jonathan was. My finger continued to throb, less so than before but persistent enough that I wanted to cut it off. In the darkness, as I drifted off, I saw Spivey's face, remembered his eyes as he warned me not to tell on him. But more than anything else, I felt the power of his hatred and wondered why I had been chosen to bear the brunt of his ridicule.

I hate it here. I hate these boys, and I hate being a Boy Scout.

CHAPTER 17

Look Me in the Eyes

FOR THE NEXT TWO MONTHS, I avoided hiking trips by lying. My parents were the easiest to fool; they didn't care one way or the other, as long as I attended the weekly meetings. Jonathan was the only one who knew how much I hated Boy Scouts. "You're going to quit, aren't you?" he asked one day in the school yard.

"I wish," I said. "I don't get you. Boy Scouts to me is like going to school but in a different uniform. I get picked on enough during the day. Why would I want to hang out with another bunch of bullies at night? I have enough problems with Seth Connelly and his gang as it is."

That afternoon, when the 2:30 P.M. bell rang and Mrs. Schiavone dismissed the class, I packed up my books and flew out of the doors. In the parking lot, I found my mother talking to Mrs. Duran. Normally, she waited for me in her car. When they saw me approach, I noticed my mother's nostrils flare as if she was suppressing an incredible urge to scream.

"There he is," said Mrs. Duran, snuffing out her cigarette on the ground with her heel. "Let me go find my sons. Nice seeing you again, Lina." As Mrs. Duran slid past me, she gripped my shoulder. "Bye, Frankie. Good luck."

In the car, my mother quietly stared out at the road ahead as I fiddled with the radio. Without warning she began. "Why didn't you tell me you've been missing hiking trips?" she asked. I stopped playing with the radio and sank back in my seat. "You know, Frank, I'm only going to put up with just so much before I explode. You made me look like a fool in front of Jonathan's mother. Do you think I'm a fool?"

"No."

"Then how come I have to hear the truth from a stranger? She knows more about my own son than I do."

"No, she doesn't," I protested.

"No?" she questioned, staring at me. "Look me in the eyes and tell me I'm wrong."

I was terrified. If I looked directly into my mother's eyes, I knew she would see the truth behind my lie. So I stared straight ahead.

"I'm waiting outside to pick up my son, and Sharon Duran comes over to me, and says, 'Lina, how is Frankie? I guess he doesn't like Boy Scouts?' And I thought to myself, why would she say that? Then she says, 'He hasn't been on the last two hikes?' I thought, what is she talking about? So I say, 'He told me the one last month was cancelled.' Then she looked at me like I was crazy. That's when I realized you've been lying to me."

"It was cancelled," I said, peeking over to look at her.

Her eyebrows arched like two broken arrows. Her eyes seemed to scorch the skin on my body. "How can you lie right to my face? You think it's nice that I have to learn the truth from a stranger? Jonathan's mother has to tell me my own son is a liar. I felt like a complete fool!"

Up ahead, I watched the traffic light turn red. I screamed and pointed to it. "Mom, the light!"

She jammed the brakes and shifted the car into PARK. I lurched forward, nearly hitting the dashboard. Then she lunged toward me, pointing her finger in my face. "You ever lie to me again, and I'm going to put you in military school. You hear me?" I crossed my forearms over my face to shield myself. "I don't care if you have walking pneumonia. You're going on the next camping trip, so help me God!"

That evening my mother recounted this story several times:

Once when Josephine came home from school. Another as Maria changed out of her work clothes, and, finally, when my father returned home for dinner. By the time we sat down to eat, my mother's anger had snowballed. "What I don't understand is why I cook and clean for this family when all that my children do is lie to me?" she continued. Josephine glared at me from across the table while Maria kept her head down, staring silently at her dish.

"All right, enough," said my father. "I'm sick of hearing this story."

My mother collapsed into her chair, crying into her hands, tomato sauce and strands of spaghetti clinging to her fingers. "I have to hear the truth from a complete stranger!"

The minutes slowly ticked by without anyone saying a single word. I thought of the shoe-box dioramas we made at school; we looked like one you might call *My Italian Family Arguing at Dinner*. Eventually, my mother's tears subsided, and the rest of us eased out of our catatonic states. Slowly we returned to our former selves and became a normal family eating dinner again. Even my mother somehow managed to finish her food. We all did. Despite everything—the tears, the yelling, and the constant threat of violence—my family always managed to eat a good meal.

Friday night, my mother held true to her threat, and I found myself riding in her Cadillac back to St. Sylvester's. My red knapsack rested on the backseat, bulging again with too much clothing and my makeshift mess kit. Earlier that day, a gnawing pain developed below the center of my rib cage. It grew steadily all afternoon. By the time we arrived at the parking lot, I felt like someone had stuck a hot poker in me. Watching all those boys preparing for the long journey ahead reminded me of how I felt the night before the last day of summer vacation.

Since the campsite was located in New Jersey, over two hours away, it was necessary to pack extra equipment and provisions for the weekend. Getting out of the car, I said good-bye to my mother, grabbed my knapsack, and looked for my patrol. Once my mother pulled away, I felt the full brunt of my anxiety.

Jonathan caught my eye from across the parking lot. He smiled as he was ushered into a station wagon.

Davis did a double take when he saw me. "Spinelli, what a surprise!"

"Hey, what can I say, my original plans fell through."

"Ha-ha," he said. "We've already been assigned cars. You better go and tell Mr. Castro you need a ride."

On the other side of the parking lot, I found Mr. Castro holding a clipboard in his hand. He looked harried. I walked right up to him. "Spinelli, how can I help you?" he said. "Do you have a ride?"

Spivey trudged up right next to me. "Out of my way, Spinhead," he said, shoving a box into my side and knocking me backward.

Mr. Castro shook his head disapprovingly. "Spivey, just put that box in my trunk so we can get on the road. Spinelli, is there something I can do for you? I'm pretty busy here. Go find your ride so we can all leave. You have one, don't you?"

Staring at Spivey as he walked away, I hesitated and then said, "Yes."

All around me, car engines started up and headlights switched on. One by one, they formed a line moving toward the parking lot exit. I backed up into the darkness next to the scrubs that lined the school. My decision had been made. I wasn't going on that camping trip. I couldn't bear the thought of spending an entire weekend trying to avoid Chris Spivey. When the last car was out of sight, the pain below the center of my rib cage finally faded.

IT WOULD HAVE BEEN UNUSUAL TO LEAVE A SCOUT BEHIND, but that was exactly what I told my parents when I called them from a pay phone. Within fifteen minutes, my father arrived and drove me back home. My mother was waiting on the landing of the second floor when I entered the house.

"I don't believe you," she said before I even had a chance to explain. "Was there anyone there, Angelo?"

"No."

"You mean they left you there by yourself?"

"I told you what happened on the phone," I said softly. "Since I decided to go at the last minute, they didn't have room available in any of the cars."

"Where was Bill?"

"I don't know. He wasn't there."

My mother stared skeptically at me for several more seconds before she turned around and walked into the kitchen. I slipped my knapsack off and stood there weighing my options. My father retreated into the den to watch television. There was nothing my mother could do. At best, she would learn the truth on Monday, but by then, it would be too late. Carrying my knapsack into the den, I collapsed on the couch and pulled my sweatshirt hood over my head. Upstairs, I heard my mother rummaging around in one of the kitchen drawers.

What followed happened quickly. I heard the sound of the rotary phone dial. At the same time, my father turned the volume up on the television to drown out the sound of my mother's voice. I began pulling the strings on my hood, alternating from left to right. After several minutes, my mother set the phone back down onto the receiver.

"Angelo," she cried out. "Angelo!"

"Goddamned woman," he mumbled as he got up from his chair. "What do you want?"

"Get up here now."

From downstairs I could hear them whispering. My mother was having words with my father, hysterical words I couldn't make out. Then my father called out, "Frank, come up here." I got up and walked to the landing. They were staring down at me from the second floor. My mother was holding her black telephone book in her hand, an excited look on her face.

"Everything is taken care of," she said. "I spoke to Bill."

"Bill who?"

"What do you mean, Bill who? Bill Fox."

"You spoke to Bill Fox?" I repeated.

"Yes, Sharon gave me his number," explained my mother.

"Bill said he had to work a late shift and that's why he wasn't there tonight. He said if he'd been there, none of this would have happened. So to make up for it, Bill is going to pick you up tomorrow morning and drive you to camp himself. Isn't that nice of him?"

I couldn't think of anything more terrifying.

CHAPTER 18

Boy Bonding

THE NEXT MORNING, my mother woke me up before dawn. Startled, I realized in a matter of seconds that I was going to camp. Then the anxiety returned, and I felt the pain below my ribs again. Quickly I dressed in my uniform and waited by the front door, staring out at the street and chewing on an English muffin.

Bill arrived on time and beeped his horn. I yelled good-bye to my mother. Walking into the cool morning, my backpack heavy on my shoulders, I yearned to be in my warm bed again, snuggling under the covers and waking up late. As I reached Bill's truck, he leaned over the passenger side and opened the door. "Put your backpack in the rear," he ordered. I walked around to the back. When I opened the door to place my knapsack on the floor, I was shocked to find the walls were lined with wood paneling. There was a large tabletop in the center with benches built along the sides. In the far corner was a small black-and-white television. The interior looked like a miniature meeting room at a Knights of Columbus hall.

I closed the door and climbed inside the truck next to Bill. Settling back in the passenger seat, I held my hands up to the vent. "You'll be warm in no time," said Bill as he pulled away from the curb. I smiled but gave no reply. I was nervous, thinking he was going to ask me what happened the night before. I hadn't yet made up my mind what I was going to say if he did.

Bill took the Staten Island Expressway and followed the signs to the Outer Bridge. Within twenty minutes, we were in New Jersey.

"So, they left you behind last night?" he asked once we passed the tollbooth.

"Uh, yeah."

"Well, that's inexcusable," he said. "Wait till I speak to Castro." I felt a twinge of pain tightening like a knot below my rib cage again.

"It's not his fault," I offered. "He didn't know. I thought I had a ride, but I was wrong. Then, when I figured it out, he was already gone."

"That's still no excuse."

I began massaging the area below my ribs with my fist to ease the pain.

"So, how do you like it so far?" asked Bill.

"It's okay."

"Did you make the rank of Scout yet?"

"Yes."

"Everyone makes Scout." He laughed. "They practically give it to you for joining. When are you going to make Tenderfoot?"

"Soon."

"Have you gotten any merit badges?"

"Yes," I said. "Well, I almost have one."

"Which one are you working on now?"

"Music."

Bill looked at me and scowled. "Music?" Then he turned and focused on the road ahead. "You should be able to get all your merit badges on these hikes. Were you on the last one? I don't remember seeing you."

"I was sick."

Bill turned his head to look at me again. "Sick, huh?"

I nodded.

"You know, before you're promoted to Tenderfoot you have

to be interviewed by the Scoutmaster in a private meeting. Did you know that?"

"A private meeting?"

"Yes, a private meeting with me," he said. "You really need to read your *Boy Scout Handbook*, Spinelli. Everything you need to know about life is in that book. How old are you?"

"Eleven," I said. "Don't you remember you came by my house to take me for ice cream right before my eleventh birthday?"

"How much do you know about life, about the birds and the bees?"

"I don't know."

I stared out the passenger window, watching the scenery whip by. It suddenly felt very warm in that truck. I unzipped my sweat jacket and considered opening the window.

"Are you hot?" he asked.

I nodded.

Bill reached over and turned down the heater. I felt his hand brush up against my knee. It seemed to linger longer than it should have. "Have you gone through puberty yet?" he asked. "That's what I meant when I said, 'the birds and the bees.' "

I remained quiet, concentrating on the sloping green fields just outside the window.

"Don't be embarrassed. You can talk to me."

I looked over at him. He was still staring ahead at the road. He turned quickly to catch my eye, then redirected his attention back toward the highway. He was grinning. "Come on," he said. "You must have reached puberty by now. I see you have a little mustache. Do you have hair down there yet?"

I remained impassive, sinking deeper into the seat and wishing I could disappear. I prayed he wouldn't look at me again and see me cringing. My face felt as if it was burning.

"What's the matter? No one ever talked to you about sex? It's all there in your *Boy Scout Handbook*."

I couldn't find the words to respond. Sex was a topic we never spoke about at home. My parents treated sex as something sinful we should hide. My mother forbade my sisters from wearing their bathing suits in front of my grandfather, for fear of insulting him with their bare skin, and my father instructed me to change out of my pajamas before I came to breakfast because he didn't think it was appropriate for a boy to show up at the table in anything other than pants. Nudity, or even the suggestion of sexuality, was something to conceal. So when Bill began speaking about sex, I was startled. A tingling sensation ran through my body, as though I had been walking on carpet in my socks and touched the television.

"Okay, do you jerk off then?" he asked.

I ignored his question and continued focusing on the sloping fields.

"You know what jerking off is?"

I lied. "Of course."

"Well, what is it then?"

I had heard that expression only once before, when my cousin Anthony took me for a ride in his car. He was a seventeen-year-old high school dropout who smoked cigarettes. My mother hated him. That day we drove around his neighborhood and picked up his friends. They started talking about this girl Stephanie, whom Anthony referred to as the Slut. The last time he took her out, Anthony said she was having her period, so she jerked him off instead. I had no idea what that meant, but I figured it was something sexual.

"You don't know what jerking off is?" asked Bill.

"It's like fucking," I mumbled finally. Saying that word "fuck" out loud to an adult felt strange.

"Fucking! No, jerking off has nothing to do with fucking." Then Bill laughed loudly. "Jerking off is when you play with yourself." Then he held up his fist and motioned up and down. "You must jerk off?"

I lied again. "All the time."

"Thank God. I was beginning to wonder about you," he said. "Hey, do you and your buddies ever get together and jerk each other off?"

"No."

"No?" he repeated. "Oh man, we have a lot to talk about when we have our little interview before you make Tenderfoot.

Your dad hasn't given you a proper education. That's a shame. This is all a part of growing up. Jerking off, hanging out with your buddies, and jerking each other off—it's all part of boy bonding." Then Bill looked directly at me and flashed a smile that made me feel he was someone I could trust. "You know, maybe if you came on more camping trips, you'd understand that. But don't worry, I'll make a man out of you yet, Spinelli."

FOR THE REST OF THE WEEKEND, I obsessed over my conversation with Bill. I became a detective searching for clues: At the mess hall, I listened to other Scouts' conversations, hoping I'd learn more about this mysterious boy bonding. Around the campfire, I watched as they roughhoused. On the two-mile hike, I carefully monitored their behavior to see whether they attempted to make secret signals. Yet I found no evidence that the other boys were meeting privately to masturbate. It all seemed unimaginable to me, yet my source was someone I thought knew boys better than anyone.

By that night I still had found nothing to suggest that boy bonding was occurring. As I lay in my sleeping bag, listening to Minitoni snore, I wondered what was wrong with me. Why didn't I know more about boys? Was it because I didn't have any brothers? Just then I heard voices approaching outside. It was James Mendola. "There's room in here."

Mendola unzipped our tent and stuck his head in. I cowered in my sleeping bag, hoping he wouldn't notice me. Through my eyelids, I felt the beam of his flashlight scan the interior.

"Hey, what's going on?" asked a sleepy Minitoni.

"Shut up, fatso, and mind your own business."

"Fuck, man. I don't want to sleep with Minitoni," whispered Metheny. "He'll probably blow farts all night."

"There's no other place to sleep," argued Mendola as he unzipped the entrance to the tent. I heard Metheny groan as he followed in after him. "Move over, fat boy."

"Hey, what are you guys doing?" asked Minitoni.

"Mind your own fucking business," said Metheny. "And no farting."

They laid down their sleeping bags on the other side of the tent. I sighed with relief, knowing they couldn't see me over Minitoni's body.

Stanley Metheny and James Mendola were both in the same eighth-grade homeroom at St. Sylvester's. In our limited interactions, neither was as mean as when they were with Chris Spivey. He was the evil link that completed their chain of cruelty. Luckily, Spivey attended public school.

As they settled into their sleeping bags, I relaxed once I was sure they hadn't noticed me. From my vantage point, I could see the silhouettes of their faces in the dark, illuminated by the moonlight through the entrance of the tent. Mendola was half-Filipino and half-Irish with a dark complexion, a wide nose, and full lips. Metheny was 100 percent German, with blond hair, hazel eyes, and angular features. Even though they came from different backgrounds, there was something very similar about them. They styled their hair the same way, parted in the middle and feathered back on the sides. They were both the same height and loved AC/DC. At school they were inseparable, and any girl with the slightest interest in boys had a crush on either one or both. Resting on my side, I listened to them talk in the dark while everyone else slept.

"Did you see the latest *Playboy*?" asked Metheny.

"No, why?"

"Fucking Marilu Henner has an awesome spread," he continued. "She's wearing these tight Spandex pants and this tight, tight, tight pink shirt that buttons up the front. What a rack! You can see her tits popping out and her bush is bulging in those Spandex pants . . . It's so fucking hot! I nearly came in my pants."

"That sounds fuckin' awesome," said Mendola. "Hey, did you ever get anywhere with Anne Marie Bonaventura?"

"She let me feel up her tits, but that's all."

"Fuck, man. I'd love to suck on her titties."

"Fuck! Now I'm getting a boner just thinking about it." Metheny laughed.

"Me, too."

"I'm telling you, you have to get the new *Playboy*. I flipped through it naked on my bedroom floor. I rubbed my boner so hard up against the rug that I came like a fucking racehorse."

"That's fucking hilarious." Mendola laughed. "Remind me not to walk barefoot on your crunchy carpet. I'll stick to coming in my gym sock."

Then they laughed so hard the others in the tent began to stir. Only I remained as still as a corpse, with one eye open, straining to see whether they were going to jerk each other off there in the dark. Their conversation continued for another fifteen minutes before I heard them both snoring softly. I stayed awake most of the night wondering whether this was what Bill referred to as "boy bonding." In that moment, it was conceivable that, if boys talked about sex as freely as Metheny and Mendola, they also met in private to masturbate.

Boy bonding suddenly made sense.

———

ON SUNDAY MORNING, THE CAMPSITE WAS DISMANTLED WITHIN A MATTER OF HOURS. The mess hall was deconstructed once breakfast was served. Tents were disassembled, rolled up, and then piled onto cars to be transported back home. Each boy was responsible for rolling up his own sleeping bag and packing his knapsack. I noticed a hole in the bottom of my knapsack, as though a mouse had eaten its way out, and I worried that it was going to get even bigger due to the weight of my clothes and that damned frying pan.

By noon, we were ordered to organize into our individual patrols outside the mess hall. We stood there in rows as the assistant Scoutmasters made their head count. All the while, Bill silently monitored our every move from the porch with his arms crossed over his chest. Once all the boys were accounted for, we marched back to the parking lot.

When we reached our destination, I just assumed that I

would be riding alone with Bill. In fact, I was looking forward to it, particularly because I was interested in continuing our conversation, now more than ever. Once we arrived at the parking lot, the other boys filed into their designated cars. I broke away from my patrol and headed straight for Bill's truck. I propped my knapsack against it and waited.

Over the hillside, I saw a small group making their way over the embankment. Bill was walking alongside Chris Spivey, James Mendola, and Stanley Metheny. As they drew closer, that pain below my ribs began to needle its way into my gut. From across the way, I saw Spivey staring at me. He mouthed the word "faggot." The gnawing sensation in my abdomen was begging me to massage it, but I didn't dare make a move as they approached.

"Spinelli, what the hell are you doing here?" asked Mendola.

Immediately, I looked to Bill for assistance.

"I drove him up here," said Bill. "You knuckleheads left him behind on Friday."

"No, we didn't," countered Spivey. "I heard Mr. Castro ask Spinelli if he had a ride."

Bill looked directly at me. "Is that true?"

"Well . . ." I said, "I decided to go at the last minute, but they didn't have any room left in any of the cars."

"What a fucking crock of shit," interjected Spivey. Mendola and Metheny burst into hysterics.

"All right, enough," said Bill. "Let's pack up the truck and get out of here." The others began stacking their knapsacks and equipment into the storage shed. When Bill noticed my knapsack up against his truck, he looked over at me and then charged like a bull. Grabbing my arm, he said, "What is that filthy knapsack doing against my truck?"

Confused, I muttered, "It's mine."

"I know whose it is," he continued, his face just inches from mine. "I want to know who told you to put it there."

I didn't have an answer.

Other boys began to circle around us like seagulls at the dump. I caught a glimpse of Spivey's eyes, gleaming with conceit. "You're one fucking disrespectful Scout," he said. Walking over to where my knapsack was, he lifted it effortlessly with one hand. "You got some nerve leaning this shitty-ass pack against your Scoutmaster's truck." The other boys concurred.

Bill was staring straight into my eyes. He seemed to look right through me. And all at once, I realized he wasn't the same person who tried to befriend me on the ride up to camp. He was someone else, or worse, he was pretending not to be my friend because he didn't want these boys to think he liked me. I started to think there were two Bills: the one who was being mean to me now, and the one who wanted to teach me to be a man. But it also seemed like the world was made up of two different types of boys—the ones who liked me, like Jonathan, and the others who hated me, like Chris Spivey and Seth Connelly. How Bill fit into this world made no sense to me at that moment.

"Wait," cried Spivey. "And what do we have here?" He now pointed to the hole in the bottom of my knapsack. First he poked his finger into it; then within seconds he'd forced his entire hand inside. I felt humiliated in front of the other boys as he rummaged around the inside of my knapsack. The pain below my ribs flared up at that very second. More boys gathered around to laugh along with him. He was creating quite a show. Even Bill was amused.

"Hey, you guys, look at this," announced Spivey, wrenching the frying pan through the now-gaping hole. Spivey discarded my knapsack on the ground like a piece of trash and waved the frying pan overhead like a trophy.

"I heard of pulling a rabbit out of a hat, but you've really gone and done it this time, Spivey." Mendola laughed.

"By Jove, I think I've got it," said Spivey with an English accent. "Hey, Spinelli, were you planning on frying up your balls with this thing?"

"All right, enough," said Bill.

Spivey ignored Bill and charged directly toward me. "Seriously, I could just clobber you over the head with this thing," continued Spivey.

"I said enough!" barked Bill. "Let's get moving. We've

wasted enough time already. Spivey and Mendola, you both ride up front with me. The rest of you clowns get in the back." I turned to Bill, bewildered by the exchange that had just taken place. Even though I was thoroughly humiliated, a part of me still thought Bill was going to make things right. Before he turned away, he stared down at me again and asked, "Are you waiting for your own personal invitation, Spinelli?"

That was all it took. I knew my place.

I filed in line with the others and headed around to the back of the truck. Spivey surprised me and came around the other side. The moment I turned the corner, he hit me square in the face with his fist. I stumbled back in shock. Only Metheny saw the whole thing, but he did not intervene. I distinctly remember hearing Bill call out Spivey's name, but Spivey didn't flinch. Instead, he just stared at me with those piercing blue eyes of his, running his hand through his long blond hair. I was in shock. I rubbed my cheek and suppressed the urge to cry. A self-assured expression came over Spivey's face. He knew I would never tell. In the span of those several seconds, I wondered why he hated me so much. I held his stare, petrified that he was going to hit me again, but he didn't.

I NEVER TOLD ANYONE ABOUT THE CONVERSATION I HAD WITH BILL, not even Jonathan. I didn't know what to think, especially after the way Bill treated me in front of the other boys that Sunday afternoon. It was bewildering that Bill could act one way with me when we were alone and, then, completely different when we were around those other boys. Unfortunately, I now had more important things to worry about. I was scared to death that Spivey was going to hurt me again.

That following Tuesday night at Boy Scouts, we were assigned to breakout sessions. I was sitting with a small group, listening to Mr. Castro discuss hypothermia. Bill surprised me by coming up from behind and hoisting me off the floor. "Everyone," he shouted. "This is a bear hug. It's a great way to immobilize your opponent." I was suffocating under the strain of

Bill's massive arms against my rib cage. The pain was so intense I thought he was going to snap me in two. "Had enough?" he shouted in my ear. Unable to speak, I nodded violently. "Okay," he said. Then he set me down. I crumpled onto the floor gasping for breath. "Good man, Spinelli," said Bill, extending his hand out to me. I took it, and he pulled me effortlessly onto my feet.

Leaning in, he whispered, "You're scheduled for your first Scoutmaster meeting this Thursday. I'll expect you at my house at eight o'clock. Have your father drop you off by eight and not a minute later." Then he released my hand and walked away.

CHAPTER 19

Making Tenderfoot

I ARRIVED AT BILL'S HOUSE ALMOST FIVE MINUTES EARLY ON THURS-DAY EVENING. It was dark and muggy on his front porch. Crickets were chirping in the grass. I heard footsteps, then Bill opened the door, and a stream of yellow light flooded the porch. Standing behind the screen door, his massive silhouette was anything but inviting. Before I went inside, I reluctantly waved good-bye to my father as he drove away.

Inside, Bill's house felt stuffy and smelled like the time we visited my mother's friend Nella at the nursing home. Her room had the distinct aroma of boiled potatoes and cabbage. I followed Bill into the living room, where he instructed me to sit on the couch.

"I have some business to finish downstairs," he said. "I'll be back in a few minutes. Wait here."

I placed my book bag on the floor and took off my sweatshirt. That was when I noticed an old woman with curly gray hair and a pale, sagging face sitting in a reclining chair in her nightgown. With a crocheted blanket over her legs, she was parked inches from the television, watching *The Newlywed Game*. Bill neglected to introduce us, but I assumed she was his mother.

I took it upon myself to say hello, but she never responded, even during a commercial. She just quietly stared at the screen. I wondered whether she was senile or demented, like my Uncle Salvatore. Often when we visited him, he would sit in front of the television and laugh. Sometimes he laughed at the television even when it wasn't on. But Mrs. Fox wasn't laughing. She was sitting there as though I was invisible.

My eyes wandered around their living room, which was decorated in early American style. The walls were paneled. There was a trophy case next to the television. An American flag hung on the far wall, next to a plaque of a bald eagle holding another American flag in its mouth. There were faded doilies on the end tables and sofa. The curtains were made from heavy, dark plaid fabric, and everywhere there was a faint smell of mildew. Even Mrs. Fox looked like an old fixture that hadn't been moved in years, collecting layers of dust. Looking around that room, I wondered what my mother would have said if she was with me. She would have never sat down on that couch.

In the trophy case there were three rows of glass shelves, each stacked with various awards, plaques, and medals Bill had earned. There was even a black-and-white photograph of Bill accepting a medal of honor in his police uniform. I learned from Jonathan that the Foxes were an Irish Catholic family made up of three sons and one daughter. Bill's father, now deceased, had been a security guard. All of Bill's brothers were policemen, and even Bill's sister, Wendy, had married a cop.

The Newlywed Game ended, and another game show began. The longer I sat there, the more concerned I was that something was wrong. I wondered whether I had been forgotten. To keep me occupied, I recited the Scout Oath over and over in my head. Once Bill had confirmed our private meeting, I began reading through the *Boy Scout Handbook* in order to prepare. Tenderfoot was the next level after Scout. To achieve this rank, a Scout had to meet several requirements, including reciting from memory the Scout Oath, Law, and Motto. A Scout had to spend at least one night on a troop campout and participate in a Scoutmaster conference. This meeting with Bill appeared perfectly legitimate, yet something was troubling me.

Moving up the ranks to Eagle Scout was the single most important part of being a Boy Scout. Yet I had no interest in becoming an Eagle Scout. In fact, I didn't even care about Tenderfoot. All I wanted to do was collect merit badges. I was obsessed with them. These small, circular pieces of cloth, embroidered with colorful logos, fascinated me. I loved the look and feel of them, and I loved wearing them. When Josephine was younger, she had been a Girl Scout. She earned many merit badges and wore them on a sash across her chest. Whenever she came home from meetings, I stared at them with envy. When she went out to play, I would sneak into her bedroom, steal the sash from her drawer, and wear it as I waved at myself in the mirror like Miss America. If anything excited me about Boy Scouts, it was the prospect of owning merit badges.

After nearly an hour, I heard the basement door open. The room suddenly filled with voices. One by one, they filed past me on their way out the front door: James Mendola, Stanley Metheny, and Chris Spivey. An unsettling panic came over me. My worst nightmare had come true. Bill followed closely behind. When Mendola saw me sitting in the living room, he stopped abruptly, pointed, and erupted with laughter. Metheny collided into him, and this set off a domino effect as Spivey came up behind them, until they were all standing there, looking at me from the foyer. Metheny and Mendola continued laughing uncontrollably, but not Spivey. He was staring at me with a mixture of astonishment and hatred. Instantly, I felt that twang of pain below my ribs. "Good night, guys," said Bill sternly as he ushered them quickly toward the front door.

Spivey craned his neck around and stared at Bill with a confused expression. Then, before he was out the door, I detected a wistful look in his eyes, an uncharacteristically wounded expression, one I thought Spivey incapable of. Ignoring him, Bill proceeded to rush them outside. When they were finally gone, I heaved a heavy sigh of relief.

"Okay, you ready, Spinelli?" asked Bill.

I got up and followed him up the stairs. Looking back, I saw

Mrs. Fox remained catatonic, in her own world and indifferent to everything that was going on around her, just like a trophy in that glass case.

Upstairs, Bill's large bedroom was divided in half, with a home office by the entrance and a bed in the far corner. The walls were paneled in the same dark wood as the living room. Over his bed was a poster of Farrah Fawcett wearing an orange bathing suit. Bill motioned for me to sit in the chair beside his gunmetal-gray desk. He switched on a small green desk lamp, and that was when I saw his gun.

Bill sat down and held out his hand. "Okay, let me have your *Boy Scout Handbook*," he said. I pulled it out of my knapsack and gave it to him. Bill began flipping through the pages. I kept staring at the gun, wondering whether it was loaded. Once he found the section he was looking for, he laid my handbook on the desk and turned it around so I could read it. "See here?" He pointed. "This is the section I was referring to the other day. Do you remember what we talked about?"

"Yes."

"Read this," he said.

The title of the section was Sexual Responsibility. My eyes scanned the page, but there was no mention of jerking off or boy bonding. Instead, it was a warning against premarital sex. As an eleven-year-old, I didn't see how this had anything to do with me. Once I was done reading, I looked up at Bill, still confused. He read my expression and stood up. I watched him walk to the other side of the room. On the wall next to his bed was a bookcase. Bill rummaged behind the books and fished out several magazines. Laying them on the bed, he began flipping through the pages. "Come here," he said.

I slowly made my way across the room. Farrah Fawcett's eyes seemed to follow me from the poster. Her smile was like no other I'd seen. *Too many teeth*, I thought to myself. When I reached Bill, I noticed the magazines on his bed contained photographs of naked men and women. The black-and-white pictures were faded. Some of the pages were torn. "You see here?"

he said, pointing to a picture of a woman holding a man's penis. "Do you know what she's doing?"

I shrugged.

"She's jerking him off," he said. "Come here and sit down next to me. I'll show you more."

Bill continued to turn the pages, revealing more and more graphic depictions of sex. There were several photographs of naked men and women kissing. There were close-ups of erect penises. I had no idea that penises came in so many different sizes and shapes. When Bill flipped over to the next page, there was a photograph of a blonde with her mouth on a man's penis. I remember thinking she wasn't very pretty, not like Farrah Fawcett. Bill tapped this photo with his finger. "See that?" he said, smiling.

I nodded.

Just then, my left leg began to spasm so uncontrollably that I felt the need to grab it so that it would stop bobbing up and down. Bill reached over and placed his hand on mine. "It's okay," he whispered. "Don't worry. That's natural." He stared at me for what felt like a very long time. His eyes once again seemed to look right through me, but unlike the haunting stare that petrified me on the last hiking trip, this time his eyes seemed to penetrate my soul. His attention was unlike any other I had experienced, and I felt comforted by his tender touch.

Bill set the magazines aside and placed my hand on his groin. I was surprised, but I wasn't afraid. It's difficult to remember how I felt exactly. I recall only images, like snapshots from a movie: Mrs. Fox sitting in her reclining chair like a frozen statue, the gun on Bill's desk, Farrah Fawcett in her orange bathing suit, the woman in the magazine holding the man's penis in her mouth, Bill standing up to remove his pants, the photograph of Bill receiving a medal of honor, dark black pubic hair, my hand wet with milky fluid, and finally, me, sitting in Bill's truck as he drove me back home.

Inside my house, I closed the door and leaned against it. In the darkness of the foyer, I heard my mother call out, "Frank, is that you? Don't forget to lock the door."

I stood there for several minutes more, replaying the events that had just taken place and thinking the whole thing was wrong but not knowing why. If I had been able to run upstairs and explain to my parents what had just happened with the same conviction I used to convince them to buy me that Evel Knievel action figure and Scramble Van, then I think my whole life would have turned out differently.

ONE WEEK LATER, BILL SHOWED UP AT MY HOUSE UNANNOUNCED. I was watching television in the den when I heard my mother cry out from the kitchen upstairs. Her voice was shrill and hysterical, as if she had just won the lottery. "Frank, Bill's here!" I stood up and walked to the front door. There he was, parked outside, waiting. He leaned out the passenger side window, smiled, and waved me over to him. My mother hurried down the stairs, holding my jacket in her hands. She slipped it on me, zipped it up the front, and said, "Go with him, but be back in time for dinner."

Bill drove to a hardware store. Soon after we entered, a man wearing an apron that read DAN'S HARDWARE strolled up and asked whether we needed help. Was he Dan? Bill described what he was looking for, and the man took us to a display of light bulbs and fixtures. As Bill made his selection, the man winked at me. He was bald with white skin and a purple birthmark over his left temple. "Are you helping your dad change lights today?" he asked.

Bill laughed and handed the man two switches and a dimmer. "We'll take these," he said. Then Bill put his arm around my shoulder, and we followed the man to the front of the store. I thought it was peculiar that Bill didn't correct him. As we reached the cash register, I wondered what it would be like if Bill were my dad. Would we run errands, go camping with the Boy Scouts, and then look at dirty magazines when we were alone? Was that what other fathers did with their sons? I didn't think so.

After Bill paid, we went back to his house. I expected to see his mother in her chair, but there was no one else home. Seeing that empty chair with the crocheted blanket hanging over it made wonder where she was. I began to perspire, thinking Bill hadn't brought me here just to change light bulbs.

"Do you want a can of soda?" he asked from the kitchen.

"No, thanks."

"Come in here and help me."

Bill had pushed the kitchen table aside to change the light bulb in the overhead lamp. He unfolded a stepladder and instructed me to hold it as he climbed up. The ladder barely moved under the weight of his body. Scanning the kitchen, I noticed the walls were covered in faded yellow-and-green wallpaper that crisscrossed, forming diamond shapes. There was a grease stain on the wall next to the stove. The linoleum table had chipped edges, and the aluminum chairs were upholstered in green vinyl.

"Do you help your dad at home?"

"Not really."

"That's a shame," he added. "Boys should help their fathers. Fathers should make their boys help them around the house. That's how boys learn to become men."

Once Bill finished, he took the ladder and carried it upstairs. I followed after him. We changed the light bulb in his bedroom, and then one in his closet. When he was done, he walked over to his bed and sat down. I knew what was going to happen next. Bill removed the magazines from behind the books and laid them out. "Come here," he said. I sat down next to Bill. We were silent for a very long time. He picked up a stack of letters from his nightstand and began sifting through them. His legs spread wide. As I watched him read his mail, his leg inched closer and closer to mine until his knee pressed up against my thigh. It stayed there for a while.

"I want to show you something," he said.

I moved in closer, and Bill put his arm around my shoulder. It felt heavy but nice. He opened a magazine and showed me more pictures. Slowly he turned the pages. Then he stopped when he got to that photograph of the woman with her mouth on the man's penis. He handed me the magazine. I stared at that blonde and this time felt myself becoming aroused. Bill then unbuckled his belt and pushed his pants past his knees. I tried not to look up from the page because I was embarrassed. It was daytime, and unlike the other night, the room was brightly lit. Glancing up, I was shocked to see Bill naked in the light.

Bill took the magazine from me. My leg began to shake again. "It's okay," he said. "Really, it's okay." Then he stood up. I felt his hands over my ears. My eyes were closed. He didn't say anything else. I knew what he wanted me to do, and I did it. I did it because I wanted him to like me. I did it because I wanted to be a normal boy, and more than anything else, I wanted his approval so that he wouldn't ever let boys like Chris Spivey or Seth Connelly hurt me.

I can still remember how it felt and tasted, but it was the smell—pungent and sweaty, like clothes in a hamper—that stayed with me the most. A few seconds later he pulled my head off and stroked his penis, holding it tightly, until the milky fluid came out all over his hand. Then he lay down on the bed and exhaled deeply.

Driving home, we rode in silence. Maybe if he had been mean, I might have run away, but he was showing me things I thought I needed to know to become a man. He was teaching me all the things my own father was incapable of.

Before I got out of the truck, Bill grabbed my shoulder. When I turned around, he said, "By the way, congratulations. You made Tenderfoot."

CHAPTER 20

Becoming a Monster

FROM THAT DAY ON, BILL AND I MET ONCE OR TWICE A WEEK. Sometimes, we ran errands, but most times we just went back to his house and he showed me new things in his magazines. At Boy Scout meetings, Bill barely paid me any attention. I told myself he didn't want anyone to think he was choosing favorites, but it still didn't make attending meetings any more bearable. All the more, it was another reason why I never learned to enjoy Boy Scouts. Still, I continued to go because I knew that Bill wanted me to, and I wanted to please him.

Eventually, we stopped going on errands altogether. He'd pick me up after school, and then we'd drive straight to his house. Sometimes his mother would be in the living room, watching television. Other times we were alone. It didn't matter. He never acknowledged her when I was with him, so I grew to ignore her myself. Once we were inside his room, I'd forget all about Mrs. Fox because we were alone. When we were alone, Bill became a different person, unlike when we were at Boy Scout meetings or running errands. Inside his bedroom, Bill was quiet, brooding, and sexual.

Every time it was the same routine: sit on his bed, look at magazines, and then came the long wait—that period in which we would sit, side by side, with those same magazines opened up on his lap. He'd stare at the pages and then at me. I watched his eyes flicker as time seemed to stand still. Then he would close his eyes so tightly I thought he might cry. He seemed to struggle with something, but in the end, his hand always reached over to touch me. Finally, the long wait was over. Once he'd gotten past that point, he'd stand up, take off his clothes, and get on the bed. Afterward, we immediately left the house. Sometimes he took me for ice cream; other times he just brought me straight home.

Over the next several weeks, I slowly began to withdraw from my usual after-school activities. I hardly played with my Evel Knievel doll and Scramble Van. When Diane and Karen came by the house, I told my mother to send them away. I even stopped calling Jonathan. Instead, I spent hours alone in the bathroom, exploring the forbidden female products stored under the sink: tampons, sanitary napkins, and vaginal douches. I became obsessed with them, taking them apart as I tried to figure out what they were used for. I even kept a tampon hidden between my mattress and box spring. At night, I'd take it out and sleep with it under my pillow.

At school, I asked Chris Reynolds why girls needed such things. He told me: "When a girl gets her period, she has to plug up the hole so that she doesn't bleed all over the place. So she can either stick a tampon up her cooch or lay a maxi-pad on her panties to soak up the blood." How he knew all this I never figured out, but it made sense. Now I understood Aunt Flo's visits better.

One morning, I stole a sanitary napkin from the bathroom. I removed the adhesive strip and affixed it to my underwear. I wore it to school just to see how it felt. I found it very uncomfortable. When I got home that afternoon, I removed it from my underwear and masturbated on it.

TWO MONTHS AFTER I MADE TENDERFOOT, Bill asked me to get my parents' permission to sleep over at his house. He told me that he often did this with the other boys and that it would be a good experience for me. My parents were so excited when I asked them. From my mother's reaction, you would have thought I'd just been awarded a full scholarship to Harvard.

For years, my parents had tried everything to get me to participate in activities that other little boys were naturally drawn to. How many Saturdays had they stood by and watched me sit on the bench as the other boys played? How many times had my coaches told them I just wasn't cut out for sports? Bill asking me to sleep over at his house was the acceptance my parents had been yearning for. Finally, someone with authority, a cop no less, was taking their son under his wing. This wasn't just an invitation; this was a sign I was fitting in.

Of course, my mother made it into a bigger deal than it actually was. Like most things, my father didn't care one way or the other as long as my mother was happy. It seemed as if we were always trying to make Mommy happy because we knew the alternative was worse. Maybe that was why my father worked more overtime than he had to, why Maria snuck food into her bedroom at night, why Josephine couldn't wait to move out, and why I always shut myself up in my room. These were the ways we coped with our mother's excessive doting, knowing it was better to exist under her radar than in her line of fire.

That Saturday, I packed up my red knapsack (my mother sewed up the hole), and my father drove me to Bill's house. Standing on the dark porch, I wondered whether Bill was going to make me wait in the living room with his mother again. Then I had this sudden overwhelming fear that Spivey, Mendola, and Metheny might be in his basement. In that second, I calculated the risk of seeing Spivey again and how my presence would only fuel his hatred toward me. I never understood boys like him, the ones who were mad at the world. For some reason, I always seemed to be the focus of their hatred.

Since the first time I visited Bill's house, I noticed that Spivey didn't attend meetings as religiously as he had in the past. Then I remembered the night he saw me sitting in the living room. The inexplicable hurt expression on his face as Bill hurried him out the door lingered in my memory.

When the front porch light went on, I took a step backward.

Looking over my shoulder at my father waiting in the car, I felt the urge to run. Sleeping over at Bill's house suddenly seemed like an awful idea. Then Bill opened the front door. The porch was flooded with yellow light, and I froze. The next thing I knew, Bill was taking my knapsack off my shoulder and I was waving good-bye to my dad.

Bill led me straight upstairs. He seemed hurried. I peeked into the living room and caught a glimpse of Mrs. Fox in her chair. This time I was sure she saw me. Without lifting her head, she peered up at me, and our eyes met for one brief second. This surprised and scared me at the same time. When I looked up at Bill, he was already inside his bedroom. I followed after him, but just before I climbed the stairs, I peeked over at Mrs. Fox again. This time she was staring at the television.

Inside Bill's room, we didn't speak. Closing the door, he undressed to his underwear. I did the same. Then we got in bed, and he turned out the light. It was only 9 P.M. I stared up at the ceiling, wondering how I was going to fall asleep. Then I rolled on my side and stared out the window. I listened to the cars drive by and thought about this relationship I had with a grown man. Spending time alone with Bill in his bedroom had become so much a part of my life. I never told anyone about our secret visits because I instinctively knew we'd get in trouble. I continued to protect Bill even as these visits became more and more unpleasant.

I don't recall how long we lay there in the dark. Bill started to stir, and then I felt his hands on my shoulders pulling me toward his body. Bill removed his underwear, and then I felt the pressure of his penis against my back. He maneuvered his arm around my chest, and with his free hand, he pulled down my underwear. Then he began to push his penis in between my buttocks. It started to hurt. With my eyes still closed, I thought about the time my family went to Disney World. We rode Space Mountain. My father sat next to me holding my hand because he knew I was frightened. I wished my father was holding my hand now.

That night was different from all the other times before. I

tried to squirm away, but Bill's arm was pressed so tightly against my chest that I couldn't move. I felt trapped, and that terrified me. Despite his persistence, Bill wasn't able to push himself inside me. Eventually he stopped. His grip relaxed, and I breathed heavily with relief. Had Bill succeeded, I might have screamed. Maybe he suspected as much, and that was why he relented. But it wasn't over yet. Grabbing my shoulders with his hands, Bill turned me around to face him. Then he pushed my head down under the covers and onto his penis. When it was all over, I opened my eyes. Bill had gotten out of bed and was in the bathroom. In the dark, I could still see the poster of Farrah Fawcett on the wall, staring, smiling, laughing . . . at me.

I began to wet my bed shortly after that night.

The first time it happened, my mother simply changed the sheets. When it happened again, she confronted me. Even though I felt I had successfully deflected her questions, something told me my mother wasn't completely satisfied with my answers. It angered me that she gave up so easily, but I knew she didn't want to hear the truth. Just as she didn't want to know why I stole that Barbie from Diane's trash. Instead, she'd rather have believed that Barbie was accidentally left behind the couch. I suspected the truth would have been too painful. If I told my parents what Bill and I were doing when we were alone, they would have been horrified. And even though they should have picked up on the clues, I lied to protect them.

The next day, when I returned home from school, I went straight to my bedroom as usual. But something didn't seem right. So I made a quick assessment: My collection of Micronaut men was aligned on my dresser, assembled for battle. My desk still contained all my drawings and writing utensils. Even the bed had been restored with a newly laundered Evel Knievel comforter. Nothing tangible seemed different yet; that made it all the more frightening. Finally, sitting down on my bed, I was startled by a strange crackling noise. Immediately, I removed the sheets and found my mother had upholstered my mattress with a thick plastic cover sheet.

Now I felt trapped by the secret I shared with Bill. Until now

I'd thought I could just keep this secret, pretend it wasn't there. I thought it wouldn't affect my life, and I would just continue to go on like before. But now I knew that wasn't true. The plastic sheets were proof. There were two realities now: the one I shared with my family and the one I had with Bill. And he was the only one who knew who I really was.

I BEGAN TO AVOID BILL'S CALLS BECAUSE I DIDN'T WANT TO SEE HIM. I didn't fully understand why, but I knew deep down inside me—in that place where the gnawing sensation developed below my ribs—that what we were doing alone in his bedroom was a sin.

After two weeks, Bill showed up at my house one day after school. My mother came rushing into my room. She instructed me to put down whatever it was that I was doing and go with him.

After the night I slept over his house, his behavior toward me became sterner and more commanding, less friendly and inviting. He hardly smiled at me at Boy Scout meetings, and that day, too, he hardly spoke as he drove down the streets of my neighborhood. He seemed to drive aimlessly. After a while, I thought he was going to kidnap me, and then I would never see my family again. But like all the other times, we ended up in his bedroom and had sex. Then he drove me home.

One Saturday, he made me kneel on the floor before him. He pressed my head down so firmly with his hands I panicked. His penis pushed my mouth wide open. I braced myself by placing my hands on his knees, trying to pull away, but he overpowered me. I was suffocating, but the more I resisted, the more he held me against my will. My eyes watered, and I began to retch. I was petrified that I might vomit, and that made me panic even more. The smell of his sweat filled my nose, and suddenly I felt a surging acidic taste fill my mouth. Bill was done.

That evening, I locked myself up in the bathroom and took a long hot bath. I let the water run so that it made my skin red, and I turned it off only when I couldn't stand the pain any longer. Then I sat there quietly, wondering how I'd gotten to this place. The world I knew, my world, seemed strange. Clearly, Bill was not my friend. I was his prisoner.

I must have been in the tub for at least an hour when Josephine began banging on the door. "What are you doing in there?" she shouted. Then I heard her laugh. That made me cringe, and I sank down under the water. Her laughter echoed in my head, reminding me of the Farrah Fawcett poster in Bill's room. It haunted me, yet no matter how I tried to convince myself that Josephine couldn't possibly know the truth or that Farrah was just a photograph on a wall, I couldn't drown out the laughter, even underwater. After several seconds, I flipped the lever with my toe and listened to the water gurgle down the drain. As soon as I stepped outside the bathroom, my sister called, "What were you doing in there?" She was standing in the doorway of her bedroom with my mother behind her. "You've been in there, like, forever."

Without a word, I walked to my room and slammed the door behind me.

That night, I wet the bed again.

About the same time, I began to have abduction nightmares. I worried that strange men in overcoats and hats, faceless men who traveled in packs, would come and get me in my bed. I started sleeping with my covers tied to the headboard so that I would be safe under my makeshift tent. I never walked around my neighborhood alone, and when I rode my bicycle, I maintained a conscious awareness of everyone around me.

⸻

AFTER EVERY SUNDAY DINNER, my parents and I would drive to Brooklyn to visit my grandfather, or Nonno, as we called him. After several weeks, my fear of abduction evolved to the point that I was convinced the tollbooth operator worked for the strange men who wore overcoats and hats. Before my father stopped to pay the toll, I'd wrap my sock over my mouth and lie on the floor of the car in order to trick the tollbooth operator into thinking my parents were delivering me to these strange men. Of course, my parents didn't know what I was doing in the backseat, and the tollbooth operator must have thought I was a peculiar child. Then once our car passed the tollbooth and drove onto the bridge, I relaxed, taking the sock from my mouth and putting it back on my foot.

Visiting my grandfather on Sundays was something I grew to enjoy. Josephine and Maria no longer accompanied us once they became teenagers. Josephine called my grandfather's apartment a "mausoleum of boredom." But I didn't feel that way, because my uncle Sal and aunt Olivia lived upstairs with their son, Alex, who was seven years my junior.

Uncle Sal was my mother's older brother. He was a paranoid schizophrenic who married my aunt despite my mother's vehement objection. The day he announced their engagement, a huge fight broke out at the dinner table. I was six years old and didn't fully understand what all the shouting was about. Later on, Josephine explained that Uncle Sal was married once before to a woman who'd left him because he had a history of violence. Despite my mother's protests, my uncle remarried and several months later, my aunt Olivia announced she was pregnant. On the drive home later that night, I remember my mother recited the rosary over and over while she sobbed.

For many years, I enjoyed being the youngest and only grandson. When I turned seven years old, I was horrified when my aunt Olivia brought home that little brown creature in a blanket. That horror grew into an insane fascination once I realized how much attention my replacement was taking away from me.

My mother was the first to notice. To get me to bond with my new cousin, my mother had me hold him one day. She explained that he was very fragile and needed extra-special care during the first few months of his life. To prove this, she removed his baby blue knitted cap and showed me a pulsating area in the back of his head where the soft swirls of his hair converged like a fingerprint. "See that?" she said. "That's the soft spot where the bones haven't come together yet. You must be careful never to touch that area because it could cause permanent brain damage." To this day, I still don't know why she felt the need to share this information with her jealous son.

On the day of Alex's christening, my aunt and uncle threw a party in their apartment. Once Alex had been fed, my aunt Olivia carried him into her bedroom and placed him in the center of their bed for a nap. Later, while everyone was enjoying coffee and cake, I slipped inside the bedroom unnoticed and tiptoed toward the bed. When I got close enough, I removed his baptism cap and watched the pulsating soft spot my mother warned me about. I stood there, staring at it, wanting only to know what it felt like and nothing more.

Leaning in closer, so that my head was eye level with his scalp, I reached out my hand. For a brief second, the pulp of my finger met Alex's velvety skin. I felt his pulse, smelled the baby powder, and then heard the shriek of my mother standing in the doorway. The events that followed were a blur. I recall being hit repeatedly. Alex cried. Then later that night, I woke up in the backseat of our car. We were home, and my father's refusal to carry me inside was the worst punishment of all.

Years later, when Alex got older, he'd rush down the stairs as soon as we arrived. Grinning from ear to ear, he'd wait by the door for me to give the word so that we could go up to his room and play. That consisted of watching television and playing with his toys. Even though he was just five years old at the time, we were very close. Some of my fondest childhood memories were the Sunday afternoons we played in his bedroom while his mother served us vanilla ice cream with Bosco chocolate syrup.

Yet our innocent playtime deteriorated. I began torturing Alex—locking him in the closet and hiding his toys—until he cried. Initially, it felt good to see his tears streaming down his cheeks. I was a god in my cousin's world. Then later, when my father drove us back home, I'd lie in the backseat with my head pressed up against the cushion, promising myself I would never make Alex cry again.

Yet on each Sunday I returned, Alex would be waiting there for me with the same wide-eyed, eager enthusiasm he displayed the week before. And before long, he would be in tears again. That's when I realized my worst fear was now a reality: I had become exactly like Bill. I had become a monster. Driving home one night, I prayed to God to make it stop. I pleaded for Bill to go away.

Chapter 21

Sleaze Torso

April 6, 1980: Bill and his partner were called to investigate a burglary. They received word from dispatch at 4 A.M. about a robbery in progress on Twelfth Avenue in Brooklyn involving a suspicious white Buick. Without lights or sirens, they turned onto the street and found a white car parked down the block. Bill got out of the police car and went around to the passenger side. His partner, Nick, approached the driver. Two Caucasian boys in their teens were sitting in the front seat.

"License and registration," asked Nick.

"Did I do something wrong, officer?" responded the driver.

Watching their transaction cautiously, Bill saw a subtle movement of the driver's hand down toward his ankle and a flash of metal reflecting off his partner's flashlight.

"He's got a weapon!" Bill cried.

The teen in the passenger seat lunged forward and grabbed Bill's arms. The driver shifted the car into gear; tires squealed. Nick hit the ground and the car charged forward. Bill's arm was trapped in the passenger-side window like a vise.

In his book, Bill stated the first thing he heard was his hip bone shatter as the car sped away. Then he tasted blood as it filled his mouth. He survived only because he was able to retrieve his gun and shoot several rounds at the tires. The car veered into a series of parked cars before it came to a halt. Bill was unconscious when they found him at the scene.

I was at a Boy Scout meeting that night when I heard a commotion in the vestibule by the entrance. Mrs. Duran burst into tears. An ominous silence fell over the entire troop. Then Mr. Castro stepped forward and called everyone to attention. "Please," he said. "I have some terrible news. Bill was badly hurt this morning, and he's in the hospital."

"He's in a goddamned coma," I heard Mrs. Duran say before her husband escorted her outside. She was trembling.

"Bill's in the intensive care unit," Mr. Castro continued. "I want you all to join me now and pray for his speedy recovery. Our Father, who art in heaven . . ."

I was too shocked to recite the words. I kept telling myself that it couldn't be as bad as Mr. Castro was making it out to be. I wanted to believe that Bill was fine or that he had just broken a few bones. I couldn't allow myself to think that he might be hurt so badly that he could possibly die. Had God misunderstood my prayers? I just wanted Bill to leave me alone. I never intended for anything more than that, and now it appeared as though I might have contributed to his death.

BOY SCOUT MEETINGS CONTINUED AS USUAL, with Mr. Castro acting as Scoutmaster. I liked meetings during those weeks when Bill was recovering in the hospital. With all the boys seated around him in a circle on the gymnasium floor, Mr. Castro often led interesting discussions on first aid and camping. Best of all, he didn't tolerate bullying, particularly from the senior Scouts, and that marked another significant change, because Spivey, Mendola, and Metheny stopped attending meetings.

Around the same time, Jonathan and I began work on our science fair project. The topic was telepathy. Jonathan came up with the idea himself. Initially, I refused to take part in it, not because it didn't intrigue me, but simply because I didn't want Seth Connelly and his gang to make fun of us. In the end, Mrs.

Giordano convinced me to join Jonathan's project when I failed to come up with an idea of my own.

The experiment involved keeping a detailed journal for two weeks. Each afternoon, we were to allocate ourselves to a quiet, undisclosed place where we were to meditate for fifteen minutes. After that, we were to write down or draw the thoughts or images that came to mind. Then at the end of the two weeks, Jonathan and I had to compare our journals to see whether there were any correlations. To prove our theory, we had to show that there were striking similarities.

The week before the science fair, we were in Jonathan's basement mapping out our journals on poster board. I thought it would be a good idea to illustrate certain entries alongside excerpts from our actual diaries. Overall, our project was a failure: we couldn't prove that, over time, our telepathic powers improved. Looking over our results, I noted a strong theme of alien abduction in Jonathan's journal while mine often took place in the forest where I was being chased by wild animals.

Upstairs I could hear Mrs. Duran singing along to the radio. "Your mom has a terrible voice," I said.

"You don't have to tell me."

A little while later, Mrs. Duran came downstairs holding a plate of brownies in one hand and a cigarette in the other. "Break time. How's it going, boys?" She came up behind Jonathan and gave him a hug. He shrugged her off. "Be nice to your mother. I bet Frankie wouldn't treat his mom like that." Then she looked over at me and winked.

"Mom, we're busy," said Jonathan.

"Okay, okay," she said, setting the plate of brownies on the table next to us. "You can be such an ungrateful little shit sometimes, Jonathan."

Shocked, I looked up in time to see her wink at me again before she went upstairs. "Your mom is so cool," I said. "She's nothing like my mom." Jonathan didn't say anything. He seemed distracted that afternoon. "Is everything okay?" I asked.

He shook his head.

"Put down that crayon." I insisted. "You've been coloring the same spot for over ten minutes."

Jonathan looked up at me. "Can I tell you a secret?"

"Yes."

"For the past few weeks, Tommy Scalici has been making me deliver his newspaper route every morning before school."

"Are you kidding?"

He nodded and wiped a tear from beneath his glasses. "I feel so stupid. I haven't told anyone. One afternoon I was walking through Emerson Hill on my way home from school. I ran into Tommy Scalici and Seth Connelly smoking pot in the woods. When they saw me, I ran, but they were fast. Seth threatened to kill me if I told anyone. Then they made me get on my hands and knees and promise. The next morning, Tommy was waiting for me outside my house with his newspaper bag. He threw it at me and told me to deliver each one as he followed behind me on his bicycle. I've been doing it ever since then."

I could not contain my outrage. "You have to tell someone! Your parents, Mrs. Giordano, anyone! You can't just keep delivering his newspapers every day. That's not right, and if you won't tell, then I will."

"No, please," he begged. "Tommy said he'd kill me if I told anyone."

"What are you going to do? Just keep delivering his stupid newspapers?"

Jonathan was weeping now. The lenses of his glasses steamed up, and he had to take them off to clean them. When he looked up at me, his squinty brown eyes reminded me of a gerbil's. It hurt me to see him cry. "There has to be someone we can tell," I said. Then it came to me. "We can talk to Mr. Castro! He'll help."

Jonathan shook his head. "No, he'll tell my dad. They're good friends, and if my dad knows, then my mom will definitely find out."

I considered his argument. Mrs. Duran would be furious if she knew her son was being bullied into delivering newspapers for Tommy. Once Mrs. Duran found out, she wouldn't be able to keep quiet. She'd probably go straight over to Tommy Scalici's house herself and scream at him right in front of his parents. That would only make Jonathan's situation worse; we both knew the only thing more hated than a sissy was a momma's boy. If that got back to everyone at school, Jonathan wouldn't be able to walk down the hall without being ridiculed.

"You're right," I said.

Jonathan sank his head down on the table. I wanted to help him so badly, but I couldn't think of anyone else we could go to. Watching him convulse with tears, I tried to imagine how difficult it must have been for him to keep this secret all this time. Not once during the past two weeks when we were working together did he indicate that something was wrong. If our science project hadn't proved we weren't telepathic, then his revelation certainly did.

I paced the basement floor. "There has to be someone who could scare Tommy off?"

"I'm doomed. At least there are only two more months left until summer."

"Stop crying. You're getting our science project all wet."

Jonathan's face was so flushed it startled me. I felt his pain, knowing that our reputations at school had always been a source of distress for both of us. In the corridors, on the playground, and even in the streets, threats of humiliation and violence hovered in the margins of our lives.

Then like a bolt of electricity, I thought of the only person I knew who could actually help. Without hesitation, I picked up the phone and dialed Information.

"Who are you calling?" asked Jonathan.

"Don't worry about it."

When the operator answered, I asked for the general number to the hospital where Bill was staying.

"You're going to call Bill?"

"Yes," I said as I dialed. Within seconds, I was connected to his room. "Bill?"

"Yeah, who's this?" There was a painful tone in his voice, a startling reminder that he had almost died.

"Bill, this is Frank."

"Frank who?"

"Frank Spinelli. I'm one of your Boy Scouts." There was a long pause followed by several deep breaths. I had an uneasy feeling that he wasn't going to remember me. "Frank Spinelli," I repeated. "You know me." Jonathan watched with a confused expression. I covered the receiver with my hand. "He doesn't remember me, Jonathan."

"Maybe he's on painkillers? My mom said he's been in a lot of pain."

"Frank," said Bill with a hint of recognition. "What's up, buddy?"

"How are you, Bill?" Hearing his voice, even though he sounded weak, filled me with relief. If Jonathan hadn't been standing there next to me, I might have started to tear up. "I'm here with Jonathan. We just wanted to call and see how you were doing."

"Oh, that was nice of you guys." He paused between words to catch his breath. "I'm doing okay."

"Bill, it sounds like you're in a lot of pain. Maybe I should let you go?"

"No, no," he insisted. "I miss you, buddy."

I clenched the receiver with my hand so that Jonathan couldn't hear. There were so many things I wanted to say, but not with him standing there next to me. The burden of carrying on this secret relationship suddenly manifested itself again, and that pain below my rib cage began to throb.

Bill struggled to continue. "I've been thinking about you."

I froze and thought how lucky I was that Jonathan and I weren't telepathically linked, because if he knew what was going on he would have died from the shock.

"Are you there?" Bill asked.

"Yes."

"You don't have to answer now, but when I get out of here, I want to take you up to my cabin. Just the two of us. You and me, buddy. Would you like that?"

I couldn't speak.

Jonathan looked on, perplexed. "What is he saying?"

"Just say yes," whispered Bill. "Then I'll know, and once I get out of here we can go away to my cabin. We'll spend a whole weekend together, alone. Will you come with me?"

Seconds ticked by. I dreamed of what that weekend would be like: Bill and me alone, in a cabin out in the woods, waking up to the smell of bacon and eggs, taking walks and fishing in a stream. It would be so magical, like a vacation without my parents, and no one would think it was strange, because he was my Scoutmaster. That was when I realized that this accident was a second chance for us both. Bill was the old person I remembered, not the scary new one he'd become.

"Yes," I said.

"That makes me so happy."

———

"SO YOU'RE THE FAMOUS FRANK I'VE BEEN HEARING SO MUCH ABOUT," said Uncle Vito, leaning up against the door with his hand slung over it like a monkey clinging to a branch.

The Saturday after the science fair, Jonathan invited me on the Day Line—a boat tour up the Hudson—with his entire family, including his uncle Vito. Since the boat departed from Manhattan, the Durans thought it would be easier if we all slept over at Uncle Vito's apartment in the West Village. Jonathan's uncle was not exactly what I expected. When he opened the door, I took a step back. He was wearing a black tank top and tight blue jeans and sported a thick mustache and dark, curly hair. Yet, the longer I stared, the more I could see the Duran resemblance: the bushy eyebrows, the soft, milky brown eyes, and the sinewy torso. Uncle Vito looked like Jonathan's father but sounded more like his mother.

"Come in," he urged. "You must be exhausted." He swung open the door and motioned me into the apartment as if he was a model on *The Price Is Right*.

His apartment was small compared to my house (not that I'd ever been in a New York apartment before). The layout was simple: the first room beyond the entrance was the kitchen, with dark wood cabinets and eggplant-colored walls. To my right, I could see the sunken living room, which was painted red. There was a large black leather couch against the far wall, a zebra-skin rug in the center of the room, and huge pieces of art—what looked like a knight's coat of arms on red velvet—hanging on all four walls. Big leafy plants in large, round ceramic pots sprouted in almost every corner of the living room. In the far corner was a dining area with a large, rectangular table and six high-back chairs fit for a medieval king. I stood at the entrance taking it all in.

"Don't be bashful now," said Uncle Vito. "I won't bite."

From the kitchen, I heard Mrs. Duran laugh. When I entered, she was choking on a thick plume of smoke. Setting down her cigarette, she bent over the sink and spit out an olive.

"Careful, Sharon," sang Uncle Vito. "We got the whole day ahead of us tomorrow." He looked over his shoulder and winked at me. "Come on in, kid. Don't mind the Dragon Lady over there. Do you want a drink?"

"Vito!" screamed Mrs. Duran. "He's just a child!"

"I meant a glass of soda, Sharon," he clarified. "What do you take me for?"

"Sorry, I thought you meant—"

"You thought I was going to corrupt a minor with a cock-tail?" he interrupted with both hands resting on his hips. "Not tonight, Sharon. Mama needs her rest. Speaking of—Jonathan, why don't you show your friend where you'll both be sleeping?"

"You're out to kill me tonight," continued Mrs. Duran as she grabbed her martini off the counter. "Kids, ignore Uncle Vito. As usual he's hell-bent on giving me a coronary because I'm making him come with us tomorrow."

"I beg your pardon," said Uncle Vito, clutching at his neck. "There is nowhere I'd rather be than with my two nephews, on a boat for three hours traveling up the scenic Hudson River. Maybe if we're lucky, we'll see a body or two floating around in the water."

Mrs. Duran looked at her husband. "See, I told you it was a bad idea to invite him."

Uncle Vito picked up a lit cigarette from a marble ashtray and flared his eyes at Mrs. Duran. "You ungrateful sister-in-law," he hissed. Whipping his head back, he noticed Jonathan and me still standing there. "Jonathan, your friend is going to grow roots if you don't show him the bedroom. Now, go! Scoot! Then, when you're done, come back here and I'll make my famous ice cream sundaes."

From the living room, we heard Jonathan's younger brother, Stevie, cheer.

"Well, then, let's hurry up," said Jonathan to me.

The apartment was on the seventeenth floor overlooking the Hudson River and the West Side Highway. As we passed the dining area, I asked whether we could go out on the terrace, since I had never been on one before. As Jonathan pulled aside the sheer metallic fabric draped over the sliding glass doors, a burst of air came into the room and we were both overwhelmed with the intoxicating smell of the city. It was a warm night, and as I pushed the curtains farther to the side, I was surprised by the spectacular view.

"Wow, it's scary up here," I said as the wind blew violently around us. "When I grow up, the first thing I'm gonna do is move into the city."

"Me, too," said Jonathan. "We can be roommates."

"Deal!"

In that instant, I felt extremely close to him and understood the value of his friendship. It was during moments like this when I felt most guilty for not confiding in him about Bill, especially after Jonathan had told me all about Tommy Scalici. That situation resolved itself once a neighbor complained to the *Staten Island Advance* that they hadn't seen Tommy delivering their paper in over a month. The *Advance* threatened to take the route away from Tommy if he didn't start making the deliveries himself. Right after that, Tommy stopped showing up at Jonathan's corner every morning.

"We better get back so we can have ice cream before my mom says it's too late."

"Lead the way." I followed Jonathan into his uncle's bedroom on the other end of the apartment. Once inside, my eyes were immediately drawn to a poster hanging over the bed. It was a naked male torso, the word SLEAZE written across the man's chest in jagged black letters. Staring at that poster, I knew there was something forbidden, not to mention unchristian, about it, yet it stirred feelings deep inside me that I'd only felt with Bill. I was drawn to it, even aroused. Jonathan, on the other hand, appeared completely oblivious and went about setting down my backpack on the floor. I had to turn away to avoid staring, so I sat down on the bed.

"Ouch-a-magouch!" I yelled. "What is this bed made of?"

Jonathan smirked. "It's not a regular mattress. It's filled with sand."

"Why would anyone want to sleep on a bed of sand?"

"I'll show you," he said, stripping off the covers. Then he climbed onto the middle of the bed and rolled back and forth. The sand shifted under the weight of his body and left an imprint in the mattress. "It contours to your body."

"I still don't see the point."

Jonathan rolled his eyes. "Uncle Vito's kind of different."

"I can see that."

"No, I mean he's *different*," Jonathan repeated. "Like gay."

"I don't follow you."

"My mom says that Uncle Vito likes men."

"You mean likes men instead of women?"

Jonathan nodded. "Come here. I want to show you something." He walked over to a set of dresser drawers and knelt. Opening the bottom drawer revealed a silk, zebra-print scarf stretched out as though it was concealing something. I squatted down to get a better look. Jonathan looked me squarely in the eyes. "You have to promise that you won't tell a soul that I showed you this."

"I swear on a stack of Sister Catherine's Bibles." I made the sign of the cross.

Then, like a magician, Jonathan whipped back the scarf to reveal an enormous, flesh-colored rubber penis that snaked around the entire drawer twice. For a second, I thought it was a dead boa constrictor. Then on closer inspection, I saw the familiar shape of the head and the contoured veins running along the shaft. It had to be four inches in diameter and about six feet long.

"Is it made of rubber?"

"I think," he said, scratching his head.

"That is so gross!"

"Touch it," he taunted. "Go ahead, it won't bite."

"No way," I said, standing up and backing away until I bumped up against the bed. "Put that scarf back and close the drawer before someone comes in and catches us."

"Chill out," he said. "If I knew you were going to freak, I wouldn't have shown it to you in the first place."

"Sorry, it's just that I don't understand why your uncle has that!"

"Who cares? I'm sure we could find even freakier things in his closet."

"No, that wouldn't be right."

Jonathan eyed me suspiciously as if I was a stranger. The truth was that I wasn't acting like myself. Normally, I would have been eager to investigate every nook and cranny of Uncle Vito's bedroom, but the penis monster and sleaze torso left me unnerved.

Looking back, I didn't understand why I felt sexually aroused. I just knew that it frightened me. When we returned to the kitchen, I avoided Uncle Vito. I felt ashamed for having violated his bedroom, and I suspected that if he looked me in the eyes, he would know what we had been up to.

———

THAT NIGHT, AS I TRIED TO FALL ASLEEP on Uncle Vito's sandbox mattress, I stared at the sleaze torso poster and imagined Bill's head attached to that body. I tried to shake off that image, but then I recalled the penis snake monster sleeping just a few feet away, nestled in the bottom of that drawer, ready to spring out at any moment and lunge for my neck.

Then I had a thought: was I gay like Uncle Vito?

No, absolutely not, I told myself.

Logically, if I was like Uncle Vito, then that would mean that Bill was gay, too. I knew that wasn't possible; Bill and Uncle Vito weren't anything alike. Uncle Vito was thin with short hair and a thick mustache. He wore tight jeans and a tank top. He spoke with his hands and often exaggerated his words. Bill, on the other hand, was a large man. He spoke in a low, commanding voice. I never saw Bill in tight pants or shirts that exposed his chest. In almost every way, Bill was the exact opposite of Uncle Vito, so he couldn't be gay. And I couldn't, either.

The only flaw in this equation was that I really didn't know what being gay was. But at the time I didn't care. So I slept lightly that night, with the sleaze torso poster overhead, the snake penis monster resting in the bottom drawer, and gay Uncle Vito in the spare room, probably wearing nothing but a zebra-print thong.

Mrs. Duran woke us up early the next morning so we could make the boat on time. At the breakfast table, I sat next to Jonathan and shared a toasted bagel, even though I could have eaten a whole one myself. "Are you sure you don't want your own, Frankie?" asked Uncle Vito.

I shook my head silently, still avoiding his eyes.

"I understand. You're watching your figure. So am I."

"Oh, Vito!" Mrs. Duran laughed.

"What? I'm serious. Those bagels are full of starch, and starch leads to saddlebags," he said, slapping his right buttock. "And that I can do without."

Jonathan snorted milk through his nostrils. It was almost impossible not to laugh around Uncle Vito because he was so animated. Maybe being silly was what made someone gay. Bill was rarely funny and never silly. In fact, he was the opposite of silly; he was serious and stern. Bill would have never patted his butt or worried about eating too much starch. Once I came to this new conclusion, I was able to relax, comforted in knowing my relationship with Bill had nothing to do with being gay. The more I thought about it, the more I realized I wanted to be more like Bill than Uncle Vito.

"If you don't mind," I said to Uncle Vito, "I think I would like another half a bagel."

"Attaboy," said Mr. Duran. "See, Vito, the kid has a hearty appetite. He's not worried about saddlebags. Right, Frankie?" Then he leaned over and whispered in my ear, "Let's leave the women to worry about getting saddlebags. Real men don't care about such things."

CHAPTER 22

Beyond Betrayal

BILL WAS DISCHARGED SIX WEEKS AFTER THE ACCIDENT. He convalesced at home and routinely attended physical therapy. We received weekly updates at Boy Scout meetings from Mr. Castro. In those weeks before Bill resumed his role as Scoutmaster, we spoke on the phone frequently. Often, he'd call me after school and asked what I'd learned or what subject I was studying. He didn't mention going away to his cabin, and I was sure he didn't remember inviting me. That left me feeling depressed. Still, I kept hoping that once he recovered fully, he would surprise me with plans to go camping alone.

One afternoon, he asked whether I would ride my bike to his house. I lied to my mother and said I was going to visit Jonathan. I don't know why I lied. My mother wouldn't have objected. She often asked me how Bill was doing. I always told her I didn't know. It was instinctual for me to keep our relationship a secret. I thought it was easier for me to lie than to admit I was going to the place that caused me so much pain. I was still so conflicted: Pre-accident, Bill had become detached, angry, and hostile toward me. Post-accident, I was consumed with guilt that somehow my prayers to get Bill to stop had almost led to his death. Though I still had a strong desire to see him again, I felt compelled to keep the truth from my family.

That day, I rode my bicycle down the hill, past Clove Lakes

Park and onto Targee Street. I sailed right past my school and pedaled until I had his house in sight. I parked across the street by the telephone pole, breathlessly waiting for a signal. Suddenly, there was movement in one of the upstairs windows. I held my breath. Then I saw a figure. *Bill.* He drew the blinds up halfway. His face was pale and thinner than I remembered, but it was him. He stuck his arm out the window and waved me off. Then he closed the blinds and disappeared. I was crushed. Questions flooded my mind: Why did he ask me to come all the way down here? Did someone come by unexpectedly? What had just happened?

I waited a few minutes longer. An unfamiliar tightness wrapped around my chest, unlike that gnawing pain below my ribs. This was more constricting. It felt rooted in anger. Standing there by the telephone pole, I never felt more foolish in my life. It dawned on me that I was just a pawn to Bill. If I had been stronger, I would have run up to his door and rung the bell. Then, when he answered, I would have demanded an explanation, but of course, I wasn't strong. I was weak, and worse, I was now invisible, someone he could abuse and then dismiss without any consideration. Bill had reverted back to his old self again. I thought the accident might have changed him. Now I knew I was wrong. He would never change.

When Bill called me the next day, I refused to speak to him.

"But it's Bill," said my mother with her hand over the receiver.

"Tell him I'm outside playing."

"Why don't you want to talk to him?" she whispered, searching my face for a reason why she had to lie. But I didn't feel the need to give her one. I remained completely silent.

Later that night, she visited me in my bedroom while I was doing homework at my desk. "Why didn't you want to speak to Bill today?" she asked.

Staring at my bedroom window, I saw her reflection in the doorway. I shrugged.

"Is there something you want to tell me?"

I shook my head.

My mother waited by the door for several more seconds. I've often wondered why it didn't seem peculiar to her that a grown man had a relationship with a young boy. Only when I showed reluctance to see him did my actions seem suspicious. I don't know how long she waited there, but when I finally turned around, she was gone.

From that day on, I became even more withdrawn. After school, I would hide in the bathroom for hours. If my sisters were home, I would find peace in my bedroom or disappear inside my closet with the door shut. I felt safe there, ensconced in the darkness alone. There, I could pretend I was somewhere else. That was when I started to wish that I would be kidnapped. I no longer worried that those strange faceless men would come and take me away—I prayed for them.

MONTHS WENT BY WITH NO WORD FROM BILL. Then, in the autumn of my eighth year at St. Sylvester's, I was in the den doing homework when I heard the familiar honk of his horn. It wasn't until that moment that I realized how much I wanted to hear that sound again. I reacted like one of Pavlov's dogs. All those feelings of anger lifted away like a curtain as I rifled through the closet to find my sneakers, hurrying so I wouldn't keep him waiting.

He was parked out front in the usual spot. Seeing his red truck that day lifted my spirits. I saw his smile peering out the passenger-side window. His face was full again. Even his skin appeared vibrant. He waved me toward him. I started to run, but before I reached the truck, I saw someone else in the passenger seat.

Jonathan.

Over the past two years, my mind had catalogued certain traumatic moments much the way you can recount an accident by looking at the scar it left behind. Though the scars inflicted by Bill were not as apparent as one from a burn or a cut, they ran just as deep. Standing outside the truck, I felt anger—anger at my best friend, not Bill. Bill was still my secret friend. I'd thought Jonathan was my best friend, but now, somehow he was my betrayer.

"Do you know Jonathan?" asked Bill.

"Yes, of course," I said, thinking it was funny how little Bill knew about me.

"Good," he said. "Are you boys up for a little adventure?"

I looked over at Jonathan. My eyes burned with hatred. "Sure," I said. "What about you, Jonathan?"

He nodded without looking in my direction.

Bill drove us to the hardware store. The man who helped Bill and me pick out light fixtures was there again. "Oh, you got two with you today," he said.

Bill smiled at the man and explained what he was looking for. Then he casually placed his hand on Jonathan's shoulder. Rage burned in my chest as I stared longingly at Bill's hand. The man directed us to another aisle, and I followed behind them, staring as Bill continued to hold on to Jonathan's shoulder, clutching it as though he was claiming him. After the hardware store, I walked back to the truck, trailing after them. Bill never took his hand off Jonathan's shoulder, and Jonathan never once looked at me.

Next, Bill drove to a grocery store. Jumping out, he said, "I need to pick up a few things. You both wait here."

While we were alone in the truck, I turned on Jonathan. "So, does Bill take you out on errands a lot?"

Jonathan stared straight ahead at the windshield. "Sometimes."

"Does he make you help him do repairs around the house, too?"

"Once in a while."

It all seemed clear now. "Does anything else go on when you're alone with Bill?" There was a long pause. I was getting closer. The interior of the truck felt as if it were closing in. Jonathan's brown eyes turned hazy. That was when I grabbed him by the shoulders and turned him to face me. He was on the verge of tears. "Answer me, Jonathan!" His face scrunched up as tears began to stream down his cheeks. Jonathan couldn't respond.

When I saw Bill exit the store, I pushed down the driver's-side lock.

Jonathan looked horrified. "What are you doing?"

"Just shut up," I said.

Bill tried the door twice, nearly dropping his grocery bags, before he realized it was locked. "Come on," he said. "Open up."

I folded my arms defiantly over my chest. Bill's face turned bright red. Jonathan began trembling. Only once before had I seen Bill's eyes that full of rage: that first night at Pouch Camp when I burned my finger on the lantern.

"What are you two up to?" he demanded, pounding on the window with his elbow. Jonathan squirmed behind me, burying his face in my back. "Okay, enough fun," warned Bill. "If you make me drop this stuff, then I'm really going to be pissed."

I sat back with my arms still folded and stared at Bill.

He studied my expression curiously. Then he shouted, "Wait until I get my hands on you two numbskulls!"

"Open it," said Jonathan.

"You open it," I yelled.

Jonathan reached over and unlocked the door. Bill swung it open and threw the bags at us. "What's wrong with you two?" he said, climbing into the truck. "You think that's funny?"

We remained quiet as Bill started the car.

"I expect more from the two of you," he said, breathing heavily. Then he pulled out of the parking lot, swerving so that Jonathan and I lurched toward the passenger-side door. Jonathan looked petrified, but I wasn't afraid. This was the first time I had ever gone against Bill.

I had been brave.

Bill drove directly to Jonathan's house. This should have made me happy. But as I watched Jonathan climb the steps up to his front door, then open it and go inside without turning back, I wanted to jump out of the truck and run after him. Bill didn't take me home next. Instead we went straight back to his house.

After he parked the car, I followed behind him as he walked through the front door carrying the groceries. All the curtains were drawn, and it was dark inside on that bright sunny afternoon. Bill set the bags down on the kitchen table while I stood in the hall. Then he walked past me and climbed the stairs. When he reached the landing, I heard him call out, "Are you waiting for an invitation?" I looked up and saw Bill unbuttoning his shirt. I made my way upstairs, counting each one. Bill was in his room now. I could hear him unbuckling his belt. When I stepped inside the doorway, he was on his bed, dressed only in his underwear.

This is where it all started.

As a child, I thought Bill and I would be friends forever, but he was never really my friend. I was his prisoner. Over two years ago, when I'd first stepped foot in his bedroom, I was lured under the pretense that I had to meet with him in private to advance in rank. He was kind to me then. Now, all I saw was his anger, and that scared me, but it didn't stop me from going inside his bedroom that very last time.

THAT NIGHT I TOLD MY FAMILY THE TRUTH ABOUT BILL, and my relationship with him ended abruptly.

My entire family was seated around the dinner table. My father was sullen, having just finished a double shift at the Environmental Protection Agency, a euphemism for the sewer department. My mother was serving pasta, something my father insisted on having every night, while my sisters argued. Josephine accused Maria of purchasing makeup and hiding it under her bed. "Enough," shouted my mother. "You're giving your father a headache." My sisters quieted down as my mother placed an enormous bowl of spaghetti in the center of the table.

As she served up three heaping forkfuls into my father's dish, he woke from a trancelike state. "Take it from the bottom! You know I hate tomato sauce."

My mother ignored him and piled his plate with sauce-soaked noodles. Then she hurried to serve the rest of us. She worked fast, doling out dinner as though she was both short-order cook and waitress. I wasn't hungry that night. My world as I knew it was falling apart.

"What's the matter?" asked my mother. "I know. You don't like pasta."

"What's his problem?" asked my father, winding his fork, collecting spaghetti, and shoving it into his mouth.

"Your son only eats hamburgers and hot dogs," said my mother, staring into my eyes. Now I'd made her angry. "Next time I'll buy you a TV dinner. They only cost a dollar fifty at the supermarket. I can feed the whole family for less than ten dollars a day. Would you like that?"

"Tomorrow night I'm going to open a can of beans," offered my father. His mouth overflowed with what looked like bloodied worms dangling from his lips. "Then you'll see how fast he'll eat pasta."

I wanted to run and hide in my bedroom, but it was too late. My mother was infuriated, and it was I who had unwittingly done this. In return, I would now bear the brunt of her anger. Turning on her heel, she left for the kitchen counter and began sawing into a long loaf of Italian bread. I glanced over at my sisters. Josephine seemed thoroughly annoyed with me while Maria's brow crinkled with pity. When my mother returned, she scattered pieces of bread on the table as though we were pigeons swarming for food. Sitting down, she reached for her napkin, whipped it open so that it snapped, and placed it on her lap. Then she scooted her chair up to the table and began attacking her dinner.

"When is the next camping trip?" she asked without looking up.

I sat there frozen.

One by one, each member of my family looked over at me, including my mother, who stared long and hard at my face, biting her lip impatiently as I remained mute. "Why is it always a war to get you to go on these camping trips?"

That precipitated an argument that involved every member of my family except me. I kept thinking about what had happened earlier that day with Bill. How could I explain everything to my family when I was so confused by it all? Then, in the midst of all the shouting, my mother stared at me . . . knowingly. Quietly, she whispered, "Is Bill touching you?" When I failed to respond, my mother excused me from the table. I didn't have to say a word.

Years later, Josephine told me that my mother became hysterical and asked my father to drive her over to Bill's house. My father convinced her otherwise. The events of that night have perplexed me for decades. Why didn't my father want to confront Bill immediately? Why didn't my sisters protect me once they learned what happened? The answer, I told myself, was that they really didn't believe me or they needed more proof.

Leaving the dinner table, I locked myself in the bathroom while the family tribunal met. I stripped down to my underwear and removed every product of feminine hygiene from the vanity. Placing them neatly in a circle around me, I hummed softly to myself, ignoring my mother's shrieking, the clanging of silverware, and the clamoring of pots and pans being dropped into the sink. I remained in the bathroom, unbothered, for over an hour. Once everything quieted down, I placed all the products back into their boxes and got dressed. From the hall, the house looked dark. Before I went inside my room, I picked up the phone and quietly dialed Jonathan's number. I needed to speak to him, tell him what I'd done, and ask for his advice. Pulling the receiver into my bedroom, I closed the door and crouched down on the floor.

Jonathan picked up. "Hello?"

"I think I'm in big trouble."

"What happened?"

"I told my parents about Bill!"

"What did you tell them?"

"Everything."

"What did they say?"

"Nothing. They just told me to go to my room."

"So I guess you won't be coming back to Boy Scouts?"

"I don't think so."

"Do you think they'll talk to Bill?"

"It doesn't look that way," I said. "But I know they won't let me see him again."

"Do you want to?"

I didn't respond, because I wasn't sure. A small part of me wanted to see Bill, but another bigger part, the one that was growing up, knew that it had to end. For all the reasons I felt inclined to see him, there was a growing realization that my attraction to him was dangerous and that confiding in my parents would sever my ties with Bill for good.

Then I heard something on the other side of the door. Quickly, I opened it and found my mother standing there, listening. "You want to tell me what's really going on?" she asked, reaching for the phone. I gripped the receiver with both hands, not wanting to let go, frightened that she would take it from me and then I would be alone with her. I needed to keep Jonathan on the phone as a witness.

"What are you talking about?" I asked.

She scrutinized my face. Her eyes burned into mine with such an unyielding intensity that I had to look away. I was afraid that she would read my fear as evidence that I was guilty of something.

"Give me the phone," she said. Reluctantly, I handed it over. She took it and hung it up. Then she quietly walked back down the hall. "Go to bed," were the last words she said before she disappeared inside her bedroom.

And that was the end of it.

THE NEXT MORNING, MY DAY BEGAN AS USUAL: I took a bath, stewing quietly in the hot, soapy water until my fingers pruned. Afterward, I dressed in my uniform, ate a buttered English muffin, and drank a glass of milk alone in the kitchen. Josephine, not my mother, drove me to school. We didn't speak in the car. "After the Love Has Gone" by Earth, Wind & Fire played on the radio.

In the school yard, I avoided Jonathan, even though I could read the concern on his face from across the yard. Later, during

American History, an announcement came over the intercom: "All altar boys, please see Father Roberts in the gymnasium at once." Matthew Seabream, Chris Reynolds, Jonathan, and I stood up. Moving up the aisle, I heard Seth cough "queer" into his fist.

Our eighth-grade teacher, Mrs. Hansen, ignored him, but by the sound of the giggling from Seth's friends in the back of the class, I knew everyone else had heard him. This time I stopped in my tracks. Briefly, I looked back at Seth. A smirk widened on his face. Then, I watched as my fellow altar boys filed out the door. I should have followed after them, but instead, I turned around and went back to my seat. Seth swiveled around in shock as I passed him.

"Mr. Spinelli, don't you have somewhere to be?" asked Mrs. Hansen curiously.

I looked over at the door. Matthew Seabream was holding it open, waiting for me.

"No," I replied. "Not anymore."

"Are you sure?" she said, standing up.

"Yes."

The class erupted with chatter. Mrs. Hansen picked up her scissors and began banging them on her desk. Seth offered me a nod of approval as I sat back down. Matthew Seabream turned to Jonathan, who then glanced over at me, perplexed. As the classroom door closed behind them, I felt myself drifting further away from the boy I used to be. If Jonathan and I were truly telepathic, he would have been able to read my mind. Once the door clicked shut, I could still see his face in the small, rectangular window, standing there with sadness in his eyes. He must have sensed it, too.

—∞∞∞—

AFTER SCHOOL THAT DAY, I took the trail up Emerson Hill on my way home. Just as I reached the clearing where a huge boulder was set against a tree, I discovered Seth and his two best friends, Bobby Staudinger and Tommy Scalici. I froze. But when they saw me, I didn't run. Seth appeared completely unfazed by my presence. He perched on the rock like a crow, smiling directly at me. "Gentlemen, it seems we have a visitor."

Tommy, who was wearing his tie wrapped around his head, stumbled back when he noticed me. "Oh shit. It's Spinelli."

"Not to worry," urged Seth. "I don't think Spinelli's looking for trouble."

I gave him a soft nod of assurance.

Bobby, with his mop of curly blond hair and wide-set blue eyes, now completely bloodshot and glassy, pulled a joint from his pocket and lit it. He took a long, slow toke before he handed it off to Seth.

"Come here," said Seth. "We don't bite."

"Yeah, we don't bite," repeated Tommy, who fell onto the ground laughing.

I inched forward. The distinct aroma of marijuana filled my nostrils, and the pungent smell made me wince.

"Here, take a hit," offered Seth.

Tommy stared at me with a dopey expression. "Yeah, go ahead. Take a hit." Just then, Bobby came up behind Tommy and pulled on his tie so that his head snapped back.

"What the fuck, man?" said Tommy. They began to wrestle, pulling at each other's shirts to reveal their white bellies, now streaked with red tracks where their hands had grazed one another's flesh.

Seth ignored them and held the joint out for me. "You know that was a cool fucking thing you did today, man."

I stepped closer.

"I mean, it's hard to take a stand, but you did that today. Right, you guys?"

Tommy and Bobby stopped wrestling long enough to answer Seth.

"Yeah, fuck altar boys," said Bobby.

"Yeah," agreed Tommy.

Then Bobby pulled Tommy's tie for the second time, and they started wrestling again.

"Yeah, fuck altar boys!" shouted Seth. Then he stood up on the rock, holding the joint above his head like a sword. "Hey, preacher, leave them kids alone!" he sang. His voice echoed through the trees. With each word, I felt myself moving closer to him, moving away from everything I thought was "queer." This was where I needed to be.

Just then, Seth took another toke off that joint. I watched his eyes roll up into his head as his chest expanded. He held his breath for several seconds and then blew out a thick stream of pungent white smoke. Looking directly into my eyes, he held it out for me again. This time I took it. The second after I inhaled, I felt my chest burn as my lungs filled up with smoke. I began to cough uncontrollably. Bobby and Tommy started to laugh. Seth hopped off the boulder and began patting me on the back. When I stopped coughing, Seth pressed his forehead firmly against mine. Our eyes were just inches apart. I smelled the smoke on his breath, saw a drop of saliva collect in the corner of his mouth, and felt the heat from his skin against my temple. "Way to go, Spinelli. Way to go."

Instantly, my head felt like it had grown to three times its size. I panicked and started to run away.

"Spinelli!" cried Seth. "Where are you going?"

"I'm sorry," I yelled back. "I'm late for dinner."

Hurrying my way through the forest, I navigated the new terrain like a drunken explorer. My head whipped from side to side, soaking in the bizarre landscape created by the distorted aperture of my eyes. The path warped, as though the ground beneath me were crumbling. I moved cautiously, with wide-legged steps. I stretched my arms out in preparation of a potential fall. Nausea rose up in my nostrils. I felt the urge to vomit, but I suppressed it and moved quickly once I saw my house up in the distance.

Inside, I climbed the stairs to my bedroom and collapsed on my mattress. The sound of firecrackers exploded as my body pressed against the plastic mattress cover. I shuddered at this sound but was relieved to be in my own room. Lying there on my bed, I felt as though I was floating, swaying from side to side as if lost at sea. Acid filled my nostrils again. This time I was sure I'd vomit. I held my hand across my mouth and began breathing heavily through my nose until the urge passed. In the distance I heard a foghorn. No, it was our telephone ringing. I heard my mother pick it up. Seconds later, there was a knock at my door.

My mother entered and said, "Jonathan's on the phone." She sounded as if she was speaking underwater. "He wants you to come over for dinner. Do you want to go? You should go. I'll have your father drive you." With each breath she took, I thought I heard bubbles gurgling to the surface. I mumbled something, and she exited the room. Slowly, the spinning subsided. I felt as though I was returning to Earth. Minutes later, my mother came back into my room. "Your father's going to drive you over to Jonathan's house now."

I raised my head off the pillow. "Okay," I whispered. "Just give me a minute."

"Were you crying?" she asked.

"No, why?"

"Your eyes are all red."

"It's just smoke from the firecrackers."

<hr>

MRS. DURAN WAS FIXING HERSELF a cup of Sanka instant coffee when I entered their house. She was pouring hot water into a mug Jonathan had made in art class, a brown, lumpy mass of clay with the word MOM scribbled in red across the front. She had to know it looked like a pile of dog crap, but she used it anyway because her son made it for her. That was something my mother would never do.

Out of the corner of my eye, I noticed Jonathan standing in the dining room. He looked guilty. I hesitated before taking another step. The entire situation suddenly seemed ominous. Paranoia set in, and I felt as though I had done something wrong.

Mrs. Duran smiled warmly at me. "Frankie, come in. I want to talk to you." I inched forward, peeking over at Jonathan, who was now cowering behind the archway that led into the kitchen. Mrs. Duran grabbed her mug in one hand and a small gold purse filled with Pall Mall cigarettes in the other. "Let's go into my bedroom."

I followed her down the hall. With each step, I felt as if I were somehow going back in time. I wondered whether at any moment I might wake up back in my own bed. Over my shoulder, I saw Jonathan skulking not too far behind.

Inside her bedroom, I noticed quaint clusters of Precious Moments figurines displayed on the dresser. Red and green throw pillows with ruffled edges were neatly arranged on the bed. On the wall over the nightstand, I noticed the Durans' wedding photo. They both looked so happy. In the photograph, Mrs. Duran wasn't wearing glasses. She had a daisy chain wrapped around her head, suspending a veil that draped down her back.

"Come sit down next to me," she said, crossing her legs Indian-style. "Jonathan, go get Mommy an ashtray." Taking a cigarette out of her gold purse, she lit the end and inhaled slowly. When Jonathan returned, he handed his mother what looked like a seashell. She cupped it in her palm and flicked the ashes from her cigarette into it. "Frankie, your mother came to see me this morning." The seriousness of her tone had a sobering effect on me. Instantly I knew why I was there. "She wanted to pull you out of school, but I convinced her not to. She agreed only because I said I would speak to you before we did anything. Your mother was very upset, and that freaked the shit out of me. What she told me is very serious. So I need you to tell me exactly what you told her."

My thoughts were racing. Honestly, I didn't know where to begin. I always liked Mrs. Duran and trusted her implicitly, even more than my own mother. But I knew that if I told her everything, my confession would lead to serious consequences for Bill. I was tied to him through the secret life we shared, and now I was the only one who could protect him. If I told her the whole truth, then this would certainly put an end to everything for good.

I watched her fidget as I stalled. She pushed her glasses up her nose, flipped her long brown feathered hair once, then twice. It occurred to me, at that moment, how much she resembled Farrah Fawcett. Although Mrs. Duran was a brunette and wore glasses, her hair was the same and so was her smile. "Frankie, you can talk to me," she whispered. "I'm not your mom. I'm Sharon." Mrs. Duran set her mug down next to me on the nightstand and held both my hands.

I wanted to tell her everything, but I also felt protective of her. Behind that tough exterior, she was still a mother, and the mother of a child whom I believed was being sexually abused. I wasn't sure whether she could handle the truth, and that made me want to lie. I stared uneasily at Jonathan, knowing he hadn't told his parents anything. How could I betray him in front of his own mother?

"I want you to trust me, okay?" she said, gently. "Frankie, are you listening to me?"

"Yes," I said. "It's just that I don't know where to start."

"Why don't you start from the beginning?"

I began with the day that Bill drove me up to camp. I explained what we spoke about and told Mrs. Duran that, after that weekend, Bill began showing up at my house regularly. Then I told her about the private Scoutmaster meeting and how Bill showed me pornographic magazines. The words poured out of me with surprising ease. I continued to speak as she listened.

When I mentioned boy bonding and jerking off, Mrs. Duran took a long, intense drag from her cigarette and blew the smoke toward the ceiling. "When you say 'jerking off,' " she interrupted, "do you mean that's what you did to him or what he did to you?"

Why does that matter? Is one worse than the other?

I became nervous and looked at Jonathan for help, but of course, he didn't meet my eyes. Instead, he stared down at the bedspread, entranced. I had a sudden thought that I should leave, but I didn't move. Though I thought I might be able to describe to Mrs. Duran what went on in Bill's bedroom when he and I were alone, hearing myself speak only made the pain below my ribs start up. I stopped talking.

"Listen to me, Frankie," she said. "It's very important that you tell me every detail. So did you do that to him or did he do it to you?" Without uttering a single word, I pointed to myself and then down at her lap. "You mean you did it to him?" she whispered slowly.

I nodded.

"Did you do anything else to him?" she asked.

I nodded again.

Mrs. Duran took another deep drag of her cigarette. Then she stifled it in the seashell ashtray. The room was filled with smoke.

"What else did you do?" she repeated, lighting another cigarette.

I stared unblinkingly into her face.

"Frankie," she said sternly, grabbing both my hands in hers and shaking them. "You have to tell me." I thought I saw tears well up in her eyes, and that made me want to cry, too. "Listen, you did nothing wrong. This is not your fault, but if you don't tell me, then your parents and I are going to confront Bill."

"No!" I shouted.

"No?" she repeated. "Well, then, tell me everything. Otherwise I'll do it. I'll get on the phone right now and call Bill."

"I can't."

"You can't what?" she threatened, reaching for the phone. "Tell me, goddamnit! Did he touch you in any other way?"

I couldn't say it out loud, so I leaned in and gently blew on her face. Her eyes glared back at me, confused at first; then, after a moment, recognition settled in. I watched her crumble, saw the blood drain out of her face as tears fell from her eyes. She clasped her hand over her gaping mouth.

"Oh my God. What did that bastard do to you?"

"I'm sorry," I whispered. "I'm so sorry."

Mrs. Duran threw her arms around me, drawing me into her. I began to cry. It felt like a lead knapsack had just been taken off my shoulders, and I collapsed in her arms, resting my head on her chest and soaking in the comfort of her long brown hair, with its faint smell of nicotine and Charlie perfume. "I'm gonna cut that bastard's heart out!" she said through gritted teeth. Then she pulled me off of her. "You did nothing wrong. You hear me?" Her voice cracked as tears continued to stream down her cheeks.

Then she looked at Jonathan. "Did Bill do anything to you?"

Jonathan shrank back against the headboard, gripping the pillow in front of him. "No, Mom. I swear. He never touched me."

Hearing Jonathan lie felt like the worst betrayal of all.

CHAPTER 23

Where Nobody Dared to Go

THE EVENTS THAT FOLLOWED my conversation with Mrs. Duran included Bill's departure from Troop 85. I'm not certain whether he was dismissed or he resigned. Either way, he was gone. I had betrayed him, and my betrayal left me depressed and isolated. Meanwhile, my family wanted to believe that my life would go on as usual, and it did, except I retreated deeper into my secret world in the bathroom, crippled by the belief that I was responsible for making Bill go away.

Mr. and Mrs. Duran confided in Mr. Castro, who told them that Bill had made sexual advances on him once. Mr. Castro had written Bill off as a closeted homosexual. He had no idea that boys were involved. Once the Durans spoke with Mr. Castro, he met with Bill privately. The police were never involved, and no charges were pressed. I'm certain Mr. Castro and the other assistant Scoutmasters felt intimidated because Bill was a highly decorated police officer. Having Bill step down must have seemed like the best solution to this problem. Once they informed my parents of this decision, they convinced them not to go to the authorities, and being good Italian Catholics, they obeyed. I didn't have to go back to Boy Scouts, even though Mr. Castro was now acting Scoutmaster.

It must have been a shock to the other boys and their families, particularly their fathers, when they learned Bill had stepped down. As the truth slowly trickled out, I imagined these families must have felt humiliated. Everyone looked up to Bill. He was, in fact, a hero. Even though he used the NYPD, the Catholic Church, and the Boy Scouts of America to infiltrate the lives of every family that made up Troop 85, the parents had to have felt deceived, knowing they'd entrusted this man with their sons.

My relationship with Jonathan changed after he lied to his mother. I could not bring myself to forgive him for that. Later I learned that Mr. Castro left Troop 85 and went on to become Scoutmaster at St. Theresa's School. The final nail in the coffin came when I learned that Jonathan joined Mr. Castro's new troop. Eventually, he went on to make Eagle Scout, fulfilling his dream.

Right before the holidays, Sister Catherine made an appearance in our homeroom. When she entered, all the students immediately stood at attention, and, in unison, sang out, "Good afternoon, Sister Catherine."

"Good afternoon," she replied. "Mrs. Hansen, may I speak to you in the hall?"

"Of course." Before she left the room, she warned us: "Not a single word from any of you."

At the same time, an announcement came over the school intercom: "Attention, all altar boys. Please see Father Roberts immediately in the gymnasium." The usual boys stood up that day, except for me and, now, Jonathan.

Seth immediately took notice. "Hey, Jon," he whispered across the room. "You're not going to queer practice today?"

"Shut up, Seth," mumbled Jonathan under his breath.

"What?" asked Seth, holding his hand up to his ear. "I *cunt* hear you."

The entire class now had their eyes trained on Jonathan, waiting to see what he was going to do next. I looked at the door. Through the small window, I could see Mrs. Hansen still talking to Sister Catherine.

"Seriously, Jon," continued Seth. "I have a bum ear. Your mother knocked me in the head with her knees last night when I was eating out her pussy."

The class now seemed divided among those who urged Seth on with clapping and laughing and those like Daisy Dickenson, who tried to protect Jonathan.

"Mind your own beeswax, zit face," snapped Seth. "Go on, Johnny boy. Tell us why you aren't going to queer practice today."

Jonathan cringed nervously in his seat. I could see his leg bobbing, and I took delight in watching him squirm, thankful that it wasn't me and feeling that he deserved it.

"Hey, Spinelli," called Seth. "Do you have any idea why Jonathan isn't going to queer practice today?"

"Seth, be quiet," insisted Daisy. "You're going to get us all in trouble."

"I said I'm not talking to you, dick-head," warned Seth again. Daisy shrank back in her chair. "Come on, Spinelli. You know Johnny. Why isn't he going to queer practice?"

I shrugged. From across the room I could see Jonathan peeking over at me, begging for help in the midst of all this chaos.

"Oh, come on now," said Seth. Then he stood up and began walking up the aisle. He was fearless, and that made him even more frightening. "You and Johnny boy here used to be best buds. You should know why he doesn't want to go to queer practice."

Josephine once told me the only way to survive Catholic school was to either be a smart-ass or a tough bitch. At thirteen, I realized you had to be both.

"Come on, Frankie boy. Why doesn't Jonathan want to go to queer practice?"

Staring across the room at Jonathan, I summoned every last bit of anger I felt toward him and said, "Maybe because he doesn't need to practice anymore?"

Silence followed as though the entire class was collectively holding their breath. Seth looked at me, his mouth hanging open, a wild look of surprise on his face. Then he howled loudly, clapping and jumping up and down. Others were laughing, too, myself included. It felt good not to be the brunt of their jokes this time. Jonathan pretended to read his novel, but I saw the hurt on his face.

Just then, Mrs. Hansen entered the classroom. She appeared visibly disturbed. Seth returned to his seat before she could notice him. Walking back to her desk, Mrs. Hansen picked up a textbook and called the class to order. "Okay, pick up your science textbooks and begin reading where we left off."

"Excuse me, Mrs. Hansen," said Daisy. "But we were reading from our English literature book before Sister Catherine arrived."

Bewildered, Mrs. Hansen looked up and stared at Daisy. "Excuse me?"

"We were reading from our English literature book," repeated Daisy.

Mrs. Hansen's cheeks grew red with embarrassment. She seemed completely confused. I could see it in her eyes. Something had left her so disoriented that she'd forgotten we were reading "The Lottery" by Shirley Jackson. "Well, then, continue reading where we left off right before Sister Catherine arrived," she replied.

As Daisy began, I watched Mrs. Hansen pace from her desk to the door and back again. I stared at her long enough for her to notice me. When our eyes met, she had the most troubled look on her face. That was when I realized she knew about Bill. Immediately, she turned away. Her eyes gazed across the entire class. When they fell upon Jonathan, she cringed, angry at the sight of a paperback in his hands. "Mr. Duran!" she shouted. "I understand our taste in literature may vary, but would it be too much trouble for you to join us in reading today?"

Out of the corner of my eye, I saw Seth cheering quietly to himself.

Daisy stopped reading. Like the rest of us, she was watching

Jonathan. Unexpectedly, he began to cry. Mrs. Hansen walked over to him. She helped Jonathan up and escorted him out of class. Right there in front of everyone, Jonathan was falling apart, and I wasn't helping.

―⸙―

BY THE TIME JUNE ROLLED AROUND, I couldn't wait to graduate. As I hoped, I won the literature award. After the ceremony, the Duran family came over to congratulate me. Mrs. Duran kissed me on the cheek and whispered, "How are you?"

"Fine."

"I want you to talk to Jonathan," she pleaded. "He misses you."

Our families moved outside into the parking lot. In those few awkward moments, they discussed the weather and vacation plans for the summer. I worked my way over to where Jonathan was standing, in a navy blue suit with a red tie.

"Well, it's over," I said. "Next stop, high school."

"Congratulations on the award."

"Thanks," I said. "Congratulations on being voted Most Shy."

"What an honor," he said sarcastically. "So are you really that excited about high school?"

"I'm glad to be done with this hellhole," I said. "Not that I'm looking forward to spending the next four years at an all-boys Catholic high school in Brooklyn, but at least I won't see anyone from good old St. Sylvester's."

"All-boys school, huh? I don't think I could handle that."

"It doesn't matter. All boys, no boys. When it comes right down to it, school is school. It's four more years of torture, and then it's off to college. That's when life really begins. I just have to get through the next four years."

The truth was that neither of us was looking forward to high school. But we were starting over again. For the past eight years, I'd spent nearly every day with the same group of boys and girls. We'd started off together practically as babies, and now, here we were, teenagers.

Seeing Jonathan at graduation and remembering when we first met, I was overcome with nostalgia. Even after all we'd been through, I still felt as though we were the same kindred spirits who treasured Stephen King novels and had experimented with telepathy.

"Hey, I got an idea," I said. "Why don't you sleep over at my house this weekend for old times' sake? Maria is taking me to see the movie *Xanadu*. You should come!"

"Okay," he said. "I'd like that."

THAT SATURDAY AFTERNOON, MARIA AND I MET JONATHAN AT THE LANE. I loved seeing movies at this particular theater because the building was a landmark. Unlike the growing number of multiplexes popping up all over Staten Island, the Lane still showed only one movie at a time.

Entering the theater that day, I was surprised by how crowded it was. An old woman with silver hair and a red vest took our tickets and escorted us all the way to the three available seats at the front of the theater. Once we sat down, the lights dimmed. The burgundy velvet curtain that draped over the screen retracted on each side, revealing a luminous projection: WELCOME TO THE LANE!

After several trailers, *Xanadu* began. From the start, I knew this movie was going to change my life forever. In the first musical number, a mural of the nine muses comes to life while the sisters dance to the music of the Electric Light Orchestra's song "I'm Alive." Immediately, I was captivated, and with every musical number that followed, I kept looking over at Jonathan, who seemed even more mesmerized. The film's finale was an extended musical number where Olivia Newton-John sings "Xanadu," with more costume changes than I had ever seen before in one musical number.

After the movie, Jonathan and I sang all the songs we could remember, making up the lyrics and thoroughly annoying my sister. We made a deal to stop singing if she agreed to drive us to the mall so we could buy the soundtrack. That night we played the album over and over on my sister's stereo. I stole two hairbrushes from the bathroom, and Jonathan and I sang the duet "Suddenly," screaming into our makeshift microphones.

Later that evening, my father set up the cot in the den while my mother made up the couch. Jonathan and I talked well into the night, lying side by side in the dark and not wanting that day to end.

"This was the most fun I've had in a long time," I said.

"Me, too."

"You know, Jonathan, I'm sorry I was such a jerk to you that day in class with Seth Connelly."

"That's okay. He instigated it."

"But that's still no excuse," I offered. "Jonathan, there is something I have to ask you. Once you told me that Bill used to come by and take you on errands. Remember that day? We were in his truck."

"Yes."

"You also said that Bill did things to you. Were you telling me the truth?"

Jonathan remained quiet for a long time. Long enough for me to think he wasn't going to answer. But then I heard him sniffle, and finally, he whispered, "Yes."

"What kind of things did you do together?"

"He used to pick me up after school, and we did the same things you told my mother you used to do with him when you were over at his house."

"Including the sex stuff?"

"Yes."

"Why didn't you tell me?"

"I was scared."

"Scared of me?"

"Scared of what you'd think of me."

"I would have never thought any less of you. I only got mad when you didn't come forward that day in your mom's bedroom."

"I couldn't."

"But why?"

"Because there was more to it than that."

"Like what?"

There was a long pause, followed by movement. In the darkness I felt Jonathan moving closer to me.

"Did Bill ever make you have sex with other boys?"

"No," I said. "Did he make you do that?"

"Forget it," said Jonathan, settling back.

"No." I reached out to grab him. My hand grazed his cheek. It felt moist with tears. "Please, Jonathan, you can tell me anything."

I heard him sobbing. The world around us seemed to slow down. Then after several more seconds, Jonathan told me a story that haunted me for years.

"One night Bill invited me to sleep over at his house. When I arrived, there were two other Scouts already there with Bill's policeman buddy, Larry O'Hare. They were hanging out in his living room. After a while, Bill went upstairs and brought down these magazines. There were naked people in them. Larry pulled his pants down and started playing with himself. Bill did the same thing. Then they told us to take off our pants and get on our hands and knees. I was so scared. The other two boys were staring at me. I didn't know what was going to happen, so I kept my eyes closed."

"What happened?"

"Bill and Larry went around, taking turns on us."

"Took turns how?" I asked.

Jonathan pushed his head into the pillow. I could hear him crying. Through the muffled sound of his tears, I heard him say, "They fucked us."

I was speechless. The feeling of remorse that coursed through my body was so powerful and sudden that all I could muster was, "I'm so sorry." When I reached out my hand to comfort him, he recoiled.

"Now you know everything," he said, lifting his head up off the pillow.

It was painful for me to hear him tell that story, but I imagined Jonathan felt relief, having finally confided in someone.

The torture of carrying that secret around for so long must have been as crippling as the actual experience itself. "I understand now," I said, "but I have to ask you one more thing."

"What?"

"Who were the other two Scouts?"

"I can't say."

"Why?"

"Because."

"Because why?"

Then Jonathan sat up. The moonlight streaked in through the sliding glass doors and outlined his face. He was looking directly at me. He no longer looked like himself, and that was the most frightening thing of all. Quietly, he whispered, "Because when Bill and Larry were done, they made the other two boys take turns on me."

Reeling from all these revelations, it took me a while to respond. "Jonathan, I understand you're upset, but you have to tell me who they were. You have to tell me!"

Jonathan fell back down on the couch, sobbing into the pillow, but I didn't care. "Jonathan, if you don't tell me, I'm going to call your mother, and I'm going to tell her everything you just told me . . ."

"All right, all right," he cried. "It was James Mendola and Chris Spivey. Are you happy now?"

It suddenly all made sense. That wounded expression on Spivey's face the first time I went to Bill's house must have been the mirror of mine when I saw Jonathan in Bill's truck the last time we were all together.

"I'm sorry I made you tell me, but I had to know." I reached out and put my hand on his shoulder. This time Jonathan did not pull away.

"Frank, are you mad at me?"

"No, not anymore."

Then we embraced. "I'm sorry," he repeated, burying his face into the hollow of my shoulder. "I'm so sorry."

I could feel his heart pounding against my chest. I pressed him closer. His tears moistened my neck. Then something strange happened. I felt the warmth of Jonathan's lips on mine. That was the first time I kissed a boy. As it was happening, I told myself it wasn't a real kiss, but I knew that wasn't true. Then Jonathan shifted his body onto the cot next to me. We embraced, and my thoughts drifted to Bill, wondering why we'd never kissed. Then I froze. Jonathan's lips felt oddly strange. When he stopped kissing me, I felt as if I was coming out of a dream. The spell was broken, and Jonathan was back on the couch again. I rolled over on my side and pretended to fall asleep.

"We'll always be friends, right?" he whispered.

"Of course," I said, but that was a lie. The truth was that Jonathan's confession angered me and our kiss only drove us further apart. If only he had told his mother what Bill had done to him, maybe things would have been better. After that night, we never spoke again.

It was comforting to think Jonathan was out of my life. Grammar school was eight long years. Now it was over. I was moving on to a high school where no one knew me. It was a chance for a new beginning. By telling my parents about Bill, I had taken the first step in ridding him from my life. Now he was gone. What remained of his memory would be erased by letting go of Jonathan, as well.

ONE WEEK LATER, I RODE MY BICYCLE TO BILL'S HOUSE, waited by the telephone pole, and stared up at his bedroom. He never came out. His truck wasn't even there, but I waited anyway. I don't know what I would have said if he'd appeared. I just wanted to see him. Standing there by the telephone pole, I no longer felt like myself. I had become dissociated. Now that Bill was no longer a part of my life, I was unable to collect the fragments that were left behind, and it was confusing to feel unrelated to myself. But, even in the midst of all this confusion, I wondered where Bill was and whether he ever thought about me. His absence left me feeling lonely. I waited for several minutes more before I got on my bicycle and rode back home from his house for the last time.

After that day, I would always blame myself for what happened. I was convinced that Bill felt the need to punish me because there was something horribly wrong with me, something I was still unaware of. For years I moved through life feeling numb, and the emptiness grew black with hatred. I became a dark teenager and, later, a cynical adult. At twenty-eight years old, when I finally admitted I was gay, it occurred to me that Bill had already known this back then. Long before I had a conscious thought that I was gay, Bill had singled me out. As a child, I threatened Bill's sexuality because I was a reminder of the very thing he loathed about himself.

PART III

CHAPTER 24

Taking the Plunge

A MONTH AFTER I MADE CONTACT WITH BILL, I took Dean's advice and met with a therapist. It was April and I was about to turn forty-one when I made an appointment with Dr. Kate McGovern. I walked the entire way from my apartment, thinking about what I was going to say. I hadn't been in therapy for over a year, and the thought of starting over again with another therapist (Kate would be my fourth) was something I wasn't looking forward to.

I arrived early and took the elevator to the fourth floor. A door at the end of the hall opened, and a tall, slender woman stepped out. We looked at each other. She smiled and motioned me toward her. As I walked down the hall, the floorboards creaked, reminding me that I was about to take that plunge off the gangplank again, headfirst into therapy.

"Hello," she said. "Come inside."

Dr. McGovern's office was a large room with the obligatory overstuffed couch. She sat in a leather chair and rested her feet on a matching black ottoman. A small coffee table separated us. The furniture behind her consisted of two large wooden pieces with cabinets and doors that closed in order to ensure the privacy of their contents. The art was minimal: a poster of a Rothko, another Expressionistic work. There were two small clocks: one behind her on the cabinet, another next to me on the couch, placed in such a way so we both knew how far into the session we were at any given time. In the past, I always kept a watchful eye on the remaining minutes. One of my biggest issues with therapy was that time was a double-edged sword: not enough when you needed it and too much when you didn't.

"To begin, I'm going to ask you a few questions," she said. Her voice was comforting and gentle. I imagined she was in her late forties. She was dressed comfortably in a white button-up shirt, light beige chinos, and penny loafers. Immediately, I saw Olga in her kind face. But Kate McGovern appeared more reserved, and unlike Olga, I imagined she had an Ivy League education, a white Protestant family, and a Latino girlfriend to piss them off.

I began.

⸺⸺

LATER THAT WEEK, MY CELL PHONE RANG. The area code was unfamiliar to me, and despite my general rule not to answer unknown callers, I picked it up anyway.

It was Jonathan.

"Oh my God, how are you?" I asked. "After I spoke to your dad, I didn't think I would hear from you. He said you were living in Denver."

"Yes," he said. "I love it here."

I was stunned. His voice was calm and sweet, like Kermit the Frog's, just as I remembered.

"I'm so sorry about your mom," I offered. "I really liked her. She was a cool lady, with such style. I loved her dark Farrah Fawcett hairdo and those round glasses."

Jonathan laughed. I recognized it as the same laugh from childhood. "That makes me so happy to hear you say that. I feel like I forgot so much of my childhood."

"I wish I could say the same."

"How have you been?"

"Good . . . mostly," I said. Then I added, "I'm a doctor living in New York. I'm gay!"

"Me, too."

We laughed at our mutual disclosure. "That didn't take long," I said. "But why beat around the bush? Hell, I wrote a book on gay men's health."

"I heard. That's amazing. I can't wait to buy it."

"Thank you," I said. "I've been traveling to promote it. Overall, it's been an exciting time for me. Recently, I came into contact with two guys who knew Father Roberts. Remember him?"

"Yes, of course."

"Well, one thing led to another, and I started to think about Bill Fox. You remember Bill, right?"

There was silence at the other end. I was sure he had hung up the phone.

"Of course I remember him," he said finally.

I noticed the change in his tone, but I continued. "I tracked him down in Pennsylvania. It seems he's adopted several boys over the past twenty-five years."

"How awful."

"What makes it worse is that he still might have children in his care."

"How did you find all this out?"

"I called him."

"You did?" he asked, as though that was the most striking thing I'd said. "You spoke to Bill Fox?"

I took a deep breath. "Jonathan, how much do you remember about what happened?"

"Honestly, my memory is very fuzzy. After I graduated from St. Sylvester's, I had a terrible time in high school. I started doing drugs and dropped out. I even ran away from home. My uncle Vito took care of me. Do you remember him?"

"Absolutely. That dildo is forever etched into my memory."

"Oh, that's right. I remember that. Well, my uncle Vito arranged an intervention. Luckily for me, he got me into rehab, and eventually, I finished high school. My parents divorced shortly after that. Then my mom died several years later. That's when I moved to Denver. I had to get away."

"I'm so sorry, Jonathan. I had no idea. Do you have a partner?"

"Yes, I've been with my partner, Mark, for nearly eight years."

"That's great." I was relieved he had someone. "Well, I hope I didn't freak your father out, but I needed to find you. I wanted to talk to you."

"When my dad called, I was like, *who?* And then he explained, and I was like, Frank Spinelli! Now that's a blast from the past. Then I looked you up online. I'm so proud of everything you've accomplished. Tomorrow, I have to buy your book. I still collect them."

"Me, too," I said. "I guess some things never change." Immediately, I was reminded of that skinny boy with tortoiseshell glasses, riding his bicycle up to my house. "Jonathan, I need your help. I want to report Bill and get those children taken away from him."

"But what can I do?" he asked. "I really don't remember what happened. I mean, I remember something happened, but I couldn't give you details."

"Do you recall that he molested us?"

Jonathan exhaled deeply into the phone. "I know something went on, but I wouldn't be able to tell you much more than that."

I found it difficult to believe that Jonathan didn't remember the past as vividly as I did. I wanted to shake him and get him to remember. I became more aggressive. "Jonathan, you don't remember sleeping over his house, the Farrah Fawcett poster over his bed, and that scary Mrs. Fox, sitting in the living room watching television?"

"I can't believe you remember all that. I'm sorry, but it all seems so fuzzy to me."

Something told me not to press him. That it was pointless to push him further. He would remember eventually. All he needed was time.

"I think we should keep in touch," I said. "I'll give you my e-mail. That way, if you remember anything, you could just write. Sometimes it's easier to write down the things we feel uncomfortable saying."

"Okay," he said. I felt him slipping away, back into my past. "It was so nice talking to you, Frank."

The next day, I received an e-mail from Jonathan. Attached were a series of photos taken with his partner, Mark, on a gay cruise. I stared at one photo in particular, where they were posed in front of a palm tree, the crystal-blue ocean behind them. Mark was a tall, fair-skinned man who wore glasses. He looked twelve years old. They had their arms over each other's shoulders. I couldn't believe how much Jonathan had changed over the years. His once dark, wavy hair had receded and gone gray along the sides. He'd grown a goatee, and those narrow cheeks had filled in. Only his eyes remained the same—forever distracted, forlorn, and hidden behind a pair of glasses. Time had changed him, Bill had changed him, and—even though we were once the best of friends who believed in telepathy and shared a love of books—he now recalled very little of the past.

In the last paragraph of his e-mail, Jonathan wrote:

> *It was good talking with you last night. Despite all the bad that happened in those years, I remember the positive things the most. I look back on it with happy memories. You were part of those happy memories, and I am glad to have had the chance to say hello again.*

WHEN I MET WITH DR. MCGOVERN THE SECOND TIME, she had a yellow notepad on her lap. The office was warm and quiet, the couch soft and cozy. I wondered how Dr. McGovern kept from falling asleep, listening to patients talk all day. Outside the window, a group of pigeons gathered on the ledge. The soft hum of the cooing was distracting. One was staring directly at me. It was completely white like a dove.

"How often did you see Bill?" she asked.

"I'd see him every week at Boy Scout meetings, but I suppose that's not what you're referring to? Honestly, I don't know how many times I saw Bill. He came by my house once or twice a week. Sometimes I didn't see him for a week or two, but then, out of the blue, he'd come over without even calling. He'd just show up."

"How'd it make you feel when he'd show up at your house?"

I stared at the pigeons again, knowing very well what Dr. McGovern was getting at. Next she'd ask me about my relationship with my parents, and then, just like all the other therapists before her, she'd nod repeatedly, as though she'd figured me out in just under two visits. Therapists always wanted to connect my molestation with my parents. I had all the textbook traits of a fucked-up gay man: domineering mother, absentee father, and sexually abusive childhood. All I needed was a crystal meth addiction to complete my unlucky hand.

Not wanting to play this game again, I stared at the pigeons instead, thinking how much I hated Dean for suggesting I go back into therapy and grateful I hadn't told Chad I made this appointment. The night I spoke to Dean at Chad's apartment I took his advice and told Chad everything. He listened, staring at me with those huge blue eyes of his, the same ones that reminded me of Mary Ingalls on *Little House on the Prairie*. The whole time I was convinced he was thinking, *What the hell did I get myself into?* When I was done, Chad just looked at me and said, "I'm sorry you have to go through this."

The process of exploring how I felt was something I grew to hate about therapy. My body felt tense sitting there on the couch. I counted the seconds on the small bronze clock and wondered how many different ways I'd answered Dr. McGovern's question before—first to Olga, then to Tim, and finally, to Roger.

"How did I feel?" I repeated. "Why's it so important to talk about how I felt as a little boy when my Scoutmaster picked me up to have sex?" I felt my cheeks heating up. I turned away, not wanting Dr. McGovern to see this side of me yet. I didn't want to explain the complex feelings of standing by the door as a little boy with my face pressed up to the screen, waiting for Bill to come.

Silently, I stared at those pigeons, thinking how beautiful the white one was. I could just hear Eric, "But you don't even like pigeons. You call them rats with feathers." Then the white one flew away and, with it, any hope I had that Dr. McGovern could help me.

"Proud," I said finally. "I felt proud, as though he'd chosen me from all the other little boys. But then afterward, I always felt shame."

"Shame because you felt what you were doing with Bill was wrong?"

"Yes," I said. "So there you have it in a nutshell, the warped nucleus of my soul—a mixture of false pride and shame. Are you happy now? Because this isn't going to help me figure out how to get those boys away from that monster."

Dr. McGovern sat up and put down her notepad. "Our time is almost up," she said. "But before you go, I'd like to say something. We need to talk more about the feelings the molestation stirred up in you as a child and now as an adult. As for the remaining boys who still live with Bill, my advice is that you seek legal counsel with a lawyer who specializes in childhood sexual abuse."

I stood up and bolted out of the room. Assailed by a deep, burning rage, I felt that if I didn't get out of the building I would melt. When I reached the street, I stood against the wall and breathed. I noticed tears on my cheeks against the cool wind. Then I wondered when I had started to cry—whether it began while I was in Dr. McGovern's office. I didn't want her to see me cry.

Walking back to my practice that morning, I convinced myself that I wasn't going to return the following week. I was done. There was no point in talking about how I felt as a child or now as an adult. Dean was wrong. He didn't know me. We hadn't even met. I had Chad now. He was all I needed, and he didn't need to feel as though he was dating some fucked-up, stereotypical gay man going through a midlife crisis.

But it's not only about you anymore.

Then I remembered that picture of Jonathan. I saw his face, those eyes, and recalled the story he told me about how he ran away from home, became a drug addict, and almost never finished high school. Bill had adopted fifteen boys. He still had three with him. When they turned forty years old, what stories would they have to tell?

That night I searched for an attorney online. I found one based in Philadelphia who specialized in working with victims of childhood sexual abuse: Jeff Brenum. I called him, and surprisingly, he answered the phone himself.

Mr. Brenum listened to my entire story and then informed me that I couldn't press charges against Bill. "Thirty years?" he confirmed. "I'm sorry, but this is well past the New York statute of limitations. If you had been molested in Pennsylvania, then that would be an entirely different story. Boys here have until their fiftieth birthday to press charges."

"Then what about the boys he's adopted?" I asked. "Is there anything we can do for them?"

"There's very little you can do. Of course, if there were other allegations involving children, particularly ones he's adopted, that would be important."

"How could I find out?"

"You could hire a private investigator to look into whether or not there have been previous allegations of child molestation made against this man by other families, but that could be costly."

"I see."

"Off the record, there is something else you could do. You could agree to meet your molester in person. Tell him you're having a difficult time understanding what you did to attract him as an adult man in such a sexual way. You could wear a wire and record the conversation."

Suddenly, I had to urinate.

When I didn't answer right away, Mr. Brenum asked, "Are you still there?"

"Yes, I'm sorry," I said, pressing firmly on my groin. "I was just thinking about what you said."

"Remember, this is completely off the record. I'm not insinuating that you should do this. You asked me what your options are."

Once I hung up, I ran into the bathroom, sat on the toilet, and waited to pee.

Could I meet Bill and wear a wiretap?

Then I recalled something Dean had said to me: "To do that, you would have to have the skills of an Academy Award–winning actress. No offense, but you're no Meryl Streep." Dean was right. I couldn't face Bill, even without a wire. Not yet.

That was when I decided I had to go back to Dr. McGovern.

CHAPTER 25

Choo-Choo Charlie

THE NEXT MORNING, I contacted Child Protective Services (CPS) in Pennsylvania. The operator connected me to the Childhood Sexual Abuse Registry. I left a detailed message, but didn't expect to hear from anyone. Twenty-four hours later, a woman from CPS named Yvonne Barlow called me.

After she introduced herself, she told me that it was difficult to open an investigation of child sexual abuse when there have been no complaints coming from within the household.

"So, you need a child to come forward before you can act?" I said sarcastically.

"I understand that's how it might sound, but that's not always the case. We investigate all charges. However, it's complicated because you don't live here, and this happened to you when you were a little boy living in New York. I am going to open an investigation. It just makes my life a bit more difficult when we don't have any accusations coming from a member of his household or a neighbor who suspects something is going on."

"Please, I have reason to believe the boys are mentally challenged. That would explain why none of them have come forward. Wouldn't that have any bearing on helping you with your investigation?"

"Yes, everything gets taken into account. I just want you to know that it's a slow process. Thank you again for contacting me. I'll be in touch."

When the mail arrived that very afternoon, I received an invitation to attend an HIV advisory board meeting in Denver at the end of the month. I considered this a good omen and immediately accepted, thinking it was time to visit Jonathan.

A STORM SETTLED OVER NEW YORK CITY. The sky was gray. Each time a patient entered the vestibule to my office, the wind swirled into the waiting area and magazines flapped open. I was scheduled to leave for Denver that afternoon. My only concern was that the flight might get cancelled due to the weather, and then I wouldn't get to see Jonathan. Once I accepted the invitation, I e-mailed him and suggested we have dinner. He was very excited at the prospect of reuniting and volunteered to make plans. "I can't wait to show you around," he wrote.

I hoped that once I had him alone and in person, I could get him to remember more about the past. I needed him to remember. If Jonathan came forward, then Ms. Barlow from CPS would have more to go on than just my statement.

I looked at my watch. A car was scheduled to pick me up in fifteen minutes. Quickly, I signed off my computer, checked over the remaining labs, and forwarded the phones to my service. Just then, Gloria walked into my office holding a fax. The letterhead read:

PENNSYLVANIA STATE POLICE

I ripped it out of her hand. It was from a Corporal Dennis Laramie. At the bottom of the fax, it read: "Dr. Spinelli, I recently received information that you may be able to assist me in an investigation in Tioga County, PA. I would appreciate it if you could contact me at your earliest convenience. Thank you."

I dialed the number.

"Thank you for getting back to me so soon," said Corporal

Laramie, clearing his throat several times. "First, I want to offer my sincerest apologies for what happened to you." He had a deep, rich, commanding voice. I imagined he was a tall man with a full head of gray hair and a thick mustache. "In Pennsylvania, we take allegations of child sexual abuse very seriously. I don't know about New York, but here in P-A, a victim has up until their fiftieth birthday to press charges against their molester."

"That is very progressive," I said. "As it was explained to me by my legal counsel, the statute of limitations in my case has expired. My concern, however, is not exclusively personal. I'm worried about the children Mr. Fox allegedly still has in his care."

"Doc," interrupted Gloria. "Your car is waiting outside to take you to the airport."

I waved her away dismissively. Just then, that familiar annoying tingling started up inside my urethra and my knees began to tremble.

"I understand, but what I wanted to tell you is that we are going to launch an investigation based on your claims. We're going to look into this. Now, I can't promise you anything, but I wanted to call and assure you that we take these allegations very, very seriously."

"Well, thank you for contacting me, Corporal Laramie."

"I'll be in touch."

I hung up and bolted past Gloria. Inside the bathroom, I started chanting immediately. "Olga Koniahin, Olga Koniahin. This is a good omen," I whispered to myself. "A very good omen. Olga Koniahin, Olga Koniahin." Within seconds, the urine came, and I stood there proudly, knowing I had convinced the police to launch an investigation. Now I needed to get Jonathan on board, as well.

THE RIDE TO THE AIRPORT WAS AS MUCH A BLUR TO ME as the view out the backseat window. Rain pelted the car, sending quivering veins of water down the glass. I needed to speak to someone. I dialed Eric.

"Oh my God," he said once I explained. "I can't believe the Pennsylvania Police called you the same day you're going to Denver. What are the chances of that?"

"It's fate," I said. "They're going to launch an investigation, and Bill will go to jail, where he belongs. I can't wait to tell Jonathan."

"Wait just a second, Choo-Choo Charlie," warned Eric. "You haven't seen this person in what . . . thirty years? Frank, he might not be as receptive to this information as you are. You're like a steam engine right now, and I don't want you to go barreling into Denver and scaring the living shit out of this guy. You have to calm down."

"Why is it you can't be excited for me?"

"I am excited. I just don't want you to walk into a situation with high expectations because, when that happens, you're setting yourself up to get hurt. And I don't want you to get hurt. I'm just looking out for my best friend."

The car pulled up to the airport drop-off. "Listen, I have to go."

"I don't give a shit," he said. "We're not done yet."

"So now you're calling the shots?"

Eric's voice climbed several octaves. "What are you talking about?"

"I don't know anymore. I feel like everyone around me is constantly warning me to be careful, and now I call to tell you that the police are launching an investigation based on my persistence, and still, you're telling me to calm down. I don't want to calm down! You used to be the most encouraging person in my life. Back in San Francisco you said, 'I promise I will see this through with you until the very end.' Now, I don't believe you meant that."

"Yes, and I also said don't jump feet first into something you don't fully understand."

"Listen, I have to go," I said, grabbing my carry-on. Then I heard a *click* as Eric disconnected.

Marching through the airport, I was enraged thinking about

my trip to San Francisco when I first read Bill's book. I had come so far since that weekend. Now, I was on the verge of bringing Bill to justice. As I made my way through security, I vowed that no one was going to get in my way—not Eric, not my family, and not even Chad. I was going to see this through to the end, even if it meant losing everyone.

CHAPTER 26

Altitude Sickness

D ENVER APPEARED AS A WIDE EXPANSE OF OPEN SPACE that was as beautiful as it was daunting. Standing in my hotel room, I stared out the window, marveling at the mountains that outlined the perimeter of the city. The endless sky above enveloped my view like the dome of an enormous snow globe.

It was late by the time I arrived, so I tried to sleep. But I couldn't stop thinking about Corporal Laramie and the police investigation. I took a sleeping pill and woke early the next morning with a throbbing headache, feeling exhausted. On the desk next to my laptop, there was a brochure listing *Things to Do in Denver*. On the back there was a list of symptoms for *High Altitude Syndrome*. I'd been in Denver less than twenty-four hours, and I already had two out of six. Inside the bathroom, I popped some aspirin and got ready for the advisory meeting.

Downstairs, I made my way to the main lecture hall, along with the other attendees. As always, I took a seat in the back and on the aisle so that I had easy access to the restrooms. Once the lights went down and the first speaker took the stage, I tried my best to pay attention. The aspirin I'd taken earlier was wearing off and left a pulsating pain over my right temple. Closing my eyes, I was transported back to 1981. Jonathan and I were in my den listening to the *Xanadu* soundtrack, singing "Suddenly" into my sisters' hairbrushes. I was amazed at how high his voice could go. Then I saw Chris Spivey's face, those cold blue eyes, and I woke up. Everywhere I looked, doctors were listening attentively. All the while, I was staring at my watch, counting down the minutes until I could go back up to my room.

JONATHAN AND I AGREED TO MEET IN THE HOTEL LOUNGE. I arrived five minutes early wearing a black fitted shirt, blue jeans, and suede boots with two-inch heels. When I turned the corner off the elevator banks, I heard a band playing "Islands in the Stream." As I entered the lounge, the music grew louder. Across the room, I saw Jonathan sitting on a couch, looking exactly as he did when we graduated from St. Sylvester's. Jarred by this memory, I felt a sudden pressure in my bladder although I knew I didn't have to pee. Throughout the day, I'd carefully rationed my fluid intake to just one cup of coffee earlier that morning and two small bottles of water over the course of the afternoon. I'd peed ten minutes before I left my hotel room. This was a phantom urge.

Weaving my way across the lounge, through dancing couples, I saw the real Jonathan emerge, looking bewildered and doddering behind oversized glasses. When he noticed me, he tapped his boyfriend's leg, and they stood up. With each step, I became more and more self-conscious, concerned that I'd worn the wrong outfit or my hair was too puffy. The entire room felt enormous, and the distance between us now seemed as long as a football field. When I finally reached them, I was surprised that Jonathan was short, shorter than me, which was comforting. We embraced, and I chuckled nervously. His body felt frail in my arms. "It's been a long time," I said as we hugged.

"Yes, it has, a very long time," he said. "Frank, this is my partner, Mark."

Mark extended his hand, but I hugged him instead. Then I stared at them for a long time.

"Would you like a drink?" asked Mark. I noticed they already had cocktails. I was relieved that we would be drinking.

Mark left for the bar to get me a margarita. Alone, Jonathan and I smiled nervously at each other. "I have to sit down," said Jonathan. "My knees suddenly feel weak."

"I'm so nervous I thought I was going to piss my pants walking across this lounge. Is everything in Denver this big?"

"Frank, you're in Rocky Mountain country."

I sat next to Jonathan, soaking in his face, each line and every gray hair. I imagined he was doing the same to me. He was all grown-up, yet his adulthood was so uncompromising that it took with it all the youthful beauty I remembered of the boy who had everything to gain in becoming a man. It was startling to think that we once looked alike, although I was always the chubby one and he was the one who needed more meat on his bones. I wondered what part Bill played in robbing him of his manhood and what Jonathan would look like if he hadn't been abused.

"This is weird," he said. "You look great. I almost didn't recognize you with the gray hair and beard, but now that I'm sitting next to you, I can see that chunky kid from St. Sylvester's."

Mark returned with drinks.

"Thank you," I said as he set them down. Immediately, I lifted my glass. "Cheers! To old friends and new ones."

I drank quickly, and, thankfully, they didn't fall far behind. After our second round of margaritas, Jonathan suggested we leave. Outside the air was chilly. We walked through Denver, past the train station. The cobblestone avenues were wide, and tall, bronze sculpted street lamps with globe fixtures illuminated the sidewalk with yellow light. The entire scene looked like a set from a Vincente Minnelli musical with quaint shops and Victorian architecture. At any moment, I expected Judy Garland to come riding past us on a trolley.

Jonathan led us into a packed Mexican cantina. The hostess seated us at a table near the front. Our waitress approached—a college girl wearing a vintage granny dress and an apron. "Can I start you fellas off with drinks?" When Jonathan ordered another round of margaritas, Mark quickly asked for three glasses of water.

"Do you speak to anyone from St. Sylvester's?" I asked.

Jonathan never looked up from his menu. "Are you kidding? I was done with that class after graduation."

"What about from Boy Scouts?"

He winced. "No," he said decisively.

"But you made it all the way to Eagle Scout, didn't you?"

"Only because Bill left," he offered. "Mr. Castro started his own troop at St. Theresa's. I became an Eagle Scout under him."

"Then who took over Troop 85?" I asked.

"Mr. Noto."

"Mr. Noto!" I yelled. "Remember?"

Then in unison, we shouted, "Got no fingers, and I got no toes, and Noto!"

I turned to Mark. "Sorry. This evening is going to be one long trip down memory lane. I apologize in advance for all the cryptic references."

"I don't mind," said Mark. "I'm happy to meet friends from Jonathan's past. He doesn't have many."

"Many? I don't have any," interjected Jonathan. "I was so excited when my father called and told me you were looking for me. Then, when we spoke on the phone, you brought back so many memories. But more than anything, I was really happy that you remembered my mom."

"Oh my God! How could anyone forget Sharon Duran?"

Jonathan looked wistfully over at Mark. "I'm disappointed Mark never got to meet her. She died of lung cancer right after my parents got divorced. With each passing year, I forget more and more about her. But you seem to remember her so vividly. That's why it was so refreshing for me to hear you reminisce about her in such a lovely way. I want Mark to hear you talk about my mom."

"Well, you came to the right place," I said proudly. After another good sip of my margarita, I set the glass down and regaled Mark with stories of Sharon Duran. "She was, without a doubt, one of the most amazing women I have ever met. She was a dynamo: petite, thin, and sexy with her feathered, long brown hair, and these small, round glasses, like Velma from *Scooby-Doo*, but not in a nerdy kind of way. No, your mother was sharp and very witty. Oh, and she always had a cigarette in her hand." I trailed off, remembering how she died. I turned to Jonathan. "I'm so sorry. I can't believe she's gone. May I ask what happened?"

"As I mentioned briefly on the phone, when I was in high school I got involved with drugs. Eventually, I ran away and was homeless for a while. I met this guy, and we became boyfriends. He was older, homeless, and also a drug addict. We lived in a train station on Long Island. Can you believe that?"

"That is unbelievable," I said. "Jonathan, the boy voted Most Shy: a homeless drug addict." Just then I noticed Jonathan staring off into the distance. I couldn't tell whether my comment had insulted him or he was just inebriated. For several more seconds we remained quiet, soaking in the reality of my remark.

After we ordered, Eric's words of warning echoed in my head. This seemed as good a time as any to take a break. "Would you guys excuse me? I have to use the facilities."

The waitress directed me to the rear of the restaurant. Fortunately, the cantina had two individual private restrooms. I entered the one marked HOMBRES and locked the door behind me. Just like everything else in Denver, the men's room was huge, roughly the size of my bedroom back in New York. Posters of Mexican wrestlers in gold frames hung on the walls. Resting on the toilet bowl tank were cylindrical glass candleholders decorated with pictures of the Virgin Mary.

I positioned myself over the toilet with my hands pressed up against the wall. Dizzy from all the tequila, I swayed from side to side. Eric's words repeated over and over in my head. I tried to shut him out by chanting.

Olga Koniahin, Olga Koniahin.

I refocused my attention on Jonathan, reminding myself why I came to Denver. I had to figure out a way to bring up Bill. He needed to remember.

Olga Koniahin, Olga Koniahin.

I urinated easily in the privacy of that restroom, drunk on tequila and staring at the Virgin Mary as I chanted Olga's name instead of saying the rosary. By the time I returned to the table, our food had arrived, along with another round of drinks. "That was quick," said Jonathan, holding his glass in his hands. He was slurring his words. His eyelids were heavy. Mark stared at him, a guarded expression on his face. I sensed they'd had an argument while I was in the restroom. I took my seat and stared down at the mishmash of refried beans, rice, and what appeared to be a burrito. I took another long sip from my drink. Despite Jonathan's obvious drunkenness, I asked, "So tell me about the intervention?"—thinking he'd answer more freely now.

Jonathan sat back in his chair, the margarita glued to his hand. "You see, I was living on the street with my boyfriend, and I knew that I had some money in an old bank account. The only problem was that I needed the passbook. So my plan was to sneak into my house during the day when everyone was at work. The only problem was that my mother was waiting for me."

"How did she know you were coming?"

"I have no idea, but the next thing I knew, my father showed up and then my uncle Vito. Thank God for Uncle Vito." Jonathan closed his eyes and sighed heavily. When he opened his eyes again, he stared directly at me. "You know, he was the only one who talked to me about being gay and drugs. If it wasn't for him, I would have run away again. He was the reason I agreed to go to rehab."

"How is your uncle?"

"He died of AIDS the year after my mom passed away."

I heard the pain in his voice. I didn't know what to say. Once again there was a long pause as conversations from the surrounding tables suddenly amplified. I heard mariachi music in the background and wondered whether it had been playing the entire time. Finally, I offered, "That must have been so tough on you to lose both your mother and your uncle Vito back-to-back."

"It was," he whispered. Mark reached over and placed his hand tenderly on the back of Jonathan's neck.

"I feel fortunate to have met him," I said. "Let's toast to Uncle Vito!"

We clinked glasses. I watched Mark, saw his concern growing

as Jonathan drank more. "Honey, why don't you have some water?" he said, sliding over a glass. Ignoring him, Jonathan stared at the margarita in his hand. He appeared sullen and detached, as if he had already departed us and was swimming in a sea of tequila, drowning in painful memories.

"Seriously," I said. "What did you think when I told you that I spoke with Bill Fox?"

"I was surprised." Jonathan set his glass down. It hit a fork, which flipped in the air before landing on the ground.

"Maybe you should slow down?" suggested Mark.

Jonathan ignored him and said, "I still don't know how you got in touch with him."

"I told you. He wrote a book."

"Yes, I found it on the Internet, but it's out of print."

"Well, I can lend you my copy if you'd like? It makes for great toilet reading."

"The nerve of him," said Jonathan. He was beginning to sound incoherent.

Mark slid Jonathan's drink out of his reach and replaced it with a glass of water. Jonathan waved at him with disgust. "So, how did you find Bill?" asked Mark, refusing to let Jonathan have his margarita back.

I leaned in. "In his book, he used actual names and their addresses. I found his sister very easily. She's lived in the same house since 1982. I simply called Information and got her number. Then I left a message on her answering machine. A day later, Bill called me."

"What did he say?" asked Jonathan. "I'm dying to know."

"We talked about a lot of things. First, he said he didn't remember me. Something about my name sounded familiar, but he couldn't place the face. Then I asked him about the boy he adopted, and he told me he adopted fifteen boys over the past twenty-five years."

"Did you confront him?"

"No, I couldn't. I was so nervous I could barely talk. He was very pleasant. Said he wanted to meet me for coffee sometime . . . Can you believe that?" Hearing my own voice left me unsettled.

The cantina felt uncomfortably warm. I sipped my drink and rested my eyes on Jonathan, who was staring at me, riveted. I took a slow inhale and continued. "Jonathan, I need to talk to you about what happened. On the phone, you said you didn't remember very much."

"It's just that it's all so fuzzy."

There was that word again, *fuzzy*. I wanted to reach over, slap him across the face, and knock the fuzziness out of his head, just as my father used to smack the side of my grandfather's old television every time the picture went static. I felt my face heating up. It hurt me to have to confront Jonathan in his fragile state, but I had to know. "You do remember being molested?" I asked, folding my hands firmly together under the table.

Jonathan squeezed his eyes closed. "I know he did something. I just can't remember the details."

"Do you remember his house, his mother, Beatrice?"

"Yes." He nodded, his eyes still shut tight. "She was that creepy old lady who sat in the living room."

"Norman Bates's mother," I interjected. My hands were now clenched around each other, forming one big fist. "Do you remember his bedroom with the Farrah Fawcett poster over the bed?"

"No . . . I mean, kind of." He opened his eyes and stared off into space. "I'm sorry. It's just that you remember so much more than I do."

Jonathan looked so much like that little boy who maintained a bewildered expression throughout grammar school that it seemed merciless of me to continue prodding him, yet I wasn't able to help myself. "Jonathan, try and remember!" I pleaded.

"It's possible Jonathan can't remember every detail," offered Mark. "It's understandable that he might have blocked out these memories."

I ignored Mark and maintained my focus on Jonathan. "You must remember the day I came over to your house and we sat on your mother's bed? Remember, I told her everything that went on between me and Bill?"

"I do remember that, because my parents hounded me that

night for hours, asking over and over if Bill had done the same to me."

"Yes, and you lied. Remember? You said Bill didn't touch you."

"Is that why you stopped being my friend and dropped out of the altar boys?"

"Funny how you remember certain things more than others."

"That's when you started hanging out with Seth Connelly and Tommy Scalici?"

"I never hung out with them."

"Yeah, but you laughed when they made fun of me. You knew Tommy was making me deliver his newspapers every morning before school, and you still laughed when they picked on me in class."

"I was mad at you. You lied to your parents. If you had only come forward, things would have been different. Your parents would have gone to the police. Maybe other boys would have come forward."

Jonathan sat up abruptly, clenching his fists. "What did you expect me to do? My mother made me invite you over that day. The next thing I know, we're sitting on her bed and telling her how you gave blow jobs to Bill. When she asked me, I froze. What did you expect? She was my mother, Frank! I was petrified. She may have been a cool lady to you and everyone else, but she was a tough mom, always getting into my business."

"And my mother wasn't?" I countered. "Don't bullshit me, Jonathan. Your mother was more understanding than mine. The truth is that you had the chance to come forward. I opened the door. Instead, you turned your back on me."

Mark placed his hand between our faces to stop the shouting. Jonathan and I sat back in our seats. I remained quiet, breathing heavily and feeling pain churn below my ribs while Jonathan chewed angrily on ice cubes. Mark removed his glasses and began rubbing his eyes with the balls of his palms.

The waitress came by and took our dishes away. "Would you guys care for any dessert?"

Mark shook his head and asked for the check.

I felt as if I was in a Mexican standoff, staring into the face of someone who was once so close to me and now was a complete stranger—but more than a stranger, a liar. I read somewhere that victims of sexual abuse often split into two categories: those who remember vividly and the others who completely shut out the painful experience of the past. I don't know why I thought I was going to be able to jar Jonathan's memory.

It dawned on me that Eric was right. Meeting Jonathan again after all these years hadn't gone as intended. Parts of Bill and some of the events we experienced as Boy Scouts had been intentionally deleted from his memory and re-edited so he could stomach the past. I'd retained a full director's cut. This night of fun, erased by confrontation, brought with it waves of shame so consuming I felt like I could just cry right there at the table like a little boy.

We didn't speak again until the waitress brought over our check. Jonathan snatched it up. We argued over who would pay, and finally, I conceded.

Despite everything, I wanted to leave Jonathan and Mark on good terms. So I thought of the only topic we hadn't discussed. "Do you remember the time my sister took us to see *Xanadu*?"

"Of course," Jonathan replied.

"I recently bought the soundtrack on iTunes."

"*Xanadu*, the movie?" asked Mark.

"Is there any other *Xanadu*?" I said, sarcastically.

Jonathan scrunched his nose. "Poor thing hasn't seen it."

"You're gay, and you haven't seen *Xanadu*? I thought that was a prerequisite, like being a fan of Cher or Liza Minnelli?"

"You're wasting your time," insisted Jonathan. "He grew up in Kansas. I've taught him everything he knows about being gay. In fact, he hadn't seen *The Wizard of Oz* until he met me. Imagine that, a boy from Kansas who'd never seen *The Wizard of Oz*."

"That's absurd."

Mark was blushing. "My parents were born-again Christians. I had no choice."

"Well, Mark, *Xanadu* just so happens to be the most amazing roller-skating musical ever made."

"With the best soundtrack of all time," added Jonathan.

Jonathan and I stared at each other and then spontaneously broke out into song, *"Suddenly the wheels are in motion."* Then we laughed out loud together.

"We sang that duet all night. Jonathan, of course, insisted on singing the Olivia Newton-John part."

"Of course you did, honey," said Mark, tapping the back of Jonathan's hand.

"Let's get out of here," I said. "It's been a long night of reminiscing."

Jonathan staggered as we headed down those same cobblestone streets. Mark caught him by the arm so he wouldn't fall. Regaining his balance, Jonathan gave him a grateful smile. I stumbled once or twice myself, but after a while the cold air had a sobering effect. They escorted me all the way to my hotel, and we said our good-byes outside the entrance.

As they made their way down the cobblestone road, I watched as the boy from Kansas helped his wobbly partner down the street. The full moon cast a shimmering glow on them like a spotlight in a musical number. For a while I stood at the hotel entrance staring after them. In my head I heard the music from "We're Off to See the Wizard."

Then I shouted out, "Good night, Scarecrow, I'll miss you most of all."

Mark looked back at me, utterly confused. When Jonathan turned around, our eyes met. In the failing light, he looked like a little boy again. But he'd stopped being a boy a long time ago.

CHAPTER 27

Alaska in Colorado

I WOKE UP THE NEXT MORNING still wearing my jeans and one of my socks. I don't remember making it back to my hotel room. The minibar was wide open, and empty wine bottles littered the floor beside the bed. I found my shirt outside the bathroom. Stepping inside, I flicked on the switch. Under the fluorescent light, I didn't recognize the man staring back at me in the mirror. The whites of my eyes were layered with a reticulum of tiny red blood vessels. I immediately switched off the light and pissed in the dark. Then I washed my face with cold water. When I noticed an empty canister of Pringles on the floor next to the toilet, I felt an incredible urge to vomit.

I showered and got back into bed. My head was throbbing. My flight would depart in four hours. Lying there in the comfort of soft sheets and fluffy pillows, I convinced myself that it would be smart to check out of the hotel early and head over to the airport. I didn't want to stay in Denver any longer than I had to. *There should be an Elite Club at the airport,* I told myself. *I can start drinking again.* This seemed like the best idea I'd had all weekend. This decision—to drink more—did not concern me at the time. Clearly, it had become a habit to help forget that annoying pain below my ribs.

In the cab, I contemplated my motives for coming, and thought about how foolish I was for expecting things to go the way I'd planned. Now my impression of Denver was tarnished by the disappointing evening I spent with Jonathan and his partner. The quaint shops and old-fashioned railroad station appeared ridiculous now in the harsh light of day—some pedestrian attempt to live in an alternate reality where Christmas existed all year long. I wanted nothing more than to return to New York, back to my reality, so that I could continue my investigation, even without Jonathan's help.

The car pulled up to the desolate airport. Inside, I whisked by the security guards. Just beyond the checkpoint, I dipped into the men's room before heading to the Elite Club. The restroom was more spacious than any airport restroom I'd ever been to in the entire New York tri state area. I was amazed by how high the ceilings were. Along the far wall was a series of stalls, more than I'd ever seen in any men's room. On the opposite side were rows of urinals—clean, white, shiny fixtures—which glistened with the undeniable promise of hygiene. In another adjoining room, there was a chain of sinks, each with its own soap dispenser and mirror. This bathroom was an architectural manifesto, the Taj Mahal of bathrooms, as if designed with paruretics in mind.

Most men's rooms have very few stalls and worse, the urinals are usually aligned in such a way that if you're standing at the sink washing your hands, you can stare directly at the men urinating behind you. Having the sinks in another adjoining room alleviates this problem. This restroom had been designed by someone like me.

Incredibly, the whole place was empty. To be sure, I knelt down and looked under the stalls for feet. There were none. I moved across the restroom toward the first stall. My heels clicked on the tile like tap shoes. I felt like Fred Astaire tapping my way offstage, except the handicapped stall was my dressing room.

Inside, I felt sheltered by the magnitude of this colossal space created for disabled people, with its four metal walls suspended from the ceiling, and roughly ten square feet in diameter. I shut the door behind me and began my routine. First, I secured my carry-on to the coat hook on the back of the door. Thinking this was going to be easy, I quickly unbuttoned my pants. I pressed my palms firmly up against the cold tile wall. A smile grew across my face as I waited for the urine to flow, but there was none. I took a slow, long inhale. Right away I saw Jonathan stumbling down the cobblestone road with Mark propping him up so that he wouldn't fall. It hurt to think about him, but I couldn't help but remember. Then I felt the hair in my nose tingle with the sudden reminder of that putrid smell of tequila, and my stomach churned.

Olga Koniahin. Olga Koniahin.

Denver had been such a failure.

Olga Koniahin. Olga Koniahin.

My head throbbed with frustration. I pressed my forehead up against the comfortingly cool tile wall. Standing there, half-naked, with my genitals exposed, I saw myself as that pathetic boy in my grammar school restroom with a bleary, red-eyed Consalvo taunting me to pee for him on command. That I even needed a ritual to pee sent a convulsion of anger rippling through my body.

Olga Koniahin, Olga Koniahin.

Suddenly, I heard someone enter the restroom. I ignored whoever it was and continued chanting quietly to myself.

Olga Koniahin . . .

I heard the shuffle of tiny feet on the tile floor, followed by the heavier steps of adult shoes. "Come on, Alaska, time to make pee-pee."

"But I don't have to go, Daddy."

"Well, try, baby. We're going to get on a big plane for a long time, and I want you to take a nap. Okay?" They entered the stall next to me. "Come on, Alaska. Let me help you." I heard the distinct sound of ruffles. "That's a good girl," he urged.

Girl!

My urethra clamped down completely when I heard the sound of tiny feet beating against the porcelain bowl like a drum. I imagined Alaska was barely five years old and wore a china-blue satin dress, white crinoline, and matching patent-leather shoes.

"But, Daddy, I don't have to go." Her sweet, high-pitched voice rose up from the stall like bubbles.

"Come on, Alaska. Please pee for Daddy. You can do it, baby," he begged patiently. His reassuring voice filled me with an inexplicable anxiety. I desperately tried to block out their voices. I needed to focus.

Olga Koniahin, Olga Koniahin.

"Alaska, if you go pee-pee, then Daddy promises to buy you ice cream."

"Oh, Daddy, really?"

Anger boiled up inside me, rising like mercury in a thermometer.

Shut up, Alaska. Olga Koniahin. Olga Koniahin . . .

"Come on, baby, concentrate."

Olga Koniahin, Olga Koniahin.

My eyes were closed tight. My forehead pressed firmly against the tile. I began pounding it softly against the wall, quietly at first so that they wouldn't hear, and then harder and louder because I knew they weren't listening. The only other discernible sounds in that restroom were coming from their stall. Meanwhile, I was chanting quietly and twisting my nipples to the point they didn't feel like nipples at all but more like rubber.

"You can do it, baby. Come on now. Pee for Daddy."

Shut up!

Hovering over the toilet, hands pressed up against the wall, I tensed every last little muscle in my groin and emitted three farts into the quiet, sterile air of the Denver International Airport, Concourse B restroom.

Alaska's laughter filled the entire restroom. Suddenly, I heard the tinkle of tiny droplets hitting toilet water like the faint echo of a distant applause. But they weren't mine.

"Good girl, Alaska," said her father, heaving with relief. "You did it! You peed for Daddy!"

The tinkling continued for several seconds, a crescendo of accomplishment as Alaska giggled enthusiastically. Finally, it came to a halt. Suffused with pride, she happily asked, "Can I have ice cream now, Daddy?"

"Yes, you can. You can have anything you want, baby."

Furious, I punched my fist against the wall, zipped up my pants, and burst out of the stall. Just as I was about to exit the restroom, I heard the sound of tiny feet tapping against the tile floor behind me. I glanced over my shoulder and saw the real Alaska—my urinary warden—as she hurried past me and opened the door.

Once I was alone in the restroom again, I turned around and walked back into the stall to begin the ritual, but my feet no longer clicked like Fred Astaire's tap shoes. Now they echoed with hollow disappointment.

———

WHEN I GOT BACK FROM DENVER, I asked Chad out to dinner. If I was going to pursue Bill, I needed to be completely honest with him about everything.

We ate at an Italian restaurant on the corner by my apartment. The weather was warm and inviting, unlike my chilly stay in Denver. Sitting outside under an umbrella, we ordered white wine and pizza. We sat in silence, staring at the passersby and holding hands under the table.

"Remember that night I first told you about Bill?" I asked. "Well, I started seeing a therapist in April."

The waitress returned with a pizza, piping hot and draped in mozzarella. I stared at Chad, trying to read his expression, but he was too busy assisting the waitress. Once she left, he said, "Why didn't you tell me this sooner?"

"Honestly, Chad, I felt like we were just starting to get serious. Then I laid my child molestation history on you at your apartment . . . I know I should have been more honest, but I didn't want to freak you out. You told me you didn't believe in therapy, and I just didn't want you to think you were dating a freak."

"I never said I didn't believe in therapy," he countered. "I just said it wasn't for me. Considering everything that's going on in your life, maybe a therapist's advice is exactly what you need." Chad served me a slice of pizza and then one for himself.

"That's not all," I added. "Before I left for Denver, I received word from the Pennsylvania State Police. They're launching an investigation based on my allegations against Bill."

Chad's face lit up. "That's great, baby. Now, why wouldn't you tell me that?"

"I don't know exactly. I received the call right before I left for the airport. I was about to call you but dialed Eric instead. We had a little fight. After that, I didn't want to tell anyone else."

"What did you fight about?"

"Stupid stuff," I said. Then I remembered the last conversation I had with Eric, how he tried to warn me and the awful things I accused him of. The gnawing pain below my ribs began to throb suddenly as if someone somewhere was sticking a pin in a voodoo doll of me. I was so acutely dreading this conversation with Chad that I'd completely forgotten about Eric. "I'm afraid I owe him an apology," I continued.

"Have you spoken to him since then?"

"No, not yet," I said. "But that's not all I have to tell you."

Chad brushed his hand through his hair. "Is this it?"

"Promise," I said, holding three fingers up to my head. "Scout's honor."

"Ha-ha," he said dryly. "Finish your story."

"Okay, part of the reason why I accepted the offer to go to Denver was so that I could visit with an old friend from grammar school named Jonathan. Bill also molested him. I had dinner with Jonathan and his partner, Mark."

"How'd it go?"

"Not so good. He doesn't remember much. Let's just say Denver wasn't a successful trip."

Chad sat up and held my hands. "I don't want you to feel you can't tell me stuff that's going on in your life. I have big issues with secrecy. My ex kept secrets, and it drove me insane. Can you understand that?"

I nodded, staring into his eyes. What I felt for Chad was clear to me. It was love, a warm and comforting closeness I'd only ever felt with friends like Eric, but now I was experiencing it with someone I felt sexually passionate about.

"So, moving forward, can you try and trust me a little more?"

Lifting three fingers to my head again, I said, "Promise."

LATER THAT NIGHT I CALLED ERIC to apologize. He asked about Denver. I told him the truth.

"Well, I'm glad you made it home safe and sound," said Eric. "I missed you, and Frank, I don't ever want you to think I'm jealous of Chad. I'm truly happy for you. And if you want my advice, give Jonathan a little time. He just might surprise you and come around."

"I'd like to believe that, but I just don't see that happening."

CHAPTER 28

Live for Right Now

SUMMER CAME ON FAST. By August, the mornings were so hot and oppressive I'd stand in my office with my arms stretched out in front of the air conditioner to dry the sweat off my body. Then I'd sit in my nook, reading over e-mails, and sipping hot coffee (yes, I have to drink it hot) until patients started to arrive.

I quickly scanned over my e-mails, searching for one from Jonathan or the Pennsylvania State Police. Over the past two months, I'd tried contacting Jonathan by e-mail and leaving messages on his voice mail. He never responded. Scrolling through the endless junk mail, I found an e-mail from Chad.

Hi, Baby,
Pick you up tomorrow at 7 P.M. I have a surprise planned.
Chad

Looking at the calendar on the wall in front of me, I stared at the heart drawn around the next day's date: our six-month anniversary. I remembered the day I drew that heart, thinking if we made it to six months then it would be a great achievement according to my gay rules of dating. It was a running joke among my friends that if two men could make it to their one-year anniversary, it was a huge accomplishment: twelve months was the equivalent of seven straight years.

After reading Chad's e-mail, I called Eric because I often gauged everything that went on in my life according to how he responded. When I told him Chad and I were celebrating our six-month anniversary, he said, "This is a huge step toward maturity."

Staring at the heart I drew on the calendar, I completely agreed.

I CALLED CORPORAL LARAMIE ON SEVERAL OCCASIONS. Each time, I was told he wasn't in. Jonathan continued to avoid me. I left several more messages on his voice mail and sent numerous e-mails. Not one reply. Finally, I tracked him down at work.

"Are you mad at me?" I asked. "Because—"

"I don't think it's a good idea for me to talk to you," he interrupted confidently. "Ever since you've come back into my life, I've been having a very difficult time."

"That's because you're beginning to remember. Isn't it?"

Jonathan remained silent, neither agreeing nor disagreeing. A dangerous dynamic was developing between us. If I pushed too hard, I might lose him for good. Yet it was a chance I was willing to take.

"I know it's hard to remember the past, but it's important that you process these feelings, not suppress them."

"Please," he whispered. "Don't call me anymore."

"Jonathan, I need you. Together, we can catch Bill. The Pennsylvania Police will pursue this case if we both come forward. Remember, the boys Bill adopted are mentally challenged."

"I have to go now."

"I'm going to do this whether you help me or not. I won't give up. Next, I'll start looking up all the other assistant Scoutmasters. Then I'll contact everyone involved who let Bill get away, including your father."

"Keep him out of this, and don't ever call me again!"

AFTER THIS SERIES OF SETBACKS, I decided to approach Dean for advice. He cautioned me that something like this couldn't be rushed. Jonathan was doing what he felt he needed to do. It was more important for me to focus on the fact that Bill was being investigated. Now it was out of my hands, and, according to Dean, the justice system could take years. Making this case an obsession was absolutely the wrong thing to do. If I allowed that to happen, it would become an addiction. This case would never move at the pace I wanted, and, ultimately, it might never get resolved.

Even though it was hard for me to accept Dean's advice, I knew he was right. He said it was more important for me to focus on my patients, with their disgusting anal warts, their oozing fissures, and their receding hairlines, and every once in a while, I should look at myself in the mirror with my white lab coat, stethoscope around my neck, and think about how hard it was to become a doctor. He wanted me to think back to that time when I thought I'd never make it, and now, here I was.

The tricky part was trusting that the police were doing everything they could, even though I was sure Bill was still molesting boys. Above all, Dean said I should focus on the good I'd done so far and avoid living in the future. It was better to live for right now, today, this instant.

CORPORAL LARAMIE FINALLY TOOK MY CALL. I was in my office taking a lunch break and decided to try him again.

"Dr. Spinelli," he said in that familiar baritone. "I've completed my investigation, and I'm sorry to tell you that I did not find any criminal activity going on at this time. So I had to throw this case back to the director of Child Welfare Services. His name is Mr. Thomas Sorensen."

"But did you find out if Bill has children in his care?"

"We were unable to verify that."

"Have there been any complaints made against Mr. Fox in the past?"

"The best thing for you to do is to contact Mr. Sorensen," he continued. "He is the one who has access to those records." Corporal Laramie's voice never fluctuated.

"But I don't understand. When I spoke to you in June, you said that the Pennsylvania State Police takes these complaints very seriously. Now you're telling me that there is nothing criminal going on and you don't have any access to records that would include complaints made against Mr. Fox in the past?"

"Dr. Spinelli, you really should contact Mr. Sorensen."

Hanging up, I removed the file box labeled THE MOLESTER from the bookshelf over my desk. It contained notes, a diary, newspaper clippings, Bill's book, and the list of men who played a crucial role during the years I was a Boy Scout. Scanning through names, my index finger stopped on Joseph Castro, the assistant Scoutmaster. I needed to speak with him. According to Mrs. Duran, he was the one who met with Bill and asked him to leave Troop 85. What did Mr. Castro say to Bill? What promises were made between those two old friends in deciding how this problem should get resolved? I had to know.

I searched online for Joseph Castro on Staten Island. There were none. Then I remembered he had a younger brother named Anthony, who graduated the same year as me from St. Sylvester's. Searching his name, I located a man, my age, living on Staten Island. The listing gave only an address, which was less than a mile from St. Sylvester's and in the same neighborhood where Jonathan grew up. It had to be him.

That Sunday I visited my parents for dinner. When my father picked me up at the ferry terminal, I asked him to drive me to the address I found online. He did so without question. I sat back, feeling the air-conditioning on my face, thinking about what I was going to do once we arrived. Looking over at my father squinting at the road ahead, it occurred to me, as we drove over Grymes Hill, that he had grown accustomed to simply carrying out requests without asking why.

When I was growing up, my father happily played the role of chauffeur. It seemed that we were always in transit together, with my father picking me up and driving me back home. My fondest memories were of going to my grandfather's house when I was very young. Driving home those Sunday nights, I'd often fall asleep in the backseat, and my father would carry me to my bed instead of waking me up. There was something magical about being transported over his shoulder, half-groggy from the long car ride. I always looked forward to the next week, when we'd visit my grandfather and I could relive that wonderful experience again. But this routine wasn't something I could plan, and when I did, it never had the same element of surprise as waking up in his arms as he climbed up the stairs.

I often wondered how my father felt once he'd learned Bill had touched me. Did he see me as someone else, not his son, or as damaged? As years passed, I watched as this feeling transitioned into guilt. That gave me license to order my father around when I got older, never fearing he would protest because he always felt guilty for not holding me in his arms after he discovered what Bill had done.

That Sunday was the first time I'd visited my parents since I'd returned from Denver. I was sure my father still didn't know what to make of Bill's book. Driving through Jonathan's old neighborhood, I suspected he knew this trip had something to do with it.

"We're here," said my father as he pulled up across the street from Anthony Castro's house.

It was just as I expected—a gray-and-white-shingled split-level duplex with a long set of stairs leading up to the entrance. It looked like every other house on the block. I imagined it was the home Anthony grew up in as a child and was now the one he chose to raise his own family in. My father and I sat in the car for several minutes in silence. He never asked me what we were doing there. I stared at the house, confirming the address against the one I'd written on a scrap of paper. Looking for a sign that someone was home, I thought about ringing the doorbell. I didn't know what I would say if Anthony answered. Suddenly, I had an idea.

"Dad, where is the closest drugstore?"

"Drugstore? There's a pharmacy less than a mile from here."

"Take me there."

Minutes later, we parked outside the Dungan Hills Drug Store. "I'll be right back," I said, jumping out of the car.

Inside, an older woman wearing cat's-eye glasses with a silver chain smiled.

"Where are your greeting cards?" I asked.

She motioned to her left.

Behind the cosmetic aisle, there was a small section of cards. Immediately, I chose a blank card with a photograph of daisies on the cover. At the cash register, I paid the woman and asked to borrow her pen. Then, back outside, my father waited in the car with the engine running. When I got in, he asked, "Where to now?"

"Back to that house."

My father responded obediently. Soon, we were parked across the street from Anthony Castro's house again. I removed the card from the brown paper bag and slipped it in my back pocket. Rushing across the street, I climbed the stairs two at a time. A pulse of anxiety flowed through my body as I reached the landing. I pulled the card out of my pocket and stuck it in the mailbox. Then I ran back to the car. In the heat of that August day, I was soaked through to my skin. "Okay, let's go," I said, strapping on my seat belt.

"Where to now?"

"Home, Jeeves."

My father smiled.

We drove in silence except for my panting. I felt an undeniable thrill that day, as though taking matters into my own hands had now empowered me. If the Pennsylvania Police hadn't uncovered enough evidence to pursue an investigation against Bill, then I was going to find it for them. Staring over at my father squinting at the road, I imagined he felt the same way, too.

During dinner that evening, Josephine argued with her husband about getting up from the table to watch the football game in the den.

"Leave him alone," called out my mother. "Sit down and finish eating."

My father turned to my mother. "What's the problem?"

"Nothing!" she shouted.

When my cell rang, I picked it up and looked at the unknown number. I left the table and walked to the back door. Instinctively, I didn't answer and let it go to my voice mail. "Frank, this is Anthony Castro. I see you left a card in my mailbox with your number. Of course I remember you. You were friends with Jonathan Duran. You two were like Butch Cassidy and the Sundance Kid. Call me. I hope all is well."

I didn't call him back that day. I don't know why. Maybe it was fear of the unknown. When I returned to the dinner table and looked around at my family, I realized the truth was that I didn't want to ruin Anthony Castro's Sunday dinner.

NEARLY ONE WEEK LATER, I was convalescing over the weekend in my apartment with a bad case of gastroenteritis.

That afternoon, Chad called to see whether I needed anything. I thanked him for being thoughtful but discouraged any contact, for fear of infecting him. After I hung up, I relaxed on my couch, flipping through channels. Fifteen minutes later, the doorman rang my intercom. *Chad.* I hurried into the bathroom, combed my hair, and washed my face. I looked like a corpse. For a brief second, I even considered applying cover-up under my eyes. Then I heard a knock. When I opened the door, Chad was standing there, holding a shopping bag. I smiled.

He took a step back. "Wow," he said, jokingly. "You really are sick."

"What did you think? I was having a sex party?"

"Not anymore," he said, walking past me and into my kitchen. "Just lie down on the couch and let me do my thing."

"Thing?" I repeated. "Since when do you have a thing?"

Chad snapped his fingers. "Go on now. Get on the couch. I've got this covered. I used to be a short-order cook."

"You?" I asked. "Wow, it's amazing what you learn about a person. Okay, I won't be a difficult patient. I'll just lie here on the couch and let you take care of me."

From the living room, I could hear Chad opening my cabinets

and talking to himself. Then I heard the stove and the clanging of pots and pans. After ten minutes, I began to smell the simmering chicken soup.

"Okay, here you go. I hope you like it." Chad was standing over the coffee table, holding a tray. I threw the books off to clear a space for him. He laid out a bowl of chicken soup, a thick slice of bread, a glass of water, and a handful of tablets.

"You didn't make this."

"Me?" he said, sitting next to me. "God, no. I hate to cook. I bought it down the street, but I did heat it up."

"Well, that was very considerate of you."

Chad took the napkin and tucked it over my collar. Then he handed me the water and some pills.

"Finally, some drugs. What are these, roofies?"

"Vitamin C and zinc. It's very important you take all of them."

"If you say so, but I won't like it."

I swallowed the vitamins and then started on the soup, which was warm and buttery with chunks of chicken. It was the first time I had eaten that day. "This is delicious." Chad picked up the remote and began changing the channel. "I was watching something," I said.

"Hush up. Save your strength." He found something on the Discovery Channel, settled back on the couch, and propped his feet up on the coffee table. Looking around, he said, "You know, you have a cute little apartment here."

"Thank you," I said, slurping up the remaining soup. I wiped my lips with the napkin and began chewing on the bread, which was hard, with tiny bits of walnuts.

Chad stood up and began walking around. "I always liked your apartment, especially the terrace. You know, you really don't see terraces like this very often."

"I know. That's why I bought this place. Haven't we had this conversation before?"

"I mean, you could probably rent it out pretty quickly."

"Rent? Why would I do that?"

Chad turned to face me. His eyes rolled up to one side, and

he pouted his lips like a little boy. "I'm just saying, it's something to consider."

"If what you're asking me to consider is moving in with you, then that's a lot to consider."

"I know it may seem soon, but you're not getting any younger. We have to think ahead."

"We just celebrated our six-month anniversary. You're screwing up my dating landmarks."

"Your what?"

"Moving in together happens after the first year."

"Who said that?"

"It's a well-known fact. Three months, six months, one year, and then three years. Those are the pivotal relationship landmarks. We can't change things around. It will only screw up the relationship. We're supposed to be building a solid foundation. You don't want a weak foundation, now, do you?"

Chad appeared thoroughly confused. "So, what you're saying is that we shouldn't move in together until we've dated for a year?"

"According to the landmark definitions, yes."

"Well, if you think about it, we met in August. Last week was actually our one-year anniversary, hence the reason why I chose to celebrate at Klee, the restaurant where we had our very first date."

"Yes, I know, and that was a wonderfully romantic surprise. Apparently, you're full of surprises: short-order cook, soup, and now moving in." I stood up and put my arms around his neck.

Chad held his hand over his mouth.

"Don't worry. It's not my mouth you need to worry about."

"Gross," he said, pulling away.

"Now, where are you going?" I asked, pulling him in closer. "Seriously, this is a big step, and it's a lot to consider, but I will totally consider it."

Chad's eyes lit up.

"But I want you to consider something, as well?"

"What's that? Not another secret, I hope?"

"No," I said. "Now put your arms around me and listen."

Up close, Chad smelled like the citrus-scented sunblock he applied religiously before he left the house. "On that table behind you is a file on Bill Fox. Right now I'm going through something that's making me feel a little crazy. Is this the kind of thing you'd want in your house? I mean, I've been working on this on my own. If we move in together, then it would be something you'd have to deal with daily. I don't think this is something you want in your life."

Chad held me tightly around the waist. "I thought we had a deal. You were going to trust me more. Remember, you made a promise?" Then he held up three fingers to his face. "Scout's honor."

"Yes, I remember," I said. "Okay, you're on." I walked over to the table and picked up Anthony Castro's contact information from the molester file. "This person went to school with me at St. Sylvester's. His brother was the assistant Scoutmaster who met with Bill after I told my parents about the molestation. Here is his phone number. I haven't called him yet."

Chad picked up my phone off the desk and handed it to me. "If I know anything about you, it's that you're determined. So why postpone the inevitable?"

I took the phone from Chad. Looking into his blue eyes, I wanted to believe he was the one, not just another in a long line of unlucky relationships. Had Chad really found a loophole in my dating landmarks, or were we tempting the gods of relationships?

I dialed Anthony Castro's number. Placing the phone up to my ear, I whispered, "I love you."

An old woman with a high-pitched voice answered, "Hello?"

I was caught off guard. "Hi, is this the Castro residence?"

"Yes, who is this?"

"Is this Mrs. Castro?"

"Yes," she responded. "Who is this?"

"Mrs. Castro, this is Dr. Spinelli. I'm looking for Anthony Castro."

"Well, this is Anthony's mother."

"Good afternoon, Mrs. Castro. I went to school with your son at St. Sylvester's. Is he home?"

"St. Sylvester's! Oh, how nice. No, Anthony isn't home. He's at the christening for the new baby. They had a baby girl. I'm home with their two-year-old son, John."

"You have a new baby granddaughter!" Chad read my frantic expression and held on to my shoulders. "I'm actually looking for your other son, Joseph," I continued. "Does he still live on Staten Island?"

"No, Joseph moved to Florida." Then I heard a voice calling out to her. "Wait a minute," she said. "They just got home. Would you like to speak to my son?"

"Yes, but just for a moment. I don't want to bother Anthony on the day of his daughter's christening."

"No, I meant Joseph," she said.

"He's there?"

"Yes," she said. "He came up for the christening."

I looked at Chad, my eyes wide with terror. Before I even had a chance to respond, I heard her shouting out his name. This was followed by a muffled conversation. Then a man took the phone. "Hello, this is Joseph Castro. Can I help you?"

<hr />

"I'M CONCERNED THAT YOU'RE CONSUMED with the journalistic aspect of this story, which is your way of avoiding the deeper feelings this is bringing up for you," stated Dr. McGovern. "I don't want you to stop your investigation, but I would like our sessions to focus more on the emotional impact all of this is having on you instead of your quest to catch Bill."

"I don't feel like I'm consumed," I countered. "I'm being diligent."

Dr. McGovern scrunched her nose like a squirrel. I wanted to tell her it irritated me when she made that face. Instead, I sat there and pouted. "Why did Joseph Castro lie to me? I just don't understand how he, of all people, could lie."

Her face relaxed. The squirrel was gone. "Regardless of

whether or not this assistant Scoutmaster confirmed or denied what happened, it doesn't change anything. Even if he'd admitted that there had been some wrongdoing and Bill was allowed to get away, you would still feel the same unresolved emotions that you struggle with now. Having him validate what happened wouldn't make it any less painful."

"He said he didn't know why Bill left. When I told him I was molested and that Jonathan became a homeless drug addict, he asked if I wanted to speak at his church about sexual abuse. Was this his way of throwing me a bone? Have me come down to some backward town in south Florida and speak to a bunch of Christians about molestation? Why would I do that?"

Dr. McGovern paused for a moment and said, "I think it would be beneficial for you to begin coming in twice a week. Usually, it's better if we meet more than once a week because then we can really begin to dig deeper. Weekly meetings only allow us to scratch the surface. It is important, now more than ever, for us to concentrate on the emotions that begin to emerge as this investigation proceeds. I don't think the recent events are a setback necessarily. You should continue your pursuit and call Child Welfare, but in here, I would like you to concentrate on the emotions."

Grabbing a tissue from the table next to me, I blew my nose. "I don't want to come here twice a week. Only crazy people need that much therapy."

Dr. McGovern pursed her lips. "Parenting children during the early years of their development has a lasting effect, more than all the years of education combined. The trust that child develops with his parents sets a precedent that a growing child will gauge all his other relationships by. When a child feels he cannot trust his parents, he begins to doubt all his adult interactions. Now you said you and Chad are planning to move in together. I think that is a major breakthrough. You're beginning to trust Chad. Now you need to start trusting me."

I looked at the clock. Thankfully, time was up.

THAT AFTERNOON I RECEIVED A CALL from Mr. Thomas Sorensen of Child Welfare in Pennsylvania.

"Before I begin, I have to preface this conversation by saying that I am not able to discuss or divulge any specifics regarding the case in question." Mr. Sorensen's voice quivered slightly. He sounded nothing like Corporal Laramie. "The reason why the Tioga County Police Department was unable to proceed with their investigation is because there have been no complaints from anyone in the Fox household."

"So, from that statement, is it safe to assume that Bill has children in his care?"

"You would be safe in your assumption," he confirmed. "You understand that if you had been molested in Pennsylvania, then we could proceed with the investigation."

"What if the boy he adopted in 1982 came forward? Would the police open an investigation against Bill Fox then?"

"Yes."

"Thank you very much, Mr. Sorensen. You have been very helpful."

"May I make a suggestion?"

"Of course."

"Go to your local police station and lodge a formal complaint against Mr. Fox."

"I appreciate your advice."

Now it seemed clear what I had to do. I had to find Nicholas. I wasn't sure how I was going to locate him. Moreover, I didn't even consider the damage I might cause in dredging up this part of his past, knowing how poorly Jonathan had reacted. What mattered most to me at that moment was that Bill be stopped.

CHAPTER 29

Autumn Perspective

AFTER WORK I SURPRISED ERIC and showed up at his apartment. I sat on his couch, eating pretzels and doodling over a picture of Joan Van Ark in *People* while Eric opened a bottle of wine. "Kate thinks I should start going to therapy twice a week," I said. Eric raised both eyebrows but remained silent. "No comment?"

Eric shrugged. "I'm listening, but if you want to know the truth, I think it's a great idea."

"Chad and I have decided to move in together."

"Well, that was bound to happen soon enough."

I bit into a pretzel and gave both dogs a piece. "I'm nervous about it. I'll be moving into his apartment. That means I'll have to put most of my stuff in storage."

"Well, you don't have much stuff."

"That's not the point. It's just that I'm the one who has to move. I'll be making most of the changes. He only has to make a little room for me in his apartment."

"But this is what you want. Isn't it?" I detected a hint of sarcasm. "And, please, stop feeding pretzels to the dogs. The salt gives them high blood pressure."

I was stunned. "I apologize, Dr. Doolittle." Standing up, I refilled my glass with more wine. With my back to Eric, I said, "I've also hired a private investigator to help me find Nicholas."

"Does Chad know you've hired a private investigator?"

I spun around. "Of course."

"Frank, did you really tell Chad?"

"No, but I will."

"Have you discussed this with Kate?"

"Eric, I don't need to ask anyone for permission," I answered immediately.

Eric gripped the armrest. He extended his head as far back as his neck would allow and breathed in deeply through his nostrils. Then he exhaled. "Of course you don't, but honestly, I don't know what to say to you. You've been here for fifteen minutes, dropping bombs left and right. My living room has become a minefield." Molly jumped off the couch and retreated with Ellie to the kitchen.

"Excuse me. I came here to confide in my best friend."

"Best friend?" Eric laughed. "Seems like your best friend is in the dark as much as Chad and your therapist. Do you hear yourself? 'I'm going to therapy twice a week. Chad and I are moving in together. Oh, I've hired a private investigator.' I'm going to be picking pieces of shrapnel out of my hair for weeks."

"Ha-ha," I said. In the kitchen I heard the dogs lapping up water from their bowl. "Well, excuse me for just being honest."

Eric sat up and leaned forward. "I'll give you honesty, if that's what you want. I think you're making the same mistakes all over again. You're keeping secrets from your boyfriend—the man you plan on moving in with—and you're being selectively honest with your therapist instead of working through the truth. And the only reason you're being *honest* with me is because you know I'm going to find out the truth eventually and I'm probably the only person you know who can't stay mad at you."

Though I had always appreciated Eric for his honesty, it felt painful to hear it now. I sat down on the couch, staring at the photograph of Joan Van Ark, who now sported a goatee, bushy eyebrows, and devil's horns.

"Hey," said Eric, placing his hand on mine. "What's really going on?"

"I'm scared he's going to get away with it again." My nose began to run, mixing with the salt from the Bavarian pretzels on my lips so that they began to sting.

"Frank, you have to prepare yourself because that is a realistic possibility," he said. "But think about how much you've accomplished. The police actually listened to you and looked into this. Okay, so they're not going to launch a full investigation, but I bet Bill is scared to death now. And you did that." Tears began to well up in Eric's eyes, and his voice started to crack. "I am so proud of you, no matter what happens, and you should be proud, too."

A WEEK LATER, I RECEIVED A MESSAGE from my real estate agent. I knew he had gotten an offer. When I called him back, he told me that a thirty-three-year-old banker from London had left a deposit. He was waiting for me to give the word before he submitted the application to my co-op board. The only problem was that I had to be out of the apartment within a week.

That night I told Chad the news.

"That's terrific, baby," he said, giving me a hug. "Are you happy?"

"Of course. It's just that it's all happening so fast."

Chad's eyes widened. "That means it's meant to be. It's all happening without any problems. You have to remain positive."

That night Chad and I made arrangements to move all my furniture to my parents' house. My mother agreed it was the best thing to do. She didn't want me to spend the money on renting a storage space. My sister had her own theory. The day the movers arrived, Josephine called me. "Mommy really lucked out this time. She got a whole new living room, bedroom, and a flat-screen television. You even gave her the artwork. I went over to her house to look around, and she practically threw me out because she was worried I was going to take something."

"I'm relieved it all worked out. Mom called me as soon as the truck arrived to ask if I had already paid and tipped the movers. I told her not to worry."

"That's our mother for you. Hey, if things don't work out with Chad, make sure you call me first. I need some new furniture."

"There won't be a next time," I assured her.

Hanging up, I started to think that maybe Chad was right. Was the key to happiness as simple as trying to maintain constant positivity? My parents raised me to think that life was an epic minefield of envious people waiting to cast evil eyes upon you. They had me believe that the future was based on luck, and according to my mother, I didn't have any. Could anything change that? It occurred to me that whenever anything good happened in my life, I questioned it. I had grown to expect a negative outcome, and when it didn't occur, I was surprised and suspicious.

As a doctor, I often told patients to listen to their inner voice; however, when that voice is leading you down the road of paranoia, remember the facts. So far, these were the facts: I had a career, my health, and a great boyfriend who loved me. I had a family and good friends. I was even able to initiate a police investigation against Bill Fox, based on something that had happened thirty years ago. And I was about to take a huge step and move in with Chad. There it was: no evil eye, no luck, just facts.

The Saturday I moved in with Chad, I was sitting on the floor in front of my hall closet, packing up the remaining items I had stored away over the years. My empty apartment echoed like a gallery whenever I spoke to myself or walked across the bare floors.

On my iPod I played Vanessa Daou's "Autumn Perspective" as I sorted through my collection of DVDs, CDs, and comic books. I packed them up, along with all my coffee table books, which included *The Films of Alfred Hitchcock* and two others on Batman and Spider-Man. The only thing left for me to do was sort through hundreds of pictures and keepsakes I'd collected from my past lives with other men. The deal I made with myself was that I could keep only what fit into a single shoe box. That included pictures, the rings my grandfather left me, my Living Dead Girl action figure, the Tiffany's dog tag Eric bought me, and my first-row ticket stub to Madonna's *Reinvention* concert. Of all the books in my collection, I chose to keep two on my new nightstand: *Anna Karenina*, which I promised to read as my New Year's resolution, and Bill's memoir.

The rest had to be thrown out.

It was easy for me to discard the other mementos now that I had a reason to. Looking into that huge, black garbage bag, I glanced one last time at photos of my various incarnations: shaved head; overly muscular Frank dancing shirtless at Gay Pride; angry, drunk, bearded Frank in San Diego with Ivan; happy, outrageous Frank on a cruise; and depressed, fat, and single Frank at Eric and Scott's apartment on New Year's Eve. It was very emotional to pack up my life this time. I had been living on my own for over five years and single for three of those. Moving in with Chad felt like a risk, but that was a chance I was willing to take.

Chad arrived later that afternoon to help me carry the last few boxes over to his apartment. He was wearing a blue button-up shirt, navy shorts, and white Adidas sneakers. "Great," I said, getting up off the floor. "I'm all sweaty and nasty and you look like you just stepped out of a J.Crew catalog."

Chad flashed his perfect white teeth and laughed. Looking around, he said, "I'm always amazed by how small apartments look when they're empty."

"Wait until you see how small your apartment is going to feel with someone else living in it."

"That sounds cozy," he said, snuggling his face into my neck. Chad was the perpetual optimist.

"I'd be careful if I were you," I said, pulling away. "I desperately need a bath. Come help me with these boxes."

Before I closed the door to my apartment, I took one last look around, as though I was the lead actor in the series finale of a long-running sitcom. There were no tears or mixed emotions, only excitement. I was making the right decision.

At Chad's apartment building, the doorman loaded up the trolley with all of my belongings and Chad wheeled it into the elevator. Outside his apartment, he said, "Okay, this is it. Your last chance to back out."

"Are you kidding?" I asked. "You're supposed to carry me over the threshold."

"Maybe after you shower."

Just as we stepped into the apartment, I heard a group shout, "Surprise!"

Michael Lyon was standing in the center of the living room, dressed in a black shirt and the same black-and-white-striped pants, surrounded by several of Chad's friends holding champagne glasses. "Congratulations," said Michael. "Have a drink."

"Did you know about this?" I asked Chad.

"I had no idea," he said. "They showed up right as I was leaving for your apartment. So I let them in, and they've been waiting here the whole time."

"That was very thoughtful of you, Michael. I'd kiss you, but I reek."

"You can kiss me later or write me a prescription for Oxycontin," he said, handing me a glass. "Everyone, I'd like to make a toast to Chad and Frank. I never thought we'd see our dear old friend Chad married off again, but here we are, and to a doctor no less. Frank, may you and Chad have a long and happy life together. Thank you for taking him off our hands. He's your problem now."

Sipping champagne, I realized I had successfully pared down my life to fit into several boxes, two suitcases, and one small shoe box. Looking around the room, it was apparent I'd collected a whole new group of friends in the process.

ONCE I WAS SETTLED INTO CHAD'S APARTMENT, I began meeting with Dr. McGovern twice a week: Monday mornings before work and Wednesday evenings. Each time I walked to her office, I worried that I had nothing to say. No sooner did my ass hit the seat than I was rambling incessantly. Therapy became the outlet

I needed to talk about Bill, my parents, Chad, and even Eric. For one guilt-free hour twice a week, there were no limits to the subjects I was able to discuss, yet they always somehow came back to Bill.

"The private investigator located Nicholas. He's living in Topeka, Kansas, and he's married with a child. I want to call him, but the only contact number I have is the Topeka Police Department. Apparently, he works there as a dispatcher."

"What would you say to him if you called?"

"You mean what would I say to him if he didn't hang up on me?"

"Why would he do that?" she asked, adjusting herself in her chair so that she was sitting on her feet.

"Think about it," I said. "Imagine if some stranger called you out of the blue and said, 'Hi, my name is Dr. Spinelli. I was a Boy Scout thirty years ago, and my Scoutmaster was a man by the name of Bill Fox. I believe he is the same man who adopted you in 1982. Oh yeah, and by the way, he molested me when I was eleven.' "

"Is that really what you would say?"

"No. I don't know what I would say. That's why I haven't called him. But I know that I will soon, because I need to hear his voice."

"What's that all about?" she asked, cocking her head to one side. "This need to hear him speak."

"Hearing his voice would make him real. For the past few months, I've been staring at a photograph of a sixteen-year-old boy on the cover of that damned book, which, by the way, sits on my nightstand. I need to put a voice to that face."

Dr. McGovern sat up, her feet now planted firmly on the floor. "You have Bill's book on your nightstand?"

"I have several: Bill's book, *The Boy Scout Handbook*, and a book that chronicles the history of pedophilia within the Boy Scouts. Oh, and a copy of *Anna Karenina*."

"And you don't think you're consumed with this investigation?"

"I see your point, but I have to remain immersed in this story. It's the only way I'll get the authorities to take me seriously."

Dr. McGovern stared at me warily. "Let's go back to your need to hear Nicholas speak. We should explore this."

"That would be interesting. I have many theories why I need to speak with Nicholas." I leaned forward. "So, Bill adopts this boy, who really isn't a boy at all. He's sixteen years old. Pedophiles generally go after the same type of boy. Bill apparently likes them young, prepubescent or on the verge of puberty, right? So why, then, would he go after a teenager, a boy who is less impressionable or less inclined to be taken in by him? Let's face it. Nicholas was on the verge of suicide. He had been through a lot of shit. This kid was no kid. He was street-smart, and the book clearly states that he did not trust Bill at first. Bill had to coax him off that ledge. He had to gain his trust. It took a long time for that adoption to go through. Bill used this time wisely to groom Nicholas properly. Grooming a sixteen-year-old street-smart boy was going to be trickier than a naïve eleven-year-old. Besides, Bill had just stepped down as Scoutmaster. Why would he risk another accusation? This teenager could have made a lot of trouble for him. They were already getting quite a bit of publicity."

"Maybe Bill never molested him?" she suggested.

"That's the logical answer. The question, then, is why did Nicholas leave Bill and go back to his mother less than a year after the adoption? Something must have happened. Bill gave him a home, an education, everything this boy ever wanted. Why leave?"

"What do you think?"

"I don't believe Bill stopped molesting children. Sure, maybe he didn't molest Nicholas. He was sixteen and too old for Bill, but child molesters don't just stop one day. I think Nicholas saw something he didn't like, and that's why he left. Unlike Beatrice, who just sat there watching television, living in a catatonic state of denial, Nicholas left and never turned back. Why else would he return to his mother, the woman who had abandoned him in the first place? Why would you go back to a life that was miserable unless you couldn't deal with your new one?"

"Well, this is all very interesting, but it's speculative."

"Do you want to hear my other theory?"

"Of course."

"I know Bill persuaded some of the older Scouts into molesting the younger ones. Jonathan admitted that when we were fourteen. My alternate hypothesis is, what if Nicholas became Bill's accomplice once he'd been fully groomed? Months go by, and then it dawns on him that what he's doing is wrong, and he runs away. Nicholas can't go to the police because he feels guilty. That's the brilliance of Bill's seduction and deception. That would explain why no other boy has come forward after all these years. It all comes down to guilt and humiliation."

Dr. McGovern stared out the window. Normally, she maintained eye contact even when I couldn't. That day, she seemed to contemplate my theories with a decisive intensity I had never seen before. "These theories are interesting, but I'm still stuck on this desire you have to hear Nicholas's voice in order to make him real. Do you have any thoughts on that piece in particular?"

"I want to talk to the boy who replaced me. How's that for honesty? Bill didn't adopt me. Maybe I want to speak to the boy whom Bill chose to keep after he left Troop 85. See what's so special about him. I'm hoping he'll answer the phone and sound like some redneck. Then I can hang up and think, 'I'm better than that.' "

Dr. McGovern laughed. "Under the circumstances, I think your feelings are understandable. Bill pitted Chris Spivey against you and then you against Jonathan. It would make sense that you feel jealous of Nicholas. However, I'm still unclear as to your motive for wanting to call him. I think in the beginning your motives were strong. You wanted to find this boy and confront him. Now things have changed for you. You seem less confrontational."

"I suppose you're right. Maybe my relationship with Chad has changed me, made me softer. Perhaps if I was still single and bitter, I would have called him by now or gotten on a plane to

Topeka. Last night, I read the *New York Times* article again. I can't imagine the pain that boy must have felt climbing out on that ledge. When the best solution you can come up with is death . . . The crowd below screaming, 'Jump, jump,' and then a sweet Irish police officer promises you the world. I don't know for sure why he left Bill. I do know that he's living in Kansas with his family. Maybe he has a little boy and takes him to baseball practice. I don't want to be the person who calls to tell him his adoptive father was a monster. If I do that, then I'm just as bad as Bill."

"Because you would be abusing him?" she offered delicately.

"Yes. I don't want to hurt anyone."

Dr. McGovern didn't say anything after that. We sat there silently as I sobbed. It was the longest time we'd spent in any session where neither of us said a word.

THAT WEEK I APPROACHED A POLICE OFFICER named Gary Ferg at the gym. He was dating a friend of mine and had the biggest biceps I'd ever seen. He was on his way out when I stopped him.

"Hey, Gary, do you have a minute? I need to ask your advice."

"Sure."

We walked to the lounge, where I recited a *TV Guide* synopsis of my story. Gary sat there quietly, shaking his head. I told him that I wanted to lodge an official complaint with the police. He offered to come by my office later in the week to take my statement himself.

"You know, most people think that cops protect one another, but when it comes to shit like this . . . molesting children," he said, still shaking his head. "I'd be glad to help. Once I get your statement, I'll pass it along to the Special Victims Unit. I guarantee you'll be hearing from them."

CHAPTER 30

Hunting Rabbits

DETECTIVE ANDREW COLLIER and his partner, Jeff Willey, from the Staten Island Special Victims Unit, arrived at my office after-hours to go over the statement I gave to Gary Ferg. Collier was wearing jeans and an unbuttoned plaid shirt over a white T-shirt. He had a receding hairline, a round face with a five o'clock shadow, and broad shoulders. His partner was older and wearing weathered jeans, construction boots, and a dungaree jacket. Together, they looked like they'd just come from a roadside bar off the turnpike.

"Sit down, detectives," I said, offering them each a seat in the waiting room.

Collier pulled out a crumpled document and a pad. "We just have a few questions," he began. "Bill Fox was your Scoutmaster, correct? And all the instances of molestation occurred on Staten Island?"

"Yes."

"When you called him, did you confront him about the molestation?"

"No, it was strictly an informal call."

"I see," he said as he jotted notes on his pad. Then, looking me squarely in the eyes, he said, "Listen, doc, I think we should arrange to wiretap a conversation between you and Bill. I know you're well aware of the statute of limitations regarding your case, but if we can get Bill to admit that he molested you, then I could take these tapes to the Pennsylvania State Police. They'd have to investigate based on this information." Imitating Elmer Fudd, Collier asked, "What do you say, doc? Are you up to hunting rabbits?"

"I say let's do it."

THE EVENING OF OCTOBER 15, Detective Collier set up the wiretap on my cell phone. In the meantime, I met with Gloria privately. She refused to leave the office while I made the call, so I gave her strict instructions to turn off her phone and not to disturb us for any reason.

I closed the door to the hall and entered my office. Collier was sitting across from my desk, ready to go. I took the seat opposite him. He inserted a microphone into my right ear. We were sitting so close to each other our knees were practically touching.

"Are you nervous?" he asked.

"Wouldn't you be?"

"I'll be here the whole time. Are you ready?"

I felt a lump in my throat, a fear so obstructing that I couldn't even swallow my own saliva. Then I heard Bill's phone ringing in my earpiece. Suddenly, a man answered.

I swallowed hard. "Hi, can I speak to Bill Fox, please?"

"Speaking," he answered in a droll, disinterested way, as if he was responding to a market researcher.

"Bill, this is Frank Spinelli. I called you several months ago. Do you remember?"

There was a pause. "The kid from Boy Scouts?" His voice lightened up. "Yeah, I remember. Sorry I never made it up to New York for that cup of coffee."

"That's okay. I was just thinking about you, and so I thought I'd give you a call. How are you doing?"

"Not so good. I just had a total knee replacement."

"Wow, a total knee," I said. Distracted, for a fleeting moment I felt sympathy. Collier made a winding motion with his hand. "That's some operation," I continued.

"Yeah, it's from an old injury I got on the force."

"Was that the one where you got dragged by the car with your arm trapped in the window?"

He chuckled. "Yeah, that's the one. You sure got some memory."

"I remember when you had that accident. They announced it at Boy Scouts. You were in the hospital for a long time. We thought you were gonna die."

"That was a bad accident. My knee has been fucked up ever since. They've been pushing me to get it replaced, but I kept putting it off. I was in the hospital all last week, and now I'll be home for a month doing physical therapy."

I glanced over at Collier. He was staring at the recording device and listening with his hand pressed up to his earpiece. He looked up at me and made the winding motion again. Startled, I resumed talking. "Bill, the reason why I called this time is because I need to talk to you about something."

"What about?"

Collier offered me an encouraging nod.

I took a deep breath and exhaled. "I need to talk to you about what went on when I was a Boy Scout. I've been living with something for many years, and I've been through a lot of therapy. It all comes down to something that involves you."

Bill didn't respond.

I looked up at Collier. He mouthed, "Say it."

"Do you have any idea what I'm referring to?" I asked.

Bill's tone instantly changed to annoyed. "No, not really."

"When I was eleven years old, you used to pick me up in your truck. You had a red truck, right?"

"Yes, that's right."

"One time you drove me up to camp because they left me behind. During that drive you talked to me about sex. You asked me if I masturbated. Does this sound familiar?"

Bill cleared his throat several times. "I can't say that it does."

"I used to run errands with you after school. One time, we

changed the light bulbs in your house. Then we had sex in your bedroom."

There was a long pause. I heard Bill breathing into the phone. Finally, he said, "I really can't say I remember any of this."

Collier wrote a prompt down on his pad and showed it to me.

I repeated it back to Bill. "Maybe you've blocked it out of your mind?" I said. "It would really help me if I could talk to you about this."

"Go ahead," he urged. His voice was low, simmering like a kettle on the stove. I detected an ominous twinge, as though he was baiting me. In my mind I heard him say, *Go ahead. Try your best. You'll never catch me.* Even with Collier there, I felt frightened. Confronted with the most horrendous accusation, Bill suddenly sounded poised, and that filled me with apprehension. I began to perspire.

Certainly he could have just hung up. That's what an innocent person would have done, right after he enjoyed a hearty laugh at the sheer absurdity of this accusation. When Bill didn't hang up, it occurred to me that he was intrigued, even aroused, and more than anything, that made me ill.

"Bill, I don't want to make trouble. In fact, I want to tell you that I am not angry. It's just that I have been dealing with this for many years, and I've tried to put this behind me. In your book, you describe how you struggled for a higher purpose. I know you are very religious. I want you to use this opportunity to tell me if you remember anything so that we can talk about it and then move on."

Collier offered me an aggressive thumbs-up.

"Honestly, I don't know what to tell you," said Bill.

I began asking him the sort of leading questions I was taught to avoid in medical school. "Do you remember having sex with me in your bedroom? The first time you showed me pornographic magazines, and then you showed me how to masturbate you."

"No, I can't say I remember that."

"Another time I slept over your house, you made me give you a blow job? You had a Farrah Fawcett poster over your bed."

"Who?"

"Farrah Fawcett, from *Charlie's Angels*."

"I don't remember."

"We had sex, and then I slept over. You sleep wearing just a T-shirt and underwear."

"Well, I do sleep like that," he admitted.

"I imagine you would remember sleeping with a little boy, too. It's not something you'd forget. We walked around in our underwear in front of your mother while she watched game shows. I remember she sat in a reclining chair in the living room. Did you let other boys sleep over?"

I heard voices in the background on Bill's end. It sounded like boys arguing. Bill covered the receiver and shouted, "Keep it down!"

"Bill, is there someone else there with you? Is this not a good time to talk?"

"I can talk."

You want to talk.

From that moment on, it became an interrogation. I questioned Bill, and he responded quickly and succinctly.

"Are those the boys you adopted?" I asked.

"Yeah, but they're teenagers now."

"How many boys did you adopt?"

"Eleven."

"How many are still living with you?"

"Two."

"Do you still talk to Nicholas?"

"Not for over three years. I only know he's married and has two kids."

"Where is he?"

"San Diego."

"I can't believe the two of you are not in contact, especially after all the trouble you went through to adopt him."

"I don't keep in contact with many of the boys once they leave," countered Bill.

"Did you adopt only boys?"

"Yeah."

"Did you ever have sex with them?"

"No," he said emphatically. Bill was growing impatient.

I looked at my watch. We had been talking for over fifteen minutes. I felt exhausted. Collier continued to stare at the recorder. Then he glanced up at me. By his expression, I knew he could see I was growing weary. This whole idea suddenly seemed pointless. Bill was not going to confess. He'd already lied several times. He was simply answering my questions. I felt as if we were playing an imaginary game of Ping-Pong, except we weren't using a ball and neither of us could win.

Collier drove his fist up against his chin as a gesture of encouragement.

I breathed in deeply. "Bill, do you remember Jonathan?"

"Who?"

"Jonathan Duran. His mother and father were very involved in Scouting."

"That name doesn't sound familiar."

Liar. You were very friendly with the Durans.

"You had sex with Jonathan, too. He told me so. Now he lives in Denver. After grammar school, he became a drug addict and ran away from home. His parents were able to get him into rehab. Eventually, he graduated."

"Honestly, I don't remember."

"Recently, I visited him in Denver. He said you molested him. Unfortunately, he won't speak to me now. That's why I called you. I need to talk to you and understand why you did this. Bill, I have no one else to turn to."

"I'd like to help you, but . . ."

"Have you ever had sex with another boy?"

"No."

"Have you ever had sex with a man?"

"No!" he said furiously.

"I know you're a Catholic, but I have to ask you, Bill, are you gay?"

His response was as equally emphatic as his others. "Gay is a choice you make. I don't believe in it."

"I figured you'd say that. How would it make you feel if I told you I was gay?"

"Well, then, I would say that was your choice."

"What would you say if I told you that, for a long time, I thought I was gay because I had sex with you when I was eleven? It took years of therapy for me to understand that what happened between us didn't make me gay. Again, I don't want to make trouble. I just want to get past this and give you an opportunity to talk to me."

"I'm sorry. It's just that I don't know what to tell you. I hope it helps you to talk about it, but you keep asking me if there's anything I want to say, and I don't have anything to tell you."

"Do you remember Father Roberts?"

"No. Should I?"

"He was a priest at St. Sylvester's. You were both the same age. I thought you guys were buddies."

"No, I don't speak to too many people from those days."

"Do you remember Sister Catherine?"

"No."

"She was the principal, an overweight nun, and very strict."

"Wait. Yeah, I remember her."

"She passed away from complications secondary to diabetes. When I was a medical student in surgery at Staten Island Hospital, she was a patient. I got to assist in amputating her leg."

"Oh God. That's awful."

"Not really."

Collier clasped his hand over his mouth to stifle his laughter. By now, I was done. There was no point in continuing. I looked over at Collier and tapped my watch to indicate I was going to end the call.

He nodded.

"Bill, I really need to go now, but if you ever want to talk, I want you to feel free to contact me any time."

"Wait, so you became a doctor? You should feel very proud about that."

Why don't you want me to go?

Collier urged me to continue.

"Don't get me wrong, Bill, I am finally happy, but I'm a forty-one-year-old man. It took me a long time to get to this place, to find someone I love. I used to think I was cursed, but I know that's not true. I was damaged. I suffered with depression because I didn't like myself very much, and I thought that I could never be loved. I hope you understand that I felt that way because of you."

Collier grabbed the phone from me and covered the receiver with his hand. "Now would be a good time to tell him anything you want, curse, yell, scream," he whispered. "Go off on him if you want. Use this opportunity, because it may be your last chance."

I shook my head. There was no point in any of that. After nearly forty minutes, I'd been unable to get Bill to confess. I saw no reason to lose my temper. He might have even found that arousing. If I'd learned anything about sexual abuse, it was that power plays a major role in why pedophiles target children. I was not about to submit to this man again. Once I made that decision, I said good-bye to Bill.

—∞∞∞—

AFTER COLLIER LEFT, I SAT WITH GLORIA in the waiting room. Once I finished telling her what happened, I sent her home. I wanted to be alone. For weeks, I had fantasized about what it was going to be like to confront Bill. I always imagined that he would deny everything, but somewhere in the back of my mind, I held out a secret hope that he had changed, found Jesus—something—and he would admit to molesting me. It was a foolish wish, yet I found myself sitting in my dark and empty waiting room feeling disappointed that Bill did not break down into tears and apologize.

Twenty minutes later, I gathered up my belongings and headed to Eric's for our weekly get-together. Knocking on his door, I heard the dogs barking.

"Shut up!" he shouted as he unbolted the lock. He didn't open the door. Instead, he left it ajar. I stepped inside and found him standing in the kitchen, pouring wine into two glasses.

"Hello," I said and proceeded to pet the dogs. Molly immediately rolled onto her back, begging me to rub her belly. "How are you?" I called out to Eric.

"Good, sit down," he instructed. "I want to hear all about it."

I abandoned Molly and moved into the living room. "You guys really should get rid of some of these magazines," I suggested. "It's beginning to look like the home of a schizophrenic shut-in."

"Why don't you shut your face and tell me what happened," ordered Eric as he set a glass of wine next to me on the end table.

I took a sip, let it swish around in my mouth, and tasted the alcohol. It felt good. I drew a deep breath. "Detective Collier came by at about five-ish to set up the wiretap."

Eric came to life and leaned forward with wide eyes. "What does he look like? Is he sexy?"

"Eric! This is serious business. Stop turning everything into a sex thing."

"Oh, okay," he said, contorting his face in a self-deprecating way. "I guess now that she's living with her boyfriend, my girl doesn't look at other men."

"As a matter of fact, I don't."

He sipped his wine, staring at me through the glass as he lifted it up to his lips.

"Okay, so he's a little sexy," I added. "Happy?"

Eric's head fell back. "Thank you," he said, setting the glass down firmly on the coffee table, startling Molly. "And we're back. Honestly, Frank, you say I've changed, but do you listen to yourself? You're with *me*. You don't have to edit yourself. I'm not Chad."

"Agreed."

Molly jumped up and curled onto Eric's lap. "Okay," he continued. "So the sexy policeman sets up the wiretap and . . ."

"And I'm sitting there thinking, holy shit! I'm going to confront Bill."

"So, who were you when you were on the phone with Bill?"

"Who was I? I was my drag persona, Urethra Franklin," I said. "What the hell kind of question is that?"

"Don't be an ass," said Eric. "Who were you in that moment?"

"Honestly, I was myself. I certainly wasn't that little boy."

"Good," he said, shaking his fist triumphantly in the air. "Were you nervous?"

"I was more than just nervous. I was scared at one point. Those old feelings emerged again, and I felt frightened, as though Bill was going to come after me. Isn't that funny?"

"No, not really."

"Eric, you would have been so proud of me. I was very specific. I gave graphic details, talked about masturbation, oral sex, and even the goddamned Farrah Fawcett poster over his bed."

Eric began rubbing his palms together. "How delicious! What did he say?"

"Eric, let me ask you something: if you're an innocent man accused of molestation, would you stay on the phone for nearly an hour, listening to graphic details?"

"What did Detective Sexy say?"

"Well, this is the part that makes me . . . concerned. After we were done, Collier said, 'I bet Bill's all fired up now. Tonight, he's going to be thinking about everything you said. He's probably all revved up.' "

"Were you excited on the phone? Last time you said you got a little aroused."

I flinched. "How embarrassing. I forgot I told you that."

"Don't get defensive," he said, rising up from the chair. "Honey, it's okay. You had sex with this man when you were eleven. He was your first love in some fucked-up way. It's natural for you to have those feelings. What he did to you was wrong, but it did feel good in the beginning, all that attention. You felt shame afterward, and that's logical because that's the way you were brought up. That's how I was brought up. I just don't want you to beat yourself up over getting aroused when you spoke to this man."

"Honestly, I didn't get aroused this time. Once I heard those boys talking in the background, all I kept thinking was, *Which one will Bill choose tonight?*"

Eric's back straightened. "Listen, what goes on in that house was happening long before you came along. Don't think for one minute that your call led Bill to molest one of those boys. In fact, I bet you might have even scared him a little."

"I don't think so, Eric."

"Ah," said Eric, pointing at me. "Have you forgotten? The fourth rule of acting: to thine own self be true?" He stood up in the center of the room. "For all the things you can't control in your life, there are a few things you can do: learn your lines, be on time, and make sure you have a good head shot." Eric smiled and opened his arms to make a grand gesture. "But presence is everything. You don't think being some hotshot doctor from New York City isn't a little intimidating?"

"Okay," I conceded. "Perhaps Bill felt a little intimidated. For the sake of those boys, I hope you're right."

"I know I'm right."

"Funny," I said. "You know what I was thinking right before I hung up? I thought, *I feel sorry for this pathetic man.* Isn't that crazy?"

Eric shook his head. "I don't think that's crazy at all."

❦

DR. MCGOVERN AND I CONTINUED TO MEET TWICE A WEEK. Initially, I didn't think I'd have enough to talk about, but it became clear there wasn't enough time in a session for me to tell her everything that was going on in my life.

"One thing you have done is that you have taken away Bill's power," she said. "Honestly, you have accomplished something most victims are unable to do. You revisited the past and confronted him." She seemed very intrigued by this concept: her eyes drifted toward the window as she pondered that thought for several moments. Then she nodded several times. "Yes, this is a huge step," she confirmed. "By talking to him, you have reconnected with your abuser, and in a way, you have rendered him powerless because now you see him as a pathetic, older man. For thirty years, you have held on to this image of him, this fantasy, of a strong, virile, fearful man, but now that's gone. Of course, you'll retain some of that fantasy, but when you look back, you'll see this new image of him. That's more than a lot of people can say. I agree with Eric: who you were while on the phone with him is very important. I think part of you was Dr. Frank Spinelli, the man who has his life together. That explains why you felt sorry for Bill. In that moment, you were in control, and you shouldn't feel ashamed, because that means you're human. Only a strong person would feel bad. Now you have to be prepared to let this all go. Our work needs to focus on the feelings that come up once you do. Only then can you begin to focus on your relationship with Chad and delve into it on a much deeper level."

"That reminds me," I said. "On a completely different note, a new patient came in today. He was this big, hairy daddy type who moved to New York recently from Ohio. He seemed nice enough at first, and then near the end of the physical, he sat up on the exam table, still in his underwear, grabbed me by the back of my neck with one hand, and tousled my hair with the other. I was caught completely off guard and embarrassed. Then, I got angry. I thought, *How disrespectful!* You know, Dr. McGovern, a year or two ago, I might have felt aroused by this man's behavior, even fantasized about having sex with him. Today, I became angry."

"Did you tell him?"

"I swatted his hand off my head and backed away. I said, 'Excuse me,' or something like that. Immediately, he tried to charm his way out of it by saying, 'Oh, don't be mad. I was just playing.' I told him to get dressed, and just as I walked out the door, I said, 'Please don't ever do that again.' "

Dr. McGovern leaned forward and smiled. "Isn't it funny how life works? This 'daddy' seems to have come down from the heavens as a reminder of those old icons of Bill that get replayed over and over throughout your life. It all seems too good to be true that this should happen now, and for you to be able to ask yourself, 'Do I want another Bill prototype, or do I want to change the trajectory of my life's path?' "

"I suppose you're right. It's a funny coincidence, but I didn't feel empowered."

"That's because you felt sorry for him."

"Yes, just like when I was on the phone with Bill. Crazy, right?"

⊸∞⊷

THE FOREST WAS DENSE WITH TREES. I was barefoot as I walked toward an old, ransacked house with a maroon truck parked outside. I wandered around back. The cellar window was cracked. I leaned to look inside, but it was dark.

Why did I come here?

A man gripped the scruff of my neck and startled me. I tried to scream, but nothing came out of my mouth.

I woke to Chad shaking me. I was gasping. In the darkness, I saw the clock read 3 A.M.

"Are you okay?" he asked. "I thought you were having trouble breathing."

Even in the safety of our bedroom, I felt an alarming disorientation. I was breathless. "Yeah, just a bad dream." For a moment, I couldn't shake the feeling of that old house. I still felt the strong grip on my neck.

"I'm sorry," said Chad. "Come here." He pulled me close and wrapped his arms around me, pressing his chest up against my back. His side of the bed smelled like warm sheets just out of the dryer. "Do you want to tell me about it?"

Gradually, my head cleared. "Not right now. Besides, I'll talk about it with Dr. McGovern. She loves to interpret my dreams."

Chad gripped my shoulders and turned me around. He stared into my eyes, searching for the truth, perhaps wondering whether he should push me to tell him more.

What I love most about Chad is his eyes—big, blue, and wondrous. Even in the dark, I could see the whole world when I looked into them. I saw us in love, moving into an apartment we'd buy together, and adopting a dog. Then, with one blink, I was transported further into the future: I saw us growing old, retiring, and traveling around the world. In another blink, I was back in our bed, staring into his blue eyes. Those two perfectly round spheres—two worlds, two lives, his and mine living as one. I hugged him tightly, nestling my chin on his shoulder, breathing in the fresh smell of the linens and never wanting to let him go.

CHAPTER 31

The Mirror Cracked

D ETECTIVE COLLIER CALLED TO TELL ME that he'd listened to the recording of the wiretap. "I think we should call Bill again."

"Are you serious?"

"Definitely. I think we're close. There's a good chance of getting a confession." His enthusiasm reignited my dwindling interest in catching Bill. "I'm telling you, I know this guy is ready to cave. Even if he doesn't confess, then we'll have more than enough information to present to the Pennsylvania Police."

Up until that day, no one with any official authority had ever been this encouraging. Right then and there, I agreed to the second wiretap.

ON NOVEMBER 20 AT 6 P.M., DETECTIVE COLLIER MET ME IN MY OFFICE. Even though he had already gone through the protocol during the first wiretap, Collier insisted on explaining it over again to me. While he spoke, my thoughts drifted. I was concerned about how Bill would react once he heard my voice.

Collier adjusted the wire to my cell phone and tested the recording device. "Okay, you ready?"

"We're doing the right thing, aren't we?"

Collier nodded. The next thing I heard was the familiar sound of Bill's phone ringing and his voice when he picked up.

"Bill, it's Frank Spinelli."

He snorted with frustration and muttered, "Hey."

"Are you busy?"

"Actually, yes, I'm in the middle of making dinner."

In the background I heard male voices carrying on a conversation. "Sorry," I said. "I won't take up much of your time. I was in Staten Island this past weekend. I thought about you and wanted to call . . . to see if you gave any thought to what we talked about."

Silence.

I glanced at Collier for help. He held his hand out and nodded slowly for me to be patient.

"Shut up and go in the other room," I heard Bill shout. "I'm on the phone." After several seconds Bill began, "Listen, I told you I can't remember that far back. There were over three hundred boys in that troop. I can't remember every one of you."

"You can't remember, or you don't want to remember? Did you have sex with every boy?"

He sounded annoyed. "I didn't say that. It's just that I can't remember that long ago. I was a cop for years. You think I remember every person I've ever shot or every person I arrested?"

"I'd think you'd remember having sex with an eleven-year-old boy. I know that would be something I'd remember. I've read accounts of other men who enjoy having sex with boys, stories very much like your own. I'm telling you this so that you understand that I didn't imagine it. It happened, and you know it."

"You need to move on. The past is past. You can't change that. You can only change the future. What are you? Like forty-five or fifty?"

"I'm forty-one to be exact."

"Well, in any case, you are a smart, successful doctor. You need to move on. You ought to put the entire incident out of your mind."

For a moment, I felt stunned. I looked at Collier. He wasn't monitoring the recorder. He was staring directly at me. Then the full import of Bill's statement struck me. I hesitated. Then I said, "I want to move on. Believe me, Bill. There is nothing I'd rather do than move past all this, but I can't. It's not that easy, you see. I almost forgot all about it. No, wait! I didn't forget. I chose to live in denial for the past thirty years, but then I discovered something. I found your book. I saw that cover with you and your son. Then it all came back to me. I thought about what you used to do to me, how those parents let you go free, and how you were allowed to adopt all those boys. I can't let it go now."

"Well, I don't know what you want me to do."

"Like I told you last time, Bill, I don't want to make trouble. I just want to hear you say it. Tell me now that it happened and you're sorry for all of it."

"Is that what you want me to say?"

"Yes."

"If what you say is true, then yeah, I would be sorry."

Did you really just say that?

I was speechless. Bill's words echoed in my ear but with no remorse. In fact, he spoke them with slight indignation.

There was so much I wanted to say, yet I couldn't. All the lines I'd rehearsed throughout the years, speaking them to myself in the mirror, all seemed suddenly useless. Memories don't change. Pedophiles don't change. They go on, year after year, molesting other little boys until someone stops them. It occurred to me that everything was now completely up to the police. I had done all I could.

"Thank you, Bill. And if you ever wish to talk to me again, you know how to reach me. Good-bye."

Collier nodded his head. "I knew he'd trip over his own words. You did good, doc. Now I'm going to take these tapes to the Pennsylvania Police. You won't have to do this again."

HOUR AFTER HOUR, I LAY IN BED AWAKE, my hands hot in between my thighs as I wished away the need to urinate. The room was dark except for the red glow of the digital clock. It read 12 A.M.

Chad was snoring gently. I found it the most comforting distraction, like a puppy listening to its mother's heartbeat. Down the hall, there was a party. I heard loud music, the sound of people singing "Happy Birthday."

I replayed my conversation with Bill over and over in my mind. I couldn't believe Bill had allowed himself to yield to my request.

If what you say is true, then yeah, I would be sorry.

As I drifted off to sleep, I saw Bill standing in my waiting room. In my dream, I punched him, saw my fist go into his mouth, and watched his head whip back like a Pez dispenser. When it snapped back, I saw my face instead but shattered like a cracked mirror.

Then I woke up.

CHAPTER 32

Home for the Holidays

"SOCIAL ANXIETY MANIFESTS IN DIFFERENT WAYS," explained Dr. McGovern. "Running late, arriving in the wrong place at the wrong time, and being unable to speak are just a few examples of how anxiety can influence dreams."

"What does that have to do with me?" I asked. "Why am I experiencing social anxiety?"

"Frank, you have a lot on your plate right now. In addition to maintaining a full-time practice and a fairly new relationship, you've just moved in with your partner and you're working with the police to apprehend the man who molested you. You don't think that's enough to keep you up at night?"

I laughed despite the seriousness of her tone.

"Part of my concern with everything that's going on with Bill is that it brings up intense anxiety. Jonathan's fuzzy recollection of the past and Bill's inability to remember that far back frustrate you. On one hand, you want to help the boys who are living with Bill, but on the other hand, there is a deeper need for you to have someone corroborate your story. So far, no one has really done that, and this stirs up intense anxiety."

"And what about my dream with Bill?"

"The one where you punch him in the face?"

"Yes."

"Let's talk about that for a moment. Do you think you found closure after your last conversation with Bill?"

I felt that gnawing sensation develop below my ribs. "Just thinking about it makes me anxious," I admitted. "It's just that I don't believe in closure. I think it's bullshit. You don't forget the past. You carry it around with you like herpes. Sometimes it flares up, and other times it remains dormant. But it doesn't go away." I began rubbing the area below my sternum with my fist.

"You don't think you felt closure with Bill? You told me that you felt sorry for him, that he was no longer brooding and sexual but more old and pathetic?"

"Yes."

Dr. McGovern sat up and planted her feet on the floor. I knew that when she did this, she was about to make an important observation. "Frank, how do you feel toward your parents?"

I shifted uneasily in my chair. "My parents? Are we really going back there?"

"Trust me."

"Okay, I suppose I'm angry with them, too. I've always been angry with them, but at a certain point you have to let go. For years, I was a very resentful young man who hated my family, particularly my mother, although my father got a free ride. I'm an adult now. I have to stop being angry or it will eat me alive. I have so much more to be grateful for: my work, Chad, and the life we have together. I won't carry that anger around with me. Otherwise, I will miss out on life." I was breathless and on the verge of tears.

"Yes. This life you have with Chad might not have been possible unless you passed through this experience. But getting back to your dream, who is it you see when you look into Bill's face?"

I thought for a moment. "Me?"

"Perhaps," she said. "You say you're not angry anymore, but if you would just allow yourself to feel that anger, then maybe you could get past it."

I pulled a tissue from the box beside me.

"I think you still harbor a great deal of anger, not only with yourself but also toward your parents, particularly with your mom."

I was crying now.

"After you told them what Bill had done, their actions—or better yet, their lack of reaction—left you feeling angry with them for not protecting you when you were little."

My chest was spasming with tears, but she continued.

"Frank, it was easier for you to get over your experience with Bill. It's easy to hate him because he was the villain. It's harder to get past the resentment you feel toward your parents because you love them. I think that dream with Bill brought up those unresolved feelings."

"I know you're right. If I didn't love my family, I wouldn't care so much. My life is all about family. We're always together for every holiday, Sunday dinner, and even on our birthdays. You know, my mother still makes us a birthday cake every year. I'm forty-one and she still has to make me dinner, and then afterward, my family sings "Happy Birthday" as my mother carries out a cake with candles on it."

"There is no doubt you love your family," she continued. "The hard part is getting over the resentment."

We remained silent for several more moments so I could collect myself. I blew my nose and disposed of the tissue into the trash can next to me.

"How has it been living with Chad?" she asked, navigating the conversation away from my dream.

"Overall it's been great, but I won't deny that it has been difficult at times. Everything has to be negotiated. I promised myself one thing before I moved in, and that was, no matter what, I was going to try and say what bothered me in the moment. No holding back. I even told Chad this, hoping he would do the same."

"How did he respond to that?"

"Let's just say we're still in negotiations."

When Dr. McGovern smiled, I felt all my anxiety fade away,

as if we were no longer doctor and patient but just two friends having a chat in her living room.

"You mentioned the dreams earlier," she interrupted. "What about your difficulty with urination and living with someone?"

My body went tense as I was reminded again where I was. "Interesting you should ask. It waxes and wanes. It's still very difficult for me to urinate in public, but the other night, we were in the apartment. I had to go really badly. Chad was in the bathroom undergoing his transformation process: He has this nightly routine that begins with a deep-cleansing facial scrub, followed by a glycolic acid peel, which he applies to his face with an eyedropper. Then he does this whole other process with his teeth. Anyway, he was in the bathroom like twenty minutes. So I just walked in, stood quietly over the toilet, and peed. I saw him glance over at me in the mirror. He said, 'Look at you, peeing in front of me.' I stared at the tile and said, 'Shut up and ignore me,' which he did. I guess that's progress?"

"Sounds like it to me."

As the holidays approached, I decided to put a hold on my pursuit of Bill. Chad and I were making plans to spend time with both our families for Christmas. One Saturday night, I received a call from my mother informing me that my father had fallen off the ladder hanging Christmas lights.

"Why was he hanging Christmas lights in his condition?" I asked.

"You know your father," she shouted into the phone, her voice trembling. "I went shopping. When I came home, I found the ladder up against the house, and he was in the den watching television. Later, I noticed he could barely walk. I asked what happened, and finally he told me he fell off the ladder. I think he hurt his hip. I don't know what to do with that man. He doesn't listen."

That Sunday when I visited my parents, I insisted that my father show me where he was injured. After nearly twenty minutes of arguing, he relented. "Goddamned people!" he shouted. "Why can't you just leave me in peace?"

Standing in the kitchen with his pants down around his ankles, wearing old, stretched-out boxer shorts, my father could barely stand on his own. His legs trembled as he tried to support himself. My mother had to brace him as I knelt down to look at his hip. I was shocked by how old he'd gotten. His once strong, muscular thighs had deteriorated into thin, flaccid limbs. There was a large bluish area of pooled blood, about the size of both my hands, over his left hip, which looked like an orange peel in texture.

I stared at the blue patch, shaking my head. "Dad, why didn't you go to the doctor?"

He ignored the question and stared straight ahead.

"You know you're on a blood thinner. You have to be very careful. Any time you fall or get hurt, you have to go to the doctor. Do you understand?"

"Goddamned people!" he yelled as he hoisted up his pants. My mother tried to help him, but he pushed her away. As he hobbled into the den, it was clear that, at seventy-seven years old, my father's body was failing him. And like so many people, he found the complex process of aging as confusing as it was depressing. I knew he still saw himself as a young, vibrant man, but he was slowing down. No matter how many times I tried to explain this to him, he never fully comprehended what was happening. Even after he'd had a heart attack and undergone bypass surgery, he repeatedly asked his doctors when he would be his old self again, denying the fact that he was growing old and ignoring us when we told him he had to take it easy.

Years passed, and I watched him sink deeper into despair. After he lost most of his hearing and the world around him slowly faded out, he became crankier. My mother tried to pull him out of his depression, but he was stubborn. This resulted in a daily ritual of arguments. Most days, she left him alone, as he wished, sitting silently in the den, watching old movies with the volume turned up so high you could hear the television from their front porch.

At 3 A.M. that night, I awoke abruptly, thirsty and hot under the covers. For a moment, I couldn't remember what I was dreaming. The room was dark. The door to the bedroom was open, revealing a dim slash of white light. I looked around. There was a dark figure crouched down at the foot of the bed. I remained quiet, trying to absorb this figure, my eyes moving anxiously over it, but the details were fading in and out. I shook my head, trying to remember what I'd taken to go to sleep.

You're losing it, kid. It's the Xanax.

I heard Chad churning beside me.

I whispered, "Are you up?"

"Yes," he groaned.

"Come here," I said, pulling him toward me. My insomnia was apparently contagious. Chad curled up against me. "I know we were planning on visiting your family in Scottsdale for the holidays, but would you mind terribly if we stayed in New York?"

"Of course not. We can spend next Christmas with Roxie and Vern."

"Really?" I asked, turning to look him in the eyes. "That would make things so much easier."

"Then it's settled."

"Hey, do you want me to tell you a story?"

Chad nodded eagerly, driving his face farther into the recess between my arm and chest.

"Okay, once upon a time, there was a little boy who wanted to be Evel Knievel"—here I made a revving noise—"and every day he practiced jumping so that one day he could jump the Grand Canyon." Driving my index and middle finger along the side of Chad's ribs, I continued. "He jumped over buses." My fingers leapt onto his shoulder. "He jumped over trains." They careened up Chad's neck. Then I changed the rev to a low putter. Chad giggled into my armpit. "He practiced every day in the hopes that, one day, he would make it to the Grand Canyon. Meanwhile, in Arizona, there was another little boy, who dreamed of living in New York City. He rode his bicycle in the desert every day." I drew a circle with my fingers on Chad's left buttock. "And he even rode his bicycle to the Grand Canyon, in the hopes that one day he could ride it all the way to New York City. And do you know what happened?"

Chad shook his head repeatedly, tickling me.

"Well, that boy from Arizona made it all the way to New York City, and there, he met the boy who wanted to jump the Grand Canyon." I reached for Chad's hand and held it in mine. "They found each other and fell in love."

Chad was silent except for the faint sound of air passing in and out of his mouth. I reached up toward the ceiling and stared at my fingers, fading in and out, hoping the Xanax would cast me adrift once again into the sea of sleep.

The dark figure crouching at the foot of the bed remained a quiet fixture in the room.

———

EVEN THOUGH WE DECIDED NOT TO TRAVEL, the holidays were still stressful. Maria and her family came up from Alabama. My mother insisted that we all stay at her house. That meant ten of us under one roof. Chad and I slept on an AeroBed in the den. To keep my sanity, I'd escape to the basement and check my e-mails. I was surprised to see one from Dean. Attached to his e-mail was a link to a leather goods store. He was shopping for a jacket to wear for an upcoming appearance. Dean wanted to know which one I preferred.

If I had to map the arc of my relationship with Dean I would have plotted that e-mail somewhere along the downward slope. This seemed inevitable considering where I was in my life. It was hard to maintain a close relationship with someone I'd never met. Yet I couldn't deny he'd helped me through a very difficult time.

"Here you are," said Chad, standing in the doorway.

"You found me."

"I thought you ran away. We're getting ready to go to midnight mass."

"We wouldn't want to miss that," I said sarcastically. "How are you holding up?"

"If I eat one more thing, I'm going to throw up."

"Don't even mention the word *food*," I said, getting up from the couch. "And thanks for being such a trooper. Even though my father won't say it, I can tell he's very happy we're all together this year."

—∞∞—

After the New Year, I called Detective Collier.

"Doc, I was just thinking about you," he said. I didn't believe him, but it was nice to hear his voice. His Staten Island accent was comforting, like running into an old friend.

"I wanted to wish you a Happy New Year and see how things are going."

"Like I said, doc, 'my phone is always on for you.' You know I mean that? Anyway, I listened to the tapes. Then I met with the head of the Boy Scouts here in Staten Island. I didn't like what I found out."

"What do you mean?"

"Apparently, Bill is still an active member of the Boy Scouts, even though he doesn't live on Staten Island. I asked this guy to come down to the police station, but he refused. And get this, he didn't want me to come to his office, either."

"That's peculiar."

"Very. Then he insisted that we meet in a public place. So he picked a bowling alley."

"Did you go?"

"Of course. I told him I was investigating Bill Fox for molesting at least two boys in 1978."

"What did he say?"

"Well, I've been a police officer for almost twenty years, and I've seen and heard just about everything, but what this guy told me was one for the books. He looked me dead in the eyes and said, 'I'm not surprised.' Just like that. He said it without flinching."

"You mean, he knew?"

"That's the way I understood it. So then I said, 'Well, if you suspected this, then why did you allow him to stay in the Scouts?' He said they allowed Bill to stay because they instituted a policy where Fox wasn't allowed to be alone with any of the Scouts. He assured me that things are different now because they teach the boys about sexual predators. This guy was pretty confident that Bill hadn't touched anyone for a long time."

"Did he know about the adoptions?"

"He knew all about it and told me that the remaining boys who still live with Fox are all teenagers, like seventeen and eighteen years old. I asked him what he thought about the adoptions, and he said he thought it was peculiar. Then again, he added that Bill had fallen on hard times. He'd been sick with a bad knee and was also having money trouble."

"So what happens now?"

"Next week, I'm going to head down there and meet with Bill."

It scared me to think Collier was going to confront Bill in person.

Collier correctly read my silence as concern and said, "Don't worry, doc. I'll be all right."

———

AS THE WEATHER TURNED RELENTLESSLY COLD, my days were spent treating the flu, sinus infections, and colds. My last conversation with Collier left me angry, more so than before. Now I was furious with the Boy Scouts for allowing Bill to continue on as a member, especially when they suspected he had molested boys.

After the last patient left that afternoon, I stayed in my office to finish writing notes. The folder from the private investigator sat on my desk collecting dust. It had been there for months, untouched but not forgotten. Several weeks before, I'd called the dispatch service where Nicholas worked, but he wasn't in that day.

Once Gloria left, I picked up the phone.

"Topeka Police," answered a woman.

"I'd like to speak to Nicholas Monroe in dispatch."

I heard several clicking sounds, as though I had been disconnected, and just as I was about to hang up, I heard a man's voice. "This is Nicholas."

"I'm Dr. Frank Spinelli. You don't know me, but I need to

speak to you. But first, I have to ask, are you the same boy who was adopted by Bill Fox?"

"Yes, that's me."

"I was a Boy Scout many years ago, over thirty to be exact. Your father was my Scoutmaster."

"Bill Fox is not my father," he corrected me.

"Excuse me. I mean your adoptive father. I've avoided calling you because I didn't want to disrupt your life. But I have to speak to you. Many years ago, Bill molested me. There were other boys. I'm sure of this, although I have no proof. The assistant Scoutmasters convinced my parents not to press charges, and Bill agreed to leave."

"Is there a number you can give me so I can call you back?" he asked. "I can't talk to you while I'm at work."

"Of course." My heart was racing. "Let me give you my cell phone number."

"I will call you back in fifteen minutes."

The daylight was fading fast. I stared at my phone, praying Nicholas would call soon. I nervously tapped my pen against the desk. Thoughts swirled around in my head. Ten minutes later, my cell rang. Quickly, I answered. "Hello."

"This is Nick Monroe." There was an echo, as if he was calling from outside. "I'm sorry I had to do that, but I'm at work. I didn't want anyone to hear this conversation." I sensed Nicholas was eager to speak with me. His voice was full of sincerity. He continued, "How did you find me?"

"Once I discovered Bill's memoir, I hired a private investigator."

"I see."

I stood up from my chair and began pacing in the dark. "It took me awhile to get up enough nerve to call you. So please hear me out. I need to know if anything happened between you and Bill Fox."

"I appreciate the lengths you've gone through to contact me, but I haven't spoken to Bill in over twenty years. We had a falling-out. You have to understand I didn't live with Bill for very long."

"Why was that?"

"My birth mother wanted me back," he explained. "Bill was angry. We haven't spoken since then."

"How long did you live with Bill?"

"Not more than a year."

"Did you know he adopted other boys?"

"I heard something about that. I'm not surprised. There were always boys around the house."

"Nicholas, I know you were sixteen when Bill adopted you. From what I read, you were very traumatized by your birth father. Bill rescued you when you were on the verge of suicide. I can't imagine what that must have been like. I suppose you have a great deal of respect for Bill and feel indebted to him. But I have to know, did he ever try anything with you?"

There was a long silence. "Well, there was some touching, which I thought was inappropriate."

"When you say touching, you mean . . ."

"Masturbation," he said flatly. "But it never went any further than that. He called it *boy bonding.*"

I nearly dropped the phone. I felt gas rising up my throat, the taste of acid in my mouth, and that familiar pressure building up in my bladder.

Boy bonding. What did Bill say to me when we were alone that first time in his truck? Do you know how to jerk off? Well, when you do it with your buddy, it's just boy bonding.

I continued, "Do you know if he touched any other boys?"

"No, like I said, I didn't live with Bill very long. Everyone who reads the book thinks we're still in touch, but that's just not the way it was. My wife is always urging me to write a book about being a foster child and our experience as foster parents."

"Do you have children?"

"Yes, we have a daughter. Our second child died when he was very young. He had a rare case of hydrocephalus. We've been foster parents to many children, but we're going to adopt a baby who has special needs. She has Prader–Willi syndrome."

"Mr. Monroe, I don't know you, but apparently you really turned your life around. I'm concerned that Bill Fox has children under his care. Don't you feel some obligation to help those boys, having been in their situation? They might not have anywhere else to go. You were lucky to have had your mother to turn to. I'm afraid these boys would comply with Bill's sexual advances as a way to maintain a roof over their heads and keep food in their mouths."

"Dr. Spinelli, have you ever been in an orphanage or a foster home?"

"No."

"Well, I have, and shit like that goes on all the time. What happened between Bill and me happened a long, long time ago. I'm married with children now. I have to think about the welfare of my family. I don't need to get mixed up with any investigation. I have a good life now. I don't need to go back there. I won't."

CHAPTER 33

Just the Way They Are

IT WAS LATE FEBRUARY. I woke up an hour before my alarm was set to go off and stared up at the ceiling. Knowing I wasn't going to fall back to sleep, I quietly got out of bed and closed the bedroom door behind me so that I wouldn't disturb Chad. Outside the living room window, I saw that it was snowing. Not just the usual New York flurries that melted as soon as they hit the asphalt, but huge, fluffy, marshmallow-sized flakes. Pressing my head against the glass, I noticed the streets and all the rooftops nearby were blanketed in white.

I missed the days when I was young and would wake up to mornings like this. Josephine and I would huddle by the television, praying they'd announce our schools were closed. The thought of climbing back in bed with Chad for a snow day of snuggling and bad television was so tempting, but those days were gone.

In the kitchen, my eyes caught the blinking red light of my cell phone indicating I had a message. It was from Detective Collier. "I met with Bill," he said. "Of course, he denied everything. He only admitted that he spoke to you and that you were pissed off because he didn't remember you. The good news is that Family Services is interested in talking to you and the boy he adopted in 1982. I said I would give them your number . . ."

I pressed END and sat down on the living room sofa. In a way,

I felt relieved, settling into what I suspected would be another dead end. Nicholas was not going to agree to speak to Family Services. I doubted any of the boys still living with Bill would ever come forward with allegations, and there would be no reason for the police to investigate further. Speaking with Family Services would result in nothing more than me retelling my story again to someone new.

Once I arrived at my office, coated in snow and ice, my toes so cold and numb that I could barely feel them, I threw off my boots and sprawled out on the floor with my feet propped up on the vent to thaw. After a while, I reached into my coat pocket and grabbed my phone to call Collier.

"Okay, before you say anything else, I have to know one thing. What does Bill look like?"

"Old," he replied definitively. "I drove to his house and parked outside. Then I called him from my car. I wanted to make sure he didn't disappear when I told him I was coming over."

"How did he react in person?"

"Unfazed."

"So what happens next?"

"I'm going to put some pressure on the local police. I want the names of the other boys who live with Bill."

I felt comforted knowing Collier still wanted to pursue this case, despite all the opposition we were encountering. "Well, be sure to keep me updated if anything new comes up."

"Of course," he said assuredly. "Call me anytime. You know my—"

"Phone is always on for you. Thank you, Detective. You have no idea, but thank you for everything."

Hanging up, I watched the snow continue to fall. I decided that it would be in my best interest if I distanced myself from the police investigation. Quietly, I lay there for several minutes until I was startled by a text message from Chad.

It read: *Happy anniversary, baby. You make me so happy. xoxo*

ONE WEEK LATER, CHAD WAS LEAVING for an overnight business trip. That morning, I received a phone call from the Tioga County Police. "Dr. Spinelli, this is State Trooper James Iverson. I was given your name by Detective Andrew Collier."

I covered the receiver with my hand. "It's about Bill," I whispered to Chad.

Iverson continued, "I've been working on this case concerning the allegations you made against Mr. Fox. I've been in contact with a boy Bill adopted. He's thirty years old now. He admitted that Bill molested him when he was a child. Now, you have to understand that most of these boys were kids nobody else wanted. Judging by Fox's past actions, it was his nature to act as hero and savior. So these boys were less inclined to come forward and say anything bad against him."

"Have the Boy Scouts been contacted? And the adoption agencies?"

"I appreciate your concern. But you have to understand that, as I proceed, I have to be cautious. It seems there were earlier findings that were never followed up on. I have to be very careful, because if I alert the wrong people, or Mr. Fox himself, then he might destroy evidence."

"What do you mean by earlier allegations?"

"All I can say is that this was not the first time our department received a complaint against Mr. Fox. I could very well step on the wrong toes as I proceed. My plan is to contact the FBI. I'm hopeful they will perform a background history on Mr. Fox. That would include speaking to you."

Chad's cell phone began ringing. "Yes, I'll be down in a minute," he whispered.

"Ultimately, what are your intentions?" I asked Trooper Iverson.

"I want to press charges against Mr. Fox and have him arrested."

My heart skipped. "That's wonderful news."

He gave me his contact information. After I hung up, I

quickly told Chad everything he said. We stood there with our mouths hanging open.

"I can't believe another boy came forward," I said.

"This is great, baby, and it's all because of you."

"Don't go on this trip."

Chad chuckled. "I don't want to go, but I have to. I'll call you when I land."

Standing at the door, I kissed him good-bye and watched him walk down the hall. "Hey," I shouted. Chad turned around. "I love you."

Chad smiled and disappeared inside the elevator. I was alone again. After living together in the same apartment for five months, I had become so deeply attached to Chad that it frightened me. Now I didn't know how I could ever live without him.

———∞∞∞———

ERIC WAS THRILLED TO HEAR THE NEWS ABOUT BILL. "Come over tonight," he suggested. "It'll be just like old times."

"What about Scott?"

"Who?"

"Your husband."

"Oh yeah, him. The governess is working tonight. Come over, and I'll make dinner. You can tell me all about the latest developments with Bill."

Later that evening, Eric and I were sitting in his living room watching reruns of *Maude* when I received a text message from Detective Collier. It read, *I haven't forgotten about you. Let's talk next week?*

"Who's that?" asked Eric.

"Detective Collier."

"The sexy one?" he asked, inching closer. "What does he want?"

"I called him earlier to tell him that the state trooper from Pennsylvania called me. I still can't believe another victim has come forward."

"You must be over the moon!" Eric threw his arms around me. "This is excellent news."

"I know, but something the state trooper said isn't sitting quite right with me."

"What did he say?"

"He told me that there were earlier findings that weren't followed up on. Then he said something about having to be cautious so that he didn't step on the wrong toes."

"What the hell does that mean?"

"Exactly. I wonder whose toes he's afraid of."

"Listen," cautioned Eric. "I can already see those gears grinding in that little head of yours. Before you get yourself all worked up over this, why don't you give this state trooper the benefit of the doubt? He must have something, or else why would he contact you?"

"I just can't help but think that the police knew something and swept it under the rug. Imagine if I'd never gotten involved."

"But you did. Now let the police do their job."

"Okay, okay. Now why don't you make yourself useful and get us some wine."

Eric winked and stood up. Halfway to the kitchen, he turned around. "Hey, whatever happened to your fancy author friend Dean?"

"I haven't spoken to him for some time. He e-mailed me a couple of months ago, asking me to help him pick out a leather jacket to wear on his book tour."

Eric's eyes widened as a smug look appeared on his face. "Oh lovely," he said. "So you went from best friend to stylist?"

"We were never best friends," I assured him. "I never even met the man. It's funny when you think about it. He was someone I only communicated with through e-mails and the occasional phone call, yet he helped change the course of my life. I guess you could say that's strange, but looking back, I wouldn't have it any other way. Helping him pick out a leather jacket is the least I could do. If he asked me to clip his toenails, I would."

"You've never offered to clip my toenails," muttered Eric, handing me a glass of wine.

"Have you seen your toenails? Your toes look like fingerling potatoes with claws."

Eric smacked me playfully. We laughed. Then I noticed his expression change. His lip began to quiver, and his eyes went hazy. "I wouldn't change your relationship with him, either," he said, snuggling close to me. "I like things just the way they are."

CHAPTER 34

Fade to Black

AFTER SUFFERING AN ACUTE, and then prolonged, attack of gout, my father scheduled a consultation with a podiatrist, who recommended a bone biopsy. He underwent surgery the first week in July.

"Your father will need a prolonged course of intravenous antibiotics," explained the surgeon. The bone was severely infected, a condition known as osteomyelitis. "Unfortunately, he will have to go to a subacute care facility because his insurance doesn't cover a visiting nurse. The good news is that he'll get physical therapy while he's there."

Maria flew up from Alabama with the children once my father was transferred to the rehab center. Except no one could lift my father's spirits. He remained hostile after surgery, frequently arguing with the staff and refusing to take part in his rehabilitation.

"Dad, you have to do what they tell you to do," I insisted.

"The only thing I have to do is pay taxes and die," replied my father.

I shook my head. That evening, I left concerned that his attitude was going to hinder his progress. My father's inability to understand the seriousness of his underlying heart condition was discouraging, and that was when I experienced the first inkling that my father might not leave the rehabilitation center alive.

Several days later, Maria returned to Alabama because the children had to go back to school. My father deteriorated rapidly the day after they left. On July 12, the doctor on call at the rehabilitation facility contacted me. "Your father is experiencing progressive shortness of breath," explained Dr. Shevamundi. "I'm going to transfer him to the emergency room."

"Yes," I said. "That's a good idea."

Standing in my living room with my cell phone up to my ear, I looked at Chad, who was listening from the bedroom doorway. "Toe surgery," I said. "This is the kind of stupid shit that's going to kill my dad. Why didn't they just chop it off? He doesn't need that toe. He's seventy-seven."

When I arrived at the emergency room later that day, I found my dad in one of the beds closest to the nurses' station. He looked pale and was breathing heavily through an oxygen mask. Wires were attached to his chest to monitor his heart rate. I reached out and held his hand. He opened his eyes, recognized me, and smiled. Then he closed his eyes again and shook his head.

"Can you believe how big Maria's boys got?" I said. "Matthew and Michael are taller than me."

He nodded, gasping. His lips were turning blue. Shivering, he pulled the mask away from his face. "I need to pee," he said. His words faltered between wheezes.

I informed a nurse, who brought over a urinal. Pulling the curtain to give my father privacy, she said, "Your mother and sister are in the waiting room." I thanked her but decided to wait until he was done, knowing my father had an enlarged prostate, which made it difficult for him to urinate.

Suddenly, an alarm began to sound, indicating his oxygen saturation was dangerously low.

"That's not good," said the nurse. "I'll go get the doctor. Your dad's going to need a catheter."

Within minutes, his condition declined as his lungs filled up with fluid. A team of physicians swarmed around his bed. A skinny, dark man emerged from the huddle and asked me whether I was his son.

"Yes, I am," I said. "I'm also a doctor."

The man's eyes went wide with panic. He addressed the other physicians in a language that sounded like gargling. Then he explained that they needed to put my father on a ventilator.

I rushed to my father's bedside. "Dad," I said. "They need to put you on a breathing machine. I'm going to get Mommy and Josephine. I'll be right back."

He nodded and closed his eyes. I never saw him open them again.

Later that evening, after I left the hospital, I rode the ferry back to Manhattan, staring out at the dull, rolling water. Moonlight shimmered on the undulating surface. I couldn't believe this was how my father's life was going to end. Like the vast ocean around me, his life had reached heights and depths he couldn't have possibly imagined, yet suddenly the limitlessness of his existence was drawing to a close, even as this boat approached the dock.

Just then, I received a text from Chad asking me about my father. I was unable to respond. I knew if I called him back, my eyes would well up, the tears would fall, and once they did, I would be unable to stop crying. Instead, I remained stoic, staring out at the waves. Minutes later, I received another text from Chad. This time it directed me to a link for the Animal Haven shelter, where an eight-week-old Beagle-mix puppy was available for adoption. His name: Hoffman. Staring at his picture, there was a familiarity in his big brown eyes, and I knew that this puppy would be ours.

My father will die. This puppy will be ours. Life goes on. It must.

As a doctor, I have had many experiences with death. I grow detached from the dead once life leaves their bodies. Perhaps that's why I was able to sit quietly, staring at my father in his coffin as my family wept. His three grandsons and one granddaughter stood at the entrance of the funeral parlor, too afraid to get a closer glimpse of their lifeless Popi. I didn't blame them. Why should they remember him that way? Like them, I wanted to recall the sarcastic, overbearing, hardworking man who devoured every day as if it was his last. Eating foods he shouldn't, drinking wine he made himself (which tasted like vinegar), and smoking cigarettes, cigars, and even a pipe whenever he chose, because life, to him, was to be lived and not feared. Each day could be his last, so he lived it surrounded with the people he loved most. Several days after the funeral, Chad and I adopted the puppy, now renamed Hoffman Angelo. Our family was now made up of three.

IN THE FALL, AS THE WEATHER COOLED DOWN, I walked Hoffman, the wind nipping at my cheeks like beestings. Leaves were changing, falling. Days passed when I didn't think of Bill. I wanted to forget him. It was my hope that one day I would become so consumed with Chad and Hoffman that the past would just fade. Yet events in the news acted as subtle reminders of Bill.

On September 26, 2009, Roman Polanski, the Academy Award–winning director of *The Pianist* and iconic films such as *Rosemary's Baby, Chinatown,* and *Repulsion,* was arrested during a raid on his hotel in Switzerland. He had been running from American authorities for a 1978 warrant issued after a statutory-rape conviction. Over the years, Polanski tried to appeal the conviction but was unsuccessful, even after the victim at the center of the case asked for the charges to be dropped.

At my next session, I confided in Dr. McGovern that for many years, I was an admirer of Polanski's work, particularly his earlier black-and-white films. Even after I learned of his arrest, I felt protective of him, and subconsciously, it bothered me that I would defend a pedophile just because I thought that, as an artist, he should not be held accountable. His art far outweighed his flaws.

"So, by that logic," she began, "should Bill not be held accountable for what he did because he was a highly decorated police officer?"

"Of course not. I know my reasoning doesn't make sense. That's why I'm so upset with myself. I should be angry that Polanski fled the country after his conviction. I should want him to pay the consequences for what he's done, regardless of how long ago it took place or how honorably he's lived his life since. I know how I should feel. Yet there is this sense that I've been tricked into feeling sorry for him, just like I used to feel sorry for Bill. I find myself defending Polanski just like I used to defend Bill. It makes me so angry."

"Have you heard from the police?"

"No, not for a while. I'm beginning to think it's over. Maybe that's why this Polanski case is bothering me so much. I just wish somebody would tell me what's going on."

"You know you don't have to wait for the police to contact you. Go over their heads if you're not satisfied."

Spurred into action, I took Dr. McGovern's advice and contacted the Pennsylvania District Attorney's office the next day. When the receptionist answered, I was ready to argue my way into speaking with the attorney handling Bill's case, but that wasn't necessary. Within minutes, Walter Sayer, the assistant district attorney, answered the phone.

"First of all, I have to say that I cannot comment on any active case, nor am I implying that there is a case open pertaining to Mr. Bill Fox. The district attorney's office does not discuss ongoing cases. Second of all, I want to personally apologize for all that you have been through, and I want to thank you for being so courageous and coming forward at this time. Mr. Fox lives in Liberty, Pennsylvania. You live in New York City. This is a part of the country you might not be familiar with, doctor. We have to proceed very carefully because jurors here lack the gumption to comprehend that a former police officer could do such a thing to a child."

"I understand that my situation is beyond the scope of the statute of limitations. Would it be reasonable to assume that another boy has come forward in order for your office to open an investigation?"

"No," he said. "We don't necessarily need to have a boy who

is currently being molested to come forward. We can act on what is 404(b) Evidence. That refers to anyone who has made a complaint of molestation. The complaint must be investigated."

"So, there were no other boys?"

"Doctor, you have to understand that this is western Pennsylvania. It's like *Deliverance* country. You don't want to mess with folks here, particularly the men. If we were to walk into a room full of boys from Liberty and ask them if they ever sucked a dick, no one would raise their hand. Now, I'm not gay, Dr. Spinelli, and I can't imagine what it must have been like for you to grow up being gay and then molested on top of that, but it's a hundred times worse if you came from Liberty."

"So, what you're saying is Bill is going to get away with it because the boys he's adopted aren't going to admit they sucked his dick?"

"I'm saying that's probably true, and more than likely, these boys would suck his dick and keep their mouths shut about it just to avoid being placed in another foster home."

"That is the worst thing I've ever heard."

"That's Liberty. I just want you to be prepared, because this process takes time," continued Mr. Sayer. "You can call me directly in a month or next week if you like. I don't mind. Cases like this usually go one of three ways: Some we process because we know the guy did it and we want to see justice served. Then there are those cases we don't take on because we think the kid lied, and that's a small percentage. Finally, there are cases where we know the guy did it, but we can't prosecute. Those are the cases I hate the most, but I want to prepare you for the possibility that, one day, you might call me, and I'll have to tell you that we're not going to prosecute Mr. Fox."

Dread came over me. Everything turned gray, just like a Roman Polanski film. I was Catherine Deneuve, enveloped in a metallic world of black-and-white. All the colors and sensations faded away. I felt helpless. It was over. Done. The credits were rolling, and the ending was bleak.

CHAPTER 35

Stroke in Evolution

I HAD A BAD HABIT OF TRYING TO DO TOO MANY THINGS AT ONCE. One afternoon, I was cleaning a patient's ears—Mr. Edwards's ears were always impacted with wax—when my cell phone began to ring in my lab coat. Unable to ignore it, I reached into my pocket as I held the speculum in his external auditory canal. I saw a Pennsylvania area code.

"Ouch," screamed Mr. Edwards, pulling on his earlobe. "What's the matter with you?"

"I'm so sorry. Let me just have another look?"

"No, I'm done for today," he said, standing up. "You've caused enough damage already."

As soon as he left, I listened to the message from Trooper Iverson. He said, "Dr. Spinelli, it's been a while since we last spoke, but I wanted to bring you up to speed on the status of our case. When you get a minute, if you can give me a call here in our barracks, I'd appreciate it."

Dialing the number, I prepared myself for the worst. I was reminded of the conversation I'd had with Mr. Sayer five months earlier. His pessimism concerning this case forced me to give up any lingering hope that Bill Fox was going to be arrested.

When Trooper Iverson answered, I immediately recalled the slow-tempered way he spoke, as though he was carefully choosing each word. "Dr. Spinelli," he said. "I wanted to update you on our case. Yesterday, we arrested Mr. Fox on twenty-one counts, including rape, child molestation, deviant sexual intercourse, and intimidation of a minor. The judge set bail at a hundred thousand. Mr. Fox declined to post and remains in prison."

I could barely squeeze out a response. "Excuse me? Could you repeat that?"

"Three victims came forward and testified," he continued. "All three were his adopted sons."

I began writing whatever words came into my mind, but was distracted by a steady throb in my temples. I was entombed in white noise. I could no longer hear Trooper Iverson.

"Dr. Spinelli, are you there?"

"I don't know what to say," I said finally. "Thank you so much for calling me. I was sure the case was going to get dropped, especially after I spoke with Mr. Sayer."

"Well, that's the thing with these cases. You have to be patient. It was only a matter of time until we collected enough evidence for the attorney general's office to agree we had a sufficient amount for an arrest warrant."

Slowly, I felt myself coming out of my state of shock. "Thank you again for all your hard work."

"We have you to thank, as well. If it wasn't for you, who knows what would have happened."

Hanging up, I stared down at the notepad. The only two words I'd written were BOY BONDING.

Chad was in Boston for work. I texted him immediately. Then I contacted so many people I lost track. I was so excited that I wanted to run into the waiting room and tell everyone my former Scoutmaster and child molester had finally been arrested. Instead, I grabbed a chart and called the next patient.

On my way home from the office, I bought a bottle of champagne and two bottles of white wine. By the time Chad arrived, I was already drunk. He slowly made his way into the apartment, stopping only to pet the dog. His reaction was nothing like I had imagined. I expected him to be as thrilled as I was. Chad's participation in this entire ordeal was crucial. Over the past three years, I'd often told him that if I hadn't had him in my life, I wouldn't have found the strength to face Bill. Was it foolish of me to think that Chad was able to sustain the intensity that I had been building up for the past thirty years? In those minutes after he opened the door, all I could feel was my own disappointment. While he unpacked, played with the dog, and then sorted through his mail, I felt a rising anger burning inside my chest.

"I've already spoken to the local newspapers. I'm thinking I should write a statement. Maybe I should call Nancy Grace?"

He remained impervious to my suggestions.

"What's the matter?"

He offered a weak smile, a condescending look he'd perfected. "Nothing."

I pointed to my glass. "Would you like a drink?"

"Sure." His succinct responses only infuriated me more. I stood up, opened the refrigerator, and stared at the bottle of champagne. For a second I considered opening it, but then I reached for the open bottle of wine instead. By the time I poured Chad a glass, he was already sitting at his computer, thoroughly engrossed in one of his favorite websites. I handed him the wine, and he drank, still staring at the computer screen.

"Cheers, Frank!" I said sarcastically. "Congratulations!"

Chad looked over his shoulder. "What? I already congratulated you earlier."

"You know this is bullshit."

Chad stared at me. He had an uncanny ability to remain at ease, as if losing his temper was a sign of weakness and retaliating with anger, an affront to his unflappable nature. "You know what's bullshit?" he said calmly. "Coming home after a long business trip and finding you drunk."

"Give me a break. Okay, so I'm drunk. I thought you were going to be home early. Forgive me for starting without you. You know, I wasn't expecting flowers from you or even a card, but you didn't even think of champagne. Anything! You know how important this is to me."

Chad stood up. He walked directly past me and into the bedroom.

"Where are you going?"

He stopped. "It's always about what I don't do for you." Then he walked in the bedroom and slammed the door.

I wanted to rip Chad's computer off his desk and throw it on the ground. I picked up a book instead and began reading. I read the same line over and over, glancing intermittently at the bedroom door, hoping Chad would come out and apologize but knowing he wasn't going to. Had I still been the old me, the man I was before I started seeing Dr. McGovern, I would have never considered giving in first during an argument. That Frank thrived on stalemate situations.

As more time passed, I began to wonder whether Chad was the least bit curious about what I was doing. I stared at the clock, counting down the seconds, hoping he'd concede first and redeem himself, but with each passing minute, I grew angrier until, finally, I stopped counting because I realized I was playing a self-defeating game.

I marched into the bedroom. Chad was lying on the bed, reading a magazine with Hoffman reclining over his abdomen. They stared at me as though they had forged an alliance of silence.

"You're a jerk. I want you to apologize for not being more excited for me, for us, about Bill's arrest."

Softly he said, "Okay, I'm sorry."

After I walked out of the room, I started to sob. Chad followed behind and hugged me. I cried on his shoulder. The outcome had finally taken its toll on both of us. It was not vindication that I felt. It was regret. Regret for those who could have been spared.

THE NEXT MORNING, I WOKE UP before my alarm went off. I had a busy day ahead of me, including a full schedule of patients and a noontime lunch presentation. I arrived earlier than usual so I'd have time to search online for reports of Bill's arrest. Surprisingly, I found articles in two local Pennsylvania newspapers. In the comment section below one of the articles I read a post from a man who identified himself as a former victim. I replied to his message and left my contact information.

At 10:30 A.M., I received a call from Chad. "I don't feel well."

"You're probably exhausted and a little dehydrated. Remember, you came home late last night after a four-hour train ride. Then we polished off a bottle of wine. Have something to eat, drink plenty of water, and no more coffee. That'll only make you feel worse. Do you have a busy day?"

"Yeah, I have a conference call in ten minutes. I'll let you know how I feel after."

"Eat something," I insisted, sounding frighteningly like my mother.

Half an hour later, I received a text from Chad: *I feel like I want to throw up*. Without a second thought, I went home. Perhaps I was channeling my mother or perhaps I'd lived with Chad long enough to know he hardly ever complained. When I arrived at the apartment ten minutes later, I found him lying in bed. A brown pool of vomit was on the floor next to him. Hoffman was in the living room, whining nervously. When he approached me, I ordered him to stay back, fearing he might lap it up. I began cleaning.

"How do you feel?" I asked as I frantically mopped up the floor with a dish towel.

"I feel like I'm having an out-of-body experience," he replied. "I barely made it through my call. I thought I'd feel better after I vomited."

I disposed of the towels directly into the washing machine. When I returned to the bedroom, I noticed Chad's left eye was closed. "What's wrong?"

"I have a headache."

I felt conflicted. On one hand, I wanted to continue acting like my mother, cleaning up the mess to restore order, while babying Chad. Perhaps I'd even make him a bowl of soup. Yet the other part of me, the doctor, clearly saw that Chad's condition was about to spiral perilously out of control. Despite my unwillingness to believe he was in serious danger, I picked up my cell phone and dialed 911. Never in my whole life had I called emergency services. When the operator answered, I stated the facts like a doctor conferring with another health-care provider. All the while, I stared cautiously at Chad, wondering whether I was wasting vital time. Then I apologized to the operator and hung up, having decided against waiting for an ambulance.

With my assistance, Chad was able to stand. I helped him get dressed and escorted him out of the apartment. While I locked the door, he began walking toward the elevator on his own. Out of the corner of my eye, I saw that with each step he veered to the left like a passenger on a tilting ship. For a second I was paralyzed with fear. Then I ran toward him, worried he might fall. In the elevator, he leaned against me with his full weight so that I could barely support the both of us.

"Chad, stay with me," I pleaded.

Once we were in the lobby, I propped him up against the concierge desk. Arlene, the doorperson on duty, rushed to help us. "Oh my Lord," she said. "Is everything all right?"

"Stay with him while I hail a cab," I begged. Fortunately, one was pulling up just as I stepped off the curb. Arlene attempted to walk Chad outside. "Thanks, I'll take it from here."

Driving across town to New York University Hospital, I called the emergency room to speak to the attending physician on call. Once we arrived, doctors and nurses descended upon us, reminding me of my former days when I worked on the trauma team. Within seconds, Chad was undressed and being examined. I stood back helplessly, watching them work while I tried to think of a simple explanation for his symptoms, something rational, but my mind was blank. I was blank. A handsome, dark-skinned physician walked over and asked me to repeat what I had just reported on the phone minutes earlier.

He stared at me inquisitively. "Are you a doctor?"

"Yes," I said. "We're both doctors."

Without uttering another word, he spun around and returned to the assemblage. I heard him say, "The patient's a doctor." I took a step back, wanting to give them the freedom to do their job without my presence looming over them. At that very second, my cell phone rang. I walked away to answer it. The number was unknown to me.

A man spoke. "You're gonna pay for what you did."

"Excuse me?" I said, confused. "What is this in reference to?"

"We both know who I'm talking about," he insisted. "You're a fuckin' faggot, and you take care of fags . . . with AIDS. You'll burn in hell for that."

The confusion evaporated quickly once the caller's intention emerged. Channeling the gumption of Barbara Stanwyck on *The Big Valley*, I said, "On the contrary. I'm actually very proud of what I do."

"Well, this won't be the last call you get. There will be more."

"I understand you're angry," I said, calmly. "If unloading your frustration on me makes you feel better, then I'm glad I was able to help."

The phone went dead as a thin, pale doctor rushed toward me and introduced himself as the neurology fellow on call. I detected a Russian accent. "We think Dr. Schroer suffered a subarachnoid hemorrhage. He has all the classic signs of a bleed: acute onset, pain behind the eye, and unsteady gait."

I stared at him with one eye and watched them wheel Chad away with the other. Instinctively, I began to follow them.

The Russian was right behind me. "They're taking him to CAT scan," he said.

I nodded and hurried to catch up.

"I have to ask, does Dr. Schroer use any drugs, like cocaine?"

"No."

"Was he having an orgasm at the time?"

"I was at work."

"He could have had an orgasm without you."

I wanted to get away from the Russian neurology fellow. I wanted to see Chad. I was concerned about how much he knew and wondered whether he was afraid. Up ahead, I saw them wheel Chad's stretcher into an elevator. I ran and squeezed in beside him. We didn't speak. I stared at his face, hoping he felt he was in good hands. When the elevator opened on the second floor, I assisted them in wheeling Chad into the CAT-scan suite. Once he was secured onto the conveyor, I whispered, "How are you?"

He winced. His left eye was still closed shut.

I crumbled inside.

A female technician walked over to us. "Sir, you'll need to wait outside." The Russian overheard her and intervened before I had a chance to turn into Gary Coleman on *Diff'rent Strokes*.

"He's with me," said the neurology fellow. "Dr. Spinelli, please come this way. They're ready to begin." I followed him into the technician's room. Through the observation window, I watched as Chad's body was slowly transported headfirst into a large metal doughnut.

The Russian urged me to have a seat. "There's nothing you can do," he said. "We'll know more in a few minutes."

I finally conceded and sat down. Suddenly, I felt exhausted.

To distract myself, I began to organize by making mental lists:

1. Collect Chad's clothing.

2. Call Eric and ask him to pick up Hoffman.

3. Call Chad's parents. No. Don't call anyone until you know what's wrong.

He's in good hands. There is nothing more I can do.

My cell phone rang again. This time it was a local number. I stepped out of the technician's room to answer it.

"Dr. Spinelli, I'm a reporter, and I'd like to ask you a few questions about Mr. Fox."

I couldn't shake the image of Chad lying on that cold metal table with his head strapped down, wondering what was happening.

It's probably just an orbital migraine. Then why was he having trouble walking?

"Dr. Spinelli, are you there?" asked the reporter.

"Sorry," I said. "You said you're a reporter?"

Behind me I heard footsteps. I turned to find the Russian. "The CAT scan is negative."

I sighed with relief.

"But I need to perform a lumbar puncture."

"Why?" I asked.

"Dr. Spinelli, are you there?" repeated the reporter.

"A negative CAT scan doesn't rule out a bleed, in light of the strong clinical picture. It could still be in the very early stages. We need to proceed quickly."

"Of course," I said to the Russian. Then I spoke into the phone. "I can't talk right now. My partner's having a stroke."

After a series of tests that included blood work, a lumbar puncture, and two negative CAT scans, Chad's doctors were unable to find a cause for his symptoms. The neurology team recommended a neurosurgical consult to assess whether Chad needed further, more invasive testing. I agreed. Soon a tall Romanian doctor arrived and examined Chad. Once he reviewed all the studies, he consulted with us in the CAT-scan suite. Without hesitation, he suggested Chad undergo a full angiogram of his head and neck. I knew what that entailed. I also knew the risks included internal bleeding, stroke, and death. Despite all my education and experience, I hesitated. They were talking about my Chad.

"We can get a second opinion," I offered.

"I don't suggest you wait," said the Romanian. Then he pulled me far enough away so that Chad couldn't hear. "Stop thinking of him as your partner and think of him as a patient. You know the facts. If this was anyone else, what would you advise?"

Fifteen minutes later, I was alone in the waiting room while the Romanian doctor I'd met twenty minutes earlier injected dye into the arteries of Chad's brain to look for blockage. Over the course of the next sixty minutes, I painfully remembered the fight Chad and I had had the night before and wished I could take back everything I'd said. I blamed myself for pushing him so hard when I should have known how tired he was having just traveled four hours by train.

My imagination, now fevered by guilt, had me doubting my initial plan not to call Chad's parents until I had something concrete to tell them. Everything suddenly seemed so bleak. We should have been celebrating. Instead, I was waiting in a hospital for the neurosurgeon to tell me what was wrong with my partner. I looked at my watch. It was already 8 P.M. I had to talk to someone. Reaching for my cell phone, I knew there was only one person in my life who would understand.

"THAT'S ALL I KNOW," I SAID. "I've told you everything. I'm waiting for the doctor to come out."

"But how did this happen?" asked my mother.

"I don't know. We still don't know what happened."

"Where are you? I'll call Josephine. We'll come to the city and wait with you."

"No, don't come. There's nothing you can do. Just talk to me. Keep me busy so I don't stare at my watch."

"Don't be ridiculous! Let me call Josephine. She's right next door. We can be in the city in twenty minutes. You shouldn't be alone."

It was comforting to know how much my mother cared about Chad. It was also the first time she'd ever responded in such a way that made me think she saw us as a real couple. I tried my best not to get emotional, but it was difficult. The parallels between this situation and my father's were obvious, although I didn't want to believe it. I suppose that was why I called my mother in the first place.

Looking up, I saw the Romanian doctor turn the corner and march toward me. "Mom, the doctor just came out. I have to go."

"Not on your life," she shouted. "I'll hold."

I stood up to greet him. "It's just as I thought," he said. "Chad had a stroke."

"What!"

"Yes, he had a small stroke in the posterior inferior cerebellar artery," he said confidently. "Come, I'll show you."

He moved with long, determined strides back to the interventional radiology suite. I hurried after him. Inside the technician's room, he pointed to a monitor. I stared at a large screen displaying the outline of Chad's head, his face replaced by a reticulum of arteries that looked like leafless white branches. "See here?" He pointed. I moved in closer. He identified a small branch that had been occluded by a clot. "That's what caused his symptoms."

"How did he get a clot there?" I asked.

The Romanian shrugged. "Chad said he was traveling for work yesterday. Perhaps he developed a clot in his leg."

"And it went from his leg all the way up to his brain?"

The Romanian scowled. Reaching for his lab coat, he said, "He'll have some residual damage. With physical therapy, he'll be able to walk with a cane."

Once Chad was moved up to the neurological intensive care unit, I stayed with him until he fell asleep. His room overlooked the East River. Across the water, I could see the old neon Pepsi-Cola sign. I remembered my father once told me that it was Joan Crawford's idea to erect the sign at that exact location as a way to remind the Manhattan residents which soda to buy. It was at times like these I missed my father the most.

I called my mother back once I got home. We spoke as I lay on my bed, alone in the dark.

"What happens next?" she asked.

"They'll start physical therapy tomorrow. It's important they begin as soon as possible. We still need to figure out where this clot came from. I don't agree with the specialist. That clot didn't come from his leg. What kills me is that Chad is the healthiest person I know. He's a naturopath. He takes vitamins, for Christ's sake. He doesn't smoke, and he hardly eats carbs. It just doesn't make sense."

"Well, at least he's stable now," she encouraged. "They'll figure out what's going on. How are you?"

"I'm okay. It's weird being alone in the apartment, no dog, no Chad."

"You're telling me. I know. It's not easy to be alone when you're used to living with someone. Sometimes I still can't fall asleep in our bed. Most nights, I sleep in your sister's old room."

"It must have been difficult for you when Dad died. I'm sorry I wasn't around more."

"I understand you have your own life. Just thank God every day because life is short. That's why I don't understand why you want to get involved with things from the past. Ever since you told me they arrested Bill, I've been worrying."

"What are you worried about?"

"Frank, his whole family is police. What if they come after you?"

"They're not going to come after me."

"How do you know?" she demanded. "You have me worried sick, wondering if someone is going to beat you up. You don't know who you're dealing with. They could be a bunch of animals. Just be careful, please."

"Mom, Bill's an old man. He didn't even post bail. No one is going to come after me. This is a good thing. You should be happy. The police told me he was molesting his sons. Aren't you proud that I was able to help put him in jail? I never told you this, but when Dad was alive, I asked him to drive me to someone's house. I left a card in their mailbox for my old assistant Scoutmaster. Daddy drove me, and didn't ask any questions. Deep down inside, I think he knew what I was doing and wanted to help."

"You know, your father always said, 'My son hates me because of Bill.' He always blamed himself. We both did."

"I don't blame you anymore."

We fell silent. It was difficult to imagine how painful it must have been for my parents to live with this guilt. I never considered for one minute that my father held himself accountable for what happened, and it was bittersweet to learn that he longed to be closer to me yet didn't have the ability to repair the damage left by Bill. But I found comfort knowing my father died mourning our disconnected relationship, rather than thinking he never really cared about it at all. Even though he was gone, I realized how much I still needed his approval. Now, I felt I finally had it.

CHAD WAS DIAGNOSED with a common congenital defect medically referred to as a patent foramen ovale (PFO). A hole between his two atria was the likely culprit that caused the clot that lodged temporarily in his brain.

As the Romanian predicted, Chad walked out of the hospital with a cane. Once he was home, however, he set it aside and never used it again. That weekend, when I saw the cane resting in the corner of our bedroom, it reminded me of the scene at the end of *Miracle on 34th Street*. Even though it was March, Christmas had come early for me. Except it wasn't a house Santa Claus left as a gift; it was Chad, fully recovered.

We visited my mother that weekend. Explaining Chad's diagnosis and miraculous recovery was difficult, but once she understood the basics, she simply looked at me and said, "What? Your love wasn't enough to fill that hole?"

"Apparently not," I said. "He still has to decide whether he's going to have the procedure to close it."

"What's there to decide?" she asked. "You can't walk around with a hole in your heart."

I looked at Chad and offered him a nod of concurrence.

He smiled politely at my mother and said, "Well, I've been walking around with this hole my entire life. I'm not convinced that's what caused the stroke."

"Then what did?"

"I'm not sure," he said. "I did have dental work the week before. Maybe the dentist dislodged the clot. He was drilling on that side of my mouth."

"Listen." I squeezed his chin. "You're closing that hole. You hear me? I'm not going to live the rest of my life wondering if you're going to have another stroke."

"Yeah," my mother shouted. "End of discussion."

"The Spinellis have spoken," I said. "Welcome to the family."

In the den later that afternoon, my mother served coffee and cake. Then she settled back in my father's armchair with a cup in her lap and Hoffman by her side. It was at that point she insisted on hearing the details of Bill's arrest. "So, who were these three boys who came forward?"

"They're his adopted sons."

"How did the police find them?"

"The Pennsylvania Police began their investigation in 2008. I don't know the exact details, but apparently, three men testified that they were molested by Bill while they lived with him."

"How could someone do such a thing?" she asked. "You adopt a boy, and then you do that to them? When is the trial?"

"First, they're going to have a preliminary hearing on April sixth. The attorney general has to present the case before a judge, who will then decide if there is enough evidence to go to trial."

My mother quietly sipped her coffee. Hoffman sat attentively at her feet, hoping she would feed him some cake. Then, she looked up at us both. "Do you have to testify?"

"No," I said. "I already spoke to the deputy attorney general. He told me that they were only going to present evidence associated with his arrest. I'm not one of the three victims, but I'm still going to the hearing."

My mother furrowed her brow. She looked at Chad and then back at me. "You're going to go all the way to Pennsylvania?"

"Yes."

She breathed in deeply. "Maybe I'll come, too," she said. "Who knows? Maybe I want to testify. I'd like to tell my side of the story." She was becoming excited. "Let me open my mouth. I'll make some noise in that courtroom. They'll have to throw me out." Then my mother settled back in her seat. She sipped her coffee and took a bite of cake while Hoffman watched her every move.

As much as I tried, I was never able to predict my mother's reactions. The more I thought about it, the more confused I became. Whatever her reasons, I found it reassuring that she wanted to come to the hearing, even though I knew she wouldn't. I suppose it brought her some degree of peace knowing Bill was in jail for the time being.

CHAPTER 36

Vertically Challenged

IN PREPARATION FOR THE UPCOMING HEARING, I asked Chad whether we should rent a car and stay overnight in Tioga County or drive up early that morning. He was working at his desk, alternating between his computer and BlackBerry.

"Hello, Earth to Chad. Are you listening?"

"Hmm?" he said. He could barely tear his eyes away from the screen before he realized how frustrated I was becoming. "The hearing. Right. I think we should just drive up that morning."

"It starts at 9 A.M. sharp. Tioga County is five hours away. We'll have to leave here by 3:30 A.M."

This information seemed to overwhelm Chad. He studied my face, the corners of his brows curling up in confusion.

"There's no train?" he asked.

"I checked. The closest train leaves you in Harrisburg, which is a forty-five-minute drive to Tioga County. We'll still have to rent a car." Chad continued to stare at me without uttering a word, without changing his expression.

I started to get angry. "If you don't want to go with me, Chad, just say so."

"No, if you want me there, then I'll go."

It was then that I concluded the world was made up of two sets of people: the Doers and the Don'ts. The Doers are proactive and two steps ahead. The Don'ts are the ones who sit by and hope someone else will take up the slack. I was beginning to think Chad, like my mother and sisters, was a Don't. Since Bill's arrest, I'd become invigorated by the prospect of attending the hearing. And even though everyone around me acted as if they wanted to help, they really didn't mean it. Like most Don'ts, they were being polite.

My mother shrouded her fear with concern by cautioning me that Bill or his family would come after me if I continued to pursue him. Maria was probably thankful she lived out of state so she had an excuse not to be by my side. Even Josephine, whom I had grown quite close to as an adult, kept me at arm's distance with regard to Bill and this case. They still lived in a world of denial, thinking that if I just let it go, it would simply go away. Even when they learned that other boys had been molested after me, I would have expected them to feel compelled to right this wrong. Instead, they let their guilt weigh them down. In a sense, they were repeating the same actions they'd committed thirty years ago—when they sat back and watched a molester go free. When it came right down to it, no one wanted to get involved, not my mother, not my sisters, not even Chad.

"How could you say that to me?" I said.

"What do you want me to say? I'm busy."

"You're always busy. There's always something going on in your life, whether it's a meeting or a conference call. The difference between you and me is that you wouldn't have to ask me to go with you if the situation was reversed." My eyes began to twitch. I squeezed them shut.

"Don't start crying now."

"I'm not crying." I rubbed my eyes. "I feel like I'm eleven years old again. You're being so passive-aggressive." Chad was sitting barely four feet away from me, yet it felt as if we were miles apart. Bill's arrest and the impending hearing hadn't brought us closer together. If anything, it had pulled us in opposite directions. "We need to come to a compromise."

"Okay," he said. "I suggest we rent a car and drive up that morning. Even if we have to leave at the crack of dawn, it's still better than sleeping over in some cheap hotel. We'll drop the dog off at the Puppy Loft the night before so we don't have to worry about him. Then we'll just leave in the morning like you suggested."

"Thank you," I said. "It will all be over soon. I promise."

Sooner or later, I knew it would come down to this. We had been ignoring the fact that the hearing would eventually happen. It wasn't until dinner was over, right after we watched the news and turned off the lights, that I began to feel that churning sensation below my ribs.

Next to me Chad tossed and turned. He moved closer and whispered, "How do you feel about seeing Bill again after all this time? It's one thing for you to talk with him on the phone. It's a completely different situation to see him in person."

"I have this ridiculous concern that I'm going to be the shortest person in the courtroom."

"What the hell does your height have to do with anything?"

"Chad, I'm practically the same height I was in grammar school. I'm worried that when I walk into that courtroom tomorrow, Bill won't see a man; he'll see a little boy."

"Why are you so obsessed with your height? It's probably one of the most attractive things about you. I don't understand why it bothers you so much."

"I told you it was ridiculous. You know there is this old Italian wives' tale that if you walk across someone's legs, you'll stop them from growing. Every time I got up from the couch, my mother would yell at me if I walked over someone's legs to get past them. I believe that being molested by Bill Fox stunted my growth."

Simultaneously, we both laughed out loud. Chad shuffled his feet under the covers, waking Hoffman. I loved making him laugh.

"It makes total Spinelli sense. It's reverse logic. You think you were stunted when, in fact, you chose not to live in denial. You became a doctor, you're in a relationship, and you're dealing with this head-on. The others, like Jonathan, Nicholas, and Bill, are in denial. If anything, *their* lives were stunted."

"I know you're right. It's something I need to work on. The

funny thing is that when I was in Denver visiting Jonathan, I immediately noticed he was short, too. You don't know how happy that made me."

Chad nuzzled and kissed my neck. "I'm not surprised, and just for the record, I don't think of you as short."

ON APRIL 6, I WOKE UP PROMPTLY and stared at the digital clock. It read 3 A.M. I had barely slept, thinking about the long drive ahead of us. Without waiting another second, I got up and began to get ready. After I showered, I put on a pair of black slacks, a solid blue shirt, and a charcoal blazer. Inside my shoes, I placed two-inch lifts. When I assessed myself in the mirror, I felt confident and tall. Then I sat in the living room, sipped coffee, and waited patiently for Chad.

When we were on the road, heading through the Lincoln Tunnel, I looked at my watch: 4:30 A.M. In New Jersey, I pulled into a coffee shop so we could buy enough rations to keep us going until we arrived at the courthouse.

The weather changed once we entered Pennsylvania. The air became cooler, even as the sun began to rise over the mountains. There was even a brief flurry. Driving the long stretch of highway, I grew anxious with each passing minute. By 8:45 A.M., I began to panic when I realized I hadn't seen an exit sign for miles. "I think I passed it," I said.

Chad sensed my rising anxiety and tried to remain calm. "It's just a few more miles," he encouraged.

Skeptical, I stared intently at the road ahead until a sign emerged indicating our exit was the next right. "To think we drove all this way, and we still might be late," I said.

"It's not much farther. The directions show the courthouse is just two miles from the off-ramp."

I turned left onto a main road that looked as if it could have been lifted from any small town. I couldn't help but notice that nothing seemed quite real. It felt as if we were on a movie set. There were rows of dilapidated homes with pickup trucks in nearly every driveway. Some houses were so beaten down by weather and disrepair that I couldn't imagine anyone lived in them. We passed a strip mall with several abandoned stores. There was one dress shop open with no mannequins in the windows, just clothing tacked onto white boards. Up ahead, an old-fashioned diner with faded blue siding and large windows was empty except for a woman standing behind the cash register.

To my left, I noticed a simple one-story building that looked like a roadside motel. "That can't be the courthouse," I said. "It's a lot smaller than I expected." We pulled up to the front and parked in the only remaining spot. It suddenly occurred to me that the courtroom was going to be packed with family members there to support Bill.

I bet they're all tall.

I looked at my watch. It was just two minutes after the hour. Rushing ahead, I opened the door to the courthouse. Inside, I found myself in a small vestibule with two doors. Like Alice in Wonderland, I chose the one to my right, hoping it would make me taller. It opened into the actual courtroom itself, which was smaller than I expected, roughly the size of my parents' living room. There was no marble floor, only cheap carpeting. The walls were covered with panel, not paint, and nearly every folding chair was occupied. I took one of the few remaining seats, in the last row next to a middle-aged woman. Once I sat down, I realized she was Bill's sister. Chad entered soon after me and sat in an empty chair by the door. Seconds later, I heard, "All rise, the Honorable Judge Carlson presiding."

Bill was no more than twenty feet away from me, dressed in an orange jumpsuit with the letters *TCP* (Tioga County Prison) printed on his back. For years, I'd kept an image of Bill in my mind, but he now looked smaller, hunched over with rounded shoulders. His gray hair was shellacked back against his scalp. When he turned slightly, I noticed he was wearing glasses. Behind them were those same blue eyes. Yet now they seemed tired and confused.

Once Judge Carlson sat down, the hearing began. I took out my cell phone and began typing notes as Deputy Attorney General Sprow presented his first witness. A man sitting in the row directly in front of me turned around and glared in my direction. He was very large and wore a flannel shirt. Next to him was someone who looked like he could be his twin. It occurred to me then that they were Bill's adopted sons. I heard Bill's sister whisper to her husband. Then he turned and gave me a stern look. Other than the lawyers, I was the only one in the courtroom wearing a suit.

The first witness was Shane Fox, the victim who'd written the comment online that I'd replied to. He looked very much like the two men sitting in front of me—large, with fair skin, dark hair, and light eyes. Shane testified that Bill adopted him in Florida when he was fourteen years old. They moved to Pennsylvania, and there the sexual activity progressed. "The night my adoption was official we had anal sex." Shane described how Bill woke him up to have sex almost every other night. He testified that when he submitted himself sexually to Bill, he was rewarded with gifts.

"What kind of gifts?" asked Sprow.

"He'd take me out to lunch," said Shane. "One time he took me to get my ear pierced."

I listened as Shane spoke in simple, short sentences, punctuated with the inflections of a little boy standing before the principal.

"It was hard falling asleep," said Shane, "because I was scared of being woken up in the middle of the night to have sex."

Bill's lawyer cross-examined Shane next. When the attorney stood up, I noticed he was wearing snakeskin boots. Immediately, he tried to throw Shane off by asking him for dates and about how old he was during various incidents. Shane struggled to remember, unable to do the math in his head. Then I remembered Trooper Iverson telling me that many of the boys Bill adopted were mentally challenged to varying degrees. Watching Shane become confused under cross-examination left me feeling frustrated. The hearing was spiraling downward.

"So you were adopted in Florida?" asked Snakeskin Boots. "By the time you moved to Pennsylvania, you were already a teenager, correct?"

Shane nodded.

"At that age, you could say the sex was consensual?"

"Objection."

I glanced over at Chad to observe his reaction. That was when I felt the skin on my face begin to tingle. After Shane's testimony, I watched him walk back with his head held down. He sat next to a woman, who whispered in his ear. Then they turned around and smiled at me.

The next witness was a redheaded young male who testified that he was never sexually molested but that Bill often showed him pornography online. Upon further questioning, he admitted that Bill had touched his erect penis once. Then he said that Bill regularly searched online for boys to adopt, considering only those who had emotional or mental disabilities. Bill's attorney was less successful at discrediting this witness on cross-examination because he was clearly not handicapped like the others, maybe not at all.

The final witness, escorted into the courtroom by a social worker, was a skinny, greasy-haired male in his twenties who appeared anxious as he took the stand. Sitting there, he repeatedly flattened his hair down and around his ears. Then he adjusted his glasses over and over again. Under oath, he testified that Bill never molested him. The man in the flannel shirt in front of me smiled and nodded eagerly. I began rubbing my temples. The burning sensation on my face felt worse as the hearing progressed. Since the first witness, I'd been feeling a sinking sensation that the entire proceeding hadn't produced enough evidence for the judge to conclude that Bill should stand trial.

But Sprow forged ahead and proceeded to read the witness's previous grand jury testimony to the courtroom. Several months earlier, this same witness had testified that Bill molested him repeatedly. The more Sprow read, the more flustered the witness became. Sprow warned him that changing his testimony now meant that he'd lied under oath to the grand jury. The witness clumsily explained that he didn't lie under oath but was confused at the time. Sprow made it clear to him that if he perjured himself, he could face prosecution. The boy glanced over at his social worker. It was obvious that he didn't know what to say. The judge excused him when there were no further questions.

Once all three witnesses testified, Sprow offered up his final argument to the court about why Bill Fox should stand trial. Bill's attorney argued against it. The judge then took a half hour to deliberate. I immediately left the courtroom with Chad and sat in our rental car.

"Look at your face," said Chad.

In the rearview mirror, I saw hives the size of quarters on my forehead and cheeks. I looked like Freddy Krueger in *Nightmare on Elm Street*.

"I don't feel good about this at all," I said.

"What are you talking about? I think it's going well."

"You do?" I said in disbelief. "Chad, one kid recanted his testimony. The second one said Bill never touched him, and the first witness was the only one who emphatically stated Bill molested him. Then Bill's attorney confused the hell out of him on the stand. And did you see Bill's lawyer is wearing snakeskin boots? What kind of an attorney wears boots? Let alone snakeskin."

"Frank, you need to relax," said Chad. "The purpose of this hearing is for the judge to listen to the evidence. If you ask me, the attorney didn't have to put all three witnesses on the stand. After the first one testified, he had more than enough evidence."

Chad's confidence was reassuring. For the entire length of the deliberation, we remained in the car with the doors locked, holding our hands up to the heater for warmth and protected from the Foxes outside. The half hour passed quickly. Before I got out of the car, I looked at myself again in the rearview mirror. Freddy Krueger was gone.

Back inside the courtroom, Deputy Attorney General Sprow introduced himself to me, along with State Trooper Iverson. Then Sprow took me aside. "I'd like to ask you a question. The judge informed me that he received an anonymous letter today, which included a photograph of Bill with some boys." He motioned to the folder in his hand. "I want to know if you sent it."

"No, I didn't."

"I didn't think so," he said. "The judge is a little concerned. Honestly, Dr. Spinelli, if this goes to trial, and we get you on the stand, Mr. Fox's attorney is going to paint you in a very unflattering way. I just want to make sure you keep your nose clean."

"I appreciate you looking out for me," I said. "I've already received one threatening phone call since this all started."

"I'm sorry to hear that. Have you notified the authorities?"

"Yes, they're looking into it. What I find encouraging is that someone thought I was important enough to be threatened. Perhaps this means that I'm on to something big?"

"I agree. It's still concerning to hear that you've received threats."

Over Sprow's shoulder, I saw the guards escort Bill back into the courtroom. His wrists and ankles were shackled and linked together. Now in full view, he no longer looked as threatening to me as when I was younger. With that sad expression and sagging cheeks, he looked more like an old bulldog chained to the fence.

At that moment, Judge Carlson entered the courtroom and everyone stood up. As he cleared his throat several times, I held my breath, anticipating the worst. If he decided there wasn't enough evidence to go to trial, I didn't want to fall apart in front of Bill's family. I knew their jubilant cheers might provoke me into crying, and I couldn't let them see me like that.

"In reviewing the evidence," said Carlson, "I feel the state has met the burden."

I was slow to grasp the meaning of his verdict, so I looked over at Chad, who stared back at me, beaming. Then I heard the judge ask Bill whether he understood.

Bill Fox was going to stand trial.

Soon after the judge departed, the police took Bill away. I practically leapt out of my chair as they escorted him to the exit. Bill stopped momentarily and whispered to the man in the flannel shirt. It looked as though he was giving him instructions. I stared at Bill, willing him to look in my direction, but he never did, or at least that's how it appeared to me.

During the long drive back to New York, I confessed to Chad that I wanted Bill to know I was there. Part of me felt foolish for that, as if I was still seeking his approval.

"Don't worry," said Chad. "I think Bill knew you were there. He might not have looked at you, but he saw you. They all did."

Chapter 37

Surprise Witness

THE NEXT SEVERAL MONTHS were less about the impending trial and more about getting my life back on track. I closed my solo practice and partnered with another physician. When I'd first started out, it was my dream to have my own practice. The office on Twenty-third Street was the gift I gave to myself for my fortieth birthday. Three years later, that didn't seem as important. My life with Chad and Hoffman was my priority. Work still took precedence over everything else, but partnering with another physician brought me something I never thought I needed before: security. I no longer felt the desire to be tethered to an office. A solo practice hinged on my presence. I had to open up the office in the morning, see patients, and then close it back up again at night. I felt as if I owned a Korean deli like the one across the street. Joining a practice was going to allow me the freedom to go on vacation and take time off in case of illness. That became more important once Chad had a stroke.

Later that month, Chad underwent the procedure to close the hole in his heart. He agreed, though he was still convinced the stroke was caused by a dental procedure. I didn't care what he thought as long as the PFO was closed. That same day I received a letter from the Pennsylvania attorney general's office informing me that Bill Fox's trial was scheduled to begin August 2. Nowhere did it mention that I was going to be called as a witness. It said only that I had to make myself available during the trial dates.

In the cardiac intensive care recovery room, I showed Chad the letter. He read it while eating Jell-O. "So, I guess we're going to the trial?"

"I really don't want to."

He looked over at me and raised his eyebrows. "Really?"

"Of course we'll go, but honestly, I've been through enough. That preliminary hearing wrecked me. I can't imagine driving out there again and going through all that. Trials are different. A jury of strangers is going to listen to this case. They don't know what I know, and it looks like I won't even be called as a witness. Then they're going to make a decision based on the testimonies of these boys, whom we both know aren't the best witnesses. I just don't think I could sit there and watch that snakeskin-wearing lawyer rip them apart. It would kill me."

Chad opened another cup of Jell-O and licked the lid. "Well, you don't have to decide now. You have two months. A lot can happen between now and then. Just look at the news. It looks like New York is going to legalize gay marriage. Who knows? You may be married before the trial begins."

"I know you didn't just propose to me in a cardiac intensive care unit."

Chad smiled. "Why not?" He chuckled. "I can't think of a better place. Your mother said it best when she inferred your love couldn't close the hole in my heart. Now it's closed. What better way to celebrate?"

DUE TO SCHEDULING CONFLICTS, Senior Deputy Attorney General Anthony Forray replaced Michael Sprow as the prosecutor. On July 31, he called me.

"How do you feel going into this trial?" I asked.

"I'm confident, but I've been a trial lawyer long enough to know that it could go either way, depending on the jury."

"Do you think I'll be called as a witness?"

"It's not likely," he said. "The only way we'll be able to call you as a witness is if Mr. Fox takes the stand."

In my limited knowledge, most of it based on famous court cases, guilty individuals hardly ever took the stand. "I don't think he will," I said.

"You never know. Mr. Fox has outsmarted people for years. He may very well take the stand because he feels he could convince a jury that he's a good man who adopted unwanted boys and was voted Father of the Year. I'll be honest with you, Dr. Spinelli. Juries have a hard time convicting a police officer, especially a highly decorated one. The witnesses are also a concern. I don't have to tell you that their mental capabilities can work in Mr. Fox's favor. I'm sure Mr. Fox's lawyer will use that to his advantage. That's why I'm having you on call, in case we need you to testify."

"Do you want me in the courtroom?" I asked hesitantly.

"Honestly, I'd prefer if you weren't there. The way I see this, jury selection will take place on Monday, and the trial begins on Tuesday. The judge has been adamant about sticking to the schedule. He doesn't want any delays. I'll likely get through all my witnesses on Tuesday."

"Really?" I asked. "It could all go that quickly?"

"Yes. Now, I'll call you Tuesday afternoon to update you on what's happening. If Mr. Fox decides to take the stand, I plan on asking him if he has ever molested anyone else. If he says no, then I'd like to have you waiting in the wings, so to speak."

I felt a heightened sense of anxiety. Mr. Forray's plan was intriguing, but unnerving. I hadn't planned on going to the trial at all, and now it seemed I could be a witness. "Does that mean you'll need me in Pennsylvania?"

"No, not right away," he said. "Once I see how fast the trial is progressing, I'll call you as soon as I'm available Tuesday afternoon. If it looks like Mr. Fox is going to testify, then I'd like you to come here as soon as possible. I expect if all goes well, you'll arrive on Wednesday in order to testify on Thursday."

"Okay, Mr. Forray. I'll do whatever you ask. I only want to help you win this case."

—∞∞∞—

ON MONDAY, AUGUST 1, I RECEIVED A CALL from Anthony Forray. He sounded very excited. "Dr. Spinelli, we've completed jury selection. Like I explained before, the judge wants no delays. We're going ahead as scheduled."

"Okay."

"I've also been told that Mr. Fox is going to take the stand on his behalf. So I'm going to need you here by tomorrow night."

Silence hung in the air as I tried to muster up something to say. "I can't believe he's going to take the stand."

"Like I said before, you never know how things are going to go. I'm not surprised Mr. Fox wants to testify. He wants to tell his side of the story. He's going to deny molesting these boys. If I can get him to open that door, ask him if he's ever molested anyone else, then I'm going to bring you out. That's why I don't want you in the courtroom, but I'll need you here by tomorrow evening."

At therapy that night, I told Dr. McGovern that I might testify after all. I read her impassive expression as the mirror image of my own. Then she smiled. "You know, this is the end of the road. All I can say is that you have to see it as the last thing you need to do. It's been a long journey, and now you have to testify. The good news is that you are a wonderful historian. All you have to do is get up there and tell the truth. What scares you the most?"

I thought about her question for a moment. "The long drive. I don't want to be in a car for five hours after a long day of work. I don't want to sleep in a cheap motel, wake up, and then wait for them to call me as a witness. I guess I'm scared of the unknown. I don't know what to expect. Do I address the jury? Do I look at Bill?"

"Do you want to look at Bill?"

"I suppose at some point we're going to have to acknowledge

each other. Honestly, Dr. McGovern, I want to go in there not as a victim or a survivor. I want to testify as a doctor, who was molested, and present myself as a clinician so that I can explain this unimaginable thing to a jury, in the hopes that they will see it through my eyes. They have a hard job ahead of them. It's difficult to look at grown men and imagine them as little boys. I want to bring my class picture from 1978 and show them what I looked like when I was eleven."

"I think you should."

"What I can't understand for the life of me is, why didn't Bill post bail? I asked the attorney, and he said that sometimes when sociopaths get caught, they feel relief at having finally been stopped. His theory is that Bill didn't make bail because he wanted to stop molesting boys. Being in jail prevents him from acting on that impulse. I want to believe his theory, because that would make Bill human."

"No. He is a monster. What it makes him is tired and old. It's your compassion as a doctor that makes you want to humanize him. Don't forget that. As for you, I don't think you have anything to worry about. You're going to be fine. Good luck."

On my walk home from therapy, I called Eric to tell him I was going to testify.

"Oh my God," he said. "You're going to be a surprise witness?"

"I knew you'd like that."

"How very Joan Collins in *Dynasty,* season finale. You have to wear a big hat with the veil and a little black dress. I'll let you borrow mine. In fact, I've got my sewing machine out right now so I can make the alterations. I know you're petite. So I'll have to take it in a little."

"I'm glad you can make jokes. Now I have to go home and tell Chad the big news. Eric, this isn't fun."

"It's not fun. I know that, but it was never supposed to be. Tomorrow you're going to work. Then afterward, you'll drive out to Pennsylvania and testify. You've been rehearsing for this moment for a very long time. Do you need me to come with you?"

"No," I said. "Chad's coming with me. I think it will be good for us to see this through to the end together."

That night I explained the plan to Chad. This time we didn't argue. There were no questions. We both understood what had to be done. Chad arranged for a hotel room while I rented the car. We planned on leaving after work and driving straight through. Forray had told me little: I didn't know what time I was going to testify. I didn't know what questions they were going to ask. All I knew was that we had to be in Pennsylvania by tomorrow evening.

In bed that night, we lay quietly side-by-side with Hoffman between us. Suddenly, we were exhausted. I found comfort in the silence. Half-asleep, I thought back to when I first met Chad and all we had been through. Although urinating in public was still somewhat of an issue, the nightmares were becoming less frequent and intimacy was slowly returning to our relationship. After Chad's stroke, it occurred to me that I had to be always conscious of what little time we had together. It seemed as if I had a new identity now that was motivated by an extreme fear of death. As I drifted off to sleep, the full story of our lives unfolded slowly until it enveloped me. In a dreamlike state, I saw us lying in bed as two old men. I tried to envision how many years we'd have together until the time came for one of us to part.

I felt Chad's hand on mine and opened my eyes. It was morning.

BEFORE I LEFT FOR WORK THAT DAY, Trooper Iverson called to confirm that I would be in Tioga County by nightfall. I assured him that Chad and I were all set to leave later that afternoon.

"If anything comes up, please call me as soon as possible," he said. His phone call left me feeling rattled.

I quickly made my way over to my office so that I could arrive early, before anyone else. I needed time alone to sort through my schedule. At my desk, I flipped through the directions to the courthouse. I printed the hotel confirmation and details for the car rental. I placed all the printed information into a folder. Everything was set.

Several hours later, I received a voice message from Trooper Iverson on my cell phone. "Dr. Spinelli, I need to follow up with you about this morning's phone call regarding our issue here in P-A. If you could give me a quick call, I'd appreciate it. I need to update you on what's going on here. If not, I'll keep trying your number."

I called him back immediately. "Hello, this is Dr. Spinelli. I'm returning Trooper Iverson's call."

"Yes, Iverson's on the phone right now, but he wants to speak to you. It's all over."

"What's over?"

"The trial. I'll have him call you back on your cell to explain."

Hearing those words, "It's over," left me tingling, but I wouldn't allow myself to read into what the officer said. I decided to take Hoffman out for a walk along Eighth Avenue. Anxiously, I marched up the street, talking out loud to myself. "What does he mean, the case is over? What happened? Is this good?" I wandered up to a French bistro and ordered coffee. Outside, I sat on a bench with Hoffman by my side, trying not to get too excited but imagining something miraculous had happened.

While I sipped my coffee, I stared at Hoffman. Gazing into those sweet, almond-colored eyes that seemed like magical orbs, I said, "You know, Hoffman, don't you?"

Then I heard my cell phone ring.

It was Forray. "It's over," he said. "Bill took a plea after Shane Fox testified. It was unbelievable. Once I had Shane on the stand, I asked him, 'Putting the sexual activity aside, do you miss your dad?' Shane replied, 'Yes, we were friends. We did everything together. I sat with him through his surgeries. I was there with him through everything.' It was heartbreaking testimony. After that you could hear a pin drop."

Bill's attorney had declined to cross-examine Shane. Instead he requested a recess. At that time, he asked Forray whether they could make a deal. When Bill returned to the courtroom, he pled no contest to three counts against each victim and one for obstruction of justice for asking the third witness to recant his testimony. According to Forray, pleading no contest in Pennsylvania was like an admission of guilt.

"I don't understand why Bill didn't take a plea earlier," said Forray. "It would have been a better strategy. The judge heard Shane's testimony. He was never cross-examined. The defense didn't even try to discredit Shane. I would imagine the judge will consider this a waste of the court's time, to have gone through all this only to plea."

"I'm shocked myself. Maybe Bill's lawyer advised him to take the plea once they heard Shane's testimony?"

"Quite honestly, the case hung on Shane's testimony. This couldn't have gone better if you ask me."

"Thank you, Mr. Forray. You've done an amazing job."

William Fox was sentenced to the maximum state prison term for each of nine misdemeanor and felony charges, adding up to a sentence of seventeen and one-half to thirty-five years in state prison. Since he was also found to be a Sexually Violent Predator, Bill is registered for life with Pennsylvania's "Megan's Law" sex offender registry.

Megan's Laws are named for Megan Kanka, a seven-year-old girl from New Jersey who was sexually assaulted and murdered in 1994 by a neighbor who, unknown to the victim's family, had been previously convicted for sex offenses against children.

Less than two years after he was sentenced, Bill died in prison on July 3, 2013.

EPILOGUE

Beverly Glass

WE WERE AT MY MOTHER'S HOUSE FOR DINNER. She had just returned from an extended visit with Maria in Alabama. "Matthew wants to study music," she announced. My sister and her husband had been visiting colleges all summer in preparation for Matthew's matriculation the next year.

"Music?" I asked, handing Chad a tray of homemade pizza.

"Be careful," my mother warned him. "I used hot peppers from the garden."

Chad piled on several slices and began eating.

"Give him some wine," she ordered me. "Drink wine. It's good for your heart, Chad."

"Please," I said. "You don't need to give him a reason to drink."

As I poured the wine, I saw Josephine and her husband walking up the path. They entered, and we greeted them.

"Mom, do you need any help downstairs?" asked Josephine.

My mother didn't respond, but my sister and I obediently followed after her.

"Did you hear Matthew wants to study music?" I whispered to Josephine.

She stopped and rolled her eyes. "I already heard the whole story," she said. "Maria wants him to be premed."

"Premed? Maria has officially turned into Mommy."

From the basement, my mother shouted at us. "Here, take the pasta!"

Josephine took the bowl from my mother. "We need more wineglasses."

"Frank, use the glasses in the china closet," ordered my mother.

"Fancy," said Josephine, placing the bowl on the table. "Frank, have you told Chad the story about the china closet?"

"No," I replied. "You tell him."

Chad sat up and smiled, eagerly waiting to hear my sister tell her tale. Josephine pulled out her chair and sat down next to him. "You're gonna love this," she began. "Apparently, when my parents got married, they were given a complete set of china and crystal by their parents. So when my mother got to New York, she told my father that he needed to buy her a china closet to put them in." Josephine pressed her hand on Chad's to emphasize her next point. "You may not know this, but Italians rarely use anything they keep in their china closet. It's completely for show."

Chad laughed.

My mother walked in and said, "Don't listen to them, Chad. My kids love to make fun of me."

"Let Josephine finish her story," urged my brother-in-law.

"Thank you," said Josephine. "Anyway, my mother got her china closet, and she was so proud of it because it's special. Why, you ask, was it special? I'll tell you." Then Josephine stood up next to me, and we gestured in unison like Vanna White. "My mother's china closet is special because it has Beverly glass."

Chad stared at us, waiting for a punch line. "That's it?"

Josephine glanced over at me and winked. "Yes, Chad, that's it. You don't think a china closet with Beverly glass is special?"

"I don't know what Beverly glass is."

Taking my cue, I opened one of the china closet doors so that he could see the beveled glass. "See," I said, pointing to the counters. "It's genuine *Beverly* glass."

Then everyone erupted with laughter, everyone except my

mother. "Are you done making fun of me? You say *beveled*, I say *Beverly*. I can't help that I have an accent!"

Josephine took her seat next to her husband. "Chad, now you know the story of my mother's china closet with the famous *Beverly* glass."

"Thank you," said Chad. "I'll never forget that story. And for what it's worth, your mom was very smart to buy something so unique."

"See," said my mother. "Chad understands. I bought that china closet because it's a collector's item."

"Exactly, what does it mean when you say it's a collector's item?" asked Josephine. "Who the hell is this collector issuing limited-edition china closets anyway?"

"Josephine, I'm telling you, that's what the man said when he sold it to me."

"He'd tell you anything to get you to buy it," said my brother-in-law.

Watching my family around the table filled me with such joy. Closing the door to my mother's infamous china closet, I caught a glimpse of myself in the beveled glass. There I was. Not some fractured, mirrored reflection of my former self, but me: short, pee-shy, a man able to make the future better than the past.

Acknowledgments

Pee-Shy is a memoir, but most names, as well as certain locations, have been changed.

I owe an enthusiastic thank-you to my agent, David Forrer, and everyone at Inkwell Management who helped me get this book published, especially Allison Hunter. Thank you to my wonderful editor and friend, John Scognamiglio (my paisano from Xaverian) at Kensington Publishing—your insights and advice were invaluable. I would also like to thank my publicist at Kensington, Vida Engstrand, for all of her hard work as well as Kristine Mills for her inventive cover design.

My deepest respect goes to the NYPD, the Pennsylvania Police Department, Child Welfare Services, the Honorable Judge Carlson, and the Pennsylvania Office of Attorney Generals, particularly Deputy Attorney Generals Michael Sprow and Anthony Forray. I'd like to extend a special thank-you to all the courageous people at GMHC. Your work is so important. Thanks to the Trevor Project, 1in6.org, and malesurvivor.org, for offering assistance to survivors of sexual abuse.

Thanks to a great support staff: Eric, Scott, Gary, Ron, Paul and Larry H. (the best CL in the world). To the gang at Chelsea Village Medical: Flo, Lesley, Lisa, Ricardo, David, Luiso, Lynne, Caroline, William, Leigh, and most of all, Bisher—I could not do what I do every day without all of you. Thanks to my early champions: Mark M., Mark P., David, the amazing Larry Flick, Jonathan (for all your help), Tom Leonardis, and the always uplifting Richard Jay-Alexander.

Loving thanks to my family: Mom, Josephine, Joe, Maria, Marc, Mitchell, Madeline, Michael, and Matthew. Dad, I miss you. In addition, I'd like to thank my West Coast family: Vern, Roxie, the Schroers, and the Branums.

My most heartfelt thanks to Cathleen Adams. During the darkest times, it was comforting to know I had you to count on. Most of all, I owe everything to my beloved husband, Chad, for his support through the worst part of this experience. It's been a long journey, and I love you and Hoffman very much.